Mr. Whistler's Gallery

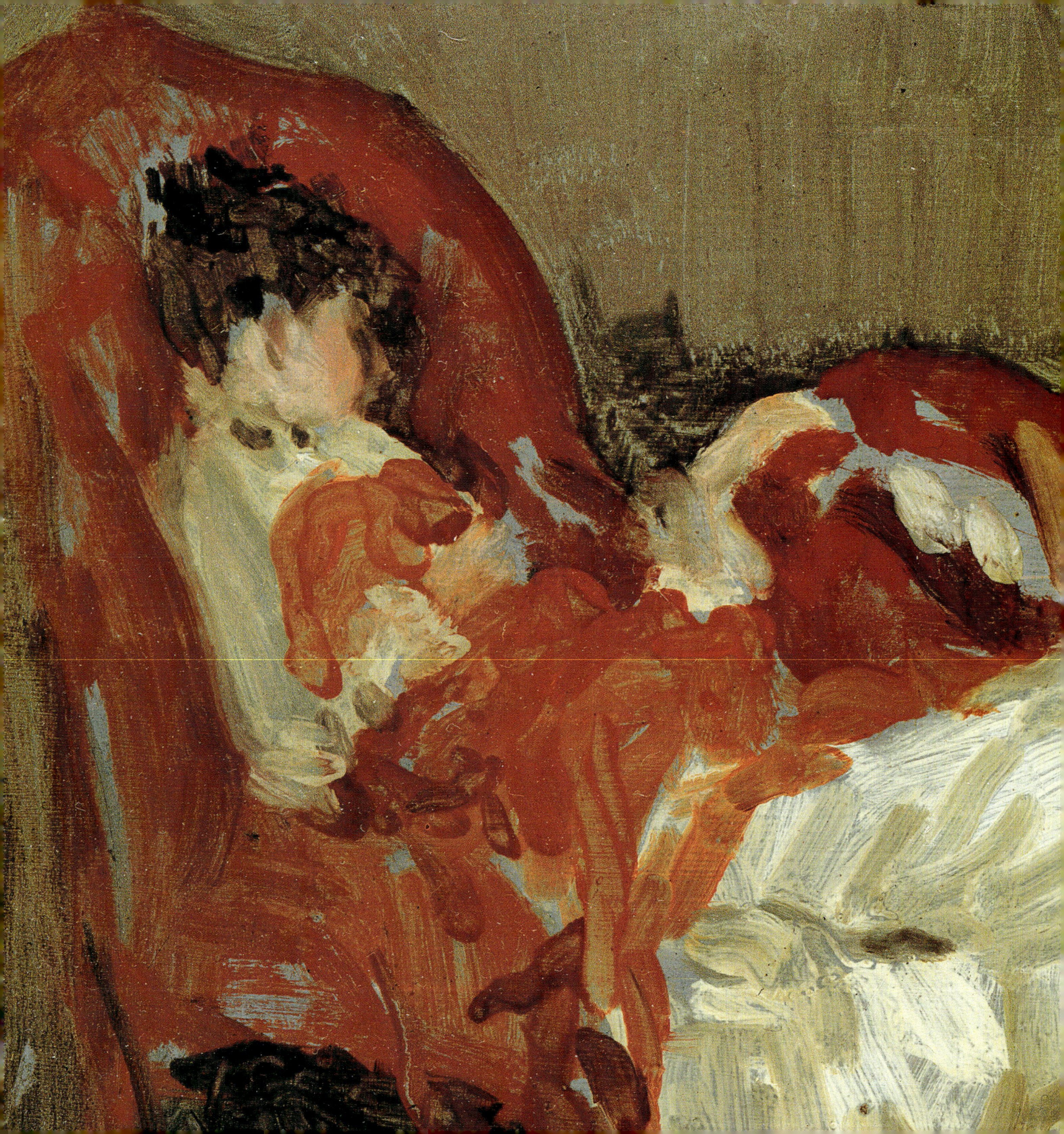

Mr. Whistler's Gallery:

Pictures at an 1884 Exhibition

Kenneth John Myers

Freer Gallery of Art, Smithsonian Institution
Scala Publishers

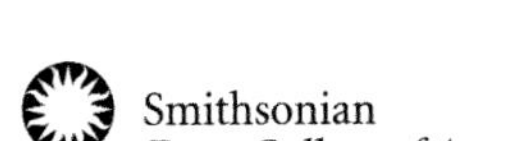

First published in 2003 by the Freer Gallery of Art, Smithsonian Institution, in association with Scala Publishers Ltd, Gloucester Mansions, 140a Shaftesbury Avenue, London WC2H 8HD.

This catalogue is published to accompany the exhibition, *Mr. Whistler's Galleries: Avant-Garde in Victorian London* (Freer Gallery of Art, November 20, 2003–April 4, 2004). *Mr. Whistler's Galleries* is a collaborative exhibition project of the Freer Gallery of Art, Smithsonian Institution, Washington, D.C., and the Virginia Museum of Fine Arts, Richmond. Publication of this book has been underwritten by the Lunder Foundation.

Head of Publications: Lynne Shaner
Managing Editor: Mariah Keller
Art Director: Kate Lydon
Designer: Misha Anikst
Produced by Scala Publishers

Printed and bound in Italy by Editoriale Lloyd s.r.l

S C A L A

Library of Congress Cataloging-in-Publication Data:
Myers, Kenneth, 1955
Mr. Whistler's gallery: pictures at an 1884 exhibition / by Kenneth Myers. p. cm. Includes bibliographical references and index. ISBN 1-85759-305-7 (pbk. : alk. paper)
1. Whistler, James McNeill, 1834-1903 — Exhibitions. 2. Art--Exhibition techniques--Exhibitions. I. Title: Mister Whistler's Gallery. II. Whistler, James McNeill, 1834–1903. III. Freer Gallery of Art. IV. Virginia Museum of Fine Arts. V. Title.
N6537.W4A4 2003 759.13--dc21

The paper used in this publication meets the minimum requirements of the American National Standard for Information Science — Permanence of Paper for Printed Library Materials, ANSI Z39.49.1984.

Frontispiece: Detail, plate 46
Page 27: Detail, plate 27

Contents

Director's Foreword

Except for a handful of scholars and antiquarians, few people know about the series of influential art installations that the American painter and printmaker James McNeill Whistler (1834–1903) organized in the London in the 1880s. But as Kenneth John Myers shows in this book, Whistler's once controversial installations played a crucial role in the development of modern standards of exhibition design. As much as any other single person, it was Whistler who promoted the idea that artworks should be hung widely apart on lightly colored walls in moderately sized but elegantly appointed rooms. The impact of Whistler's ideas has been so profound that we often assume that the now commonplace preference for spare installations is somehow natural or inevitable. One measure of Whistler's influence is the shock many of us feel when we visit an older style installation, like the ones at Sir John Soane's Museum in London, or the Isabella Stewart Gardner Museum in Boston, or even the Barnes Collection in Philadelphia. Myers's research challenges our assumptions as to how art should be displayed by enabling us to imagine ourselves as visitors to one of the most influential of Whistler's installations, the *Arrangement in Flesh Colour & Grey* that he designed for the exhibition of sixty-seven of his paintings and drawings at the Dowdeswells' gallery in London in 1884.

Whistler's ideas about the display of art had an especially profound effect on a young Detroit art collector named Charles Lang Freer (1854–1919), the founder and principal benefactor of this museum. Freer did not see the 1884 exhibition at the Dowdeswells' gallery. Nor did he see any of the other London installations that Whistler designed in the 1880s. But in 1889 Freer did see a version of the 1884 Dowdeswells' exhibition in New York. Installed in the Hermann Wunderlich Gallery, the New York exhibition included sixty-two paintings and drawings. As in London in 1884, all the artworks were hung in "flat gold frames, on walls of pink silk, with nothing to keep them company or to distract attention from them but two Chinese vases in 'crushed strawberry' and 'sang de boeuf'" (*The Critic*, 16 March 1889). Freer visited the Wunderlich exhibition shortly after it opened, absorbed ideas for the design of the new home he was planning to build in Detroit, and purchased one of the watercolors, *Grey and silver—Liverpool* (F1889.3). It was the first painting by Whistler that Freer ever bought. Eleven months later, Freer set off on his first trip to London. On March 4, 1890 he rang Whistler's doorbell, explained that he was a visiting American, and was admitted to a thrilling interview with the Master. Freer and Whistler talked for an hour. Freer left Whistler's studio with fresh ideas for the decoration of the house in Detroit that he had already begun to build, ten wonderful Whistler etchings of Amsterdam, his first Whistler pastel, a new friend, and the beginning of a life-long interest in Asian art. By the time he died in 1919, Freer had acquired more than twelve hundred works by Whistler including the world famous *Harmony in Blue and Gold: The Peacock Room* and approximately thirty-four of the sixty-seven paintings and drawings that Whistler had shown at the Dowdeswell's gallery in 1884.

Freer's close friendship with Whistler shaped both his collecting interests and his understanding as to how art should be displayed. As Freer's collection grew, he added Whistlerian-style exhibition spaces to his home in Detroit, spaces which subsequently served as models for the galleries that he and his architect designed for his museum in Washington. As one walks through the Freer Gallery of Art today, the scale, shape, height, color, and lighting of the galleries all express ideas and values that Freer took from Whistler.

Publication of *Mr. Whistler's Gallery: Pictures at an 1884 Exhibition* and the organization of the related exhibition *Mr. Whistler's Galleries: Avant-Garde in Victorian London* are the highlights of the Freer's year-long commemoration of the centenary of Whistler's death in 1903. Many people have contributed to the success of these projects. I especially want to thank Michael Brand, Kathleen Morris, and the rest of our colleagues at the Virginia Museum of Fine Arts who have collaborated with us on the exhibition; Cheryl Sobas, exhibition coordinator at the Freer; and David Park Curry and Kenneth John Myers, co-curators of the exhibition.

Julian Raby
Director, Freer Gallery of Art and Arthur M. Sackler Gallery

Author's Acknowledgments

I dedicate this book to my parents, Nathaniel Charles Myers, Jr., and Frances Jean Goldberg Myers. Their love has sustained me in good times and bad, does so today, and will do so hereafter.

In the spring of 2000, I proposed that the Freer commemorate the centenary of Whistler's death in 1903 by creating a new version of the influential *Flesh Colour & Grey* exhibition he designed in 1884. My first thanks go to Milo C. Beach, former director of the Freer, Thomas W. Lentz, former deputy director, and Vidya Dehejia, former chief curator and acting director, each of whom enthusiastically supported my proposal. I especially want to thank Dr. Raby, current director, for suggesting that we expand the project to include a new version of a second Whistler exhibition, and for giving me the opportunity to write this book.

Several friends read all or part of the manuscript. My deepest thanks go to Anne Harrell of Virginia Commonwealth University, Alan Wallach of the College of William and Mary, and Debra Diamond of the Freer and Sackler Galleries. My research was made immeasurably easier by Nigel Thorpe, Director of the Centre for Whistler Studies at the University of Glasgow, who provided me with pre-publication access to the magisterial on-line edition of Whistler's correspondence that the Centre launched in June 2003. My greatest scholarly debt is to Margaret F. MacDonald, Principal Research Fellow at the Centre, co-author of one of the two indispensable catalogues raisonné to Whistler's paintings and drawings, and sole author of the other, who allowed me to read her unpublished essay on the 1884 exhibition and helped with the identification of several paintings. Interns Kate Hutchinson, Eileen Kim, Katherine Leland, Kathryn Haesller, Jessica Apuzzo, and Sunni Morgan, together with volunteer Pete Koltnow each played a key role in collecting information, tracking down images, and proofing the manuscript. I could not have completed the book without the help of Josephine Rodgers who among all her other responsibilities managed to get all the reproductions to the printer in time—a thankless task much like herding cats.

Colleagues at the Freer and Sackler galleries have been very generous of their time and expertise. A researcher is only as good as the library support he or she is lucky enough to receive. Much thanks to Mike Smith, Yue Shu, and Reiko Yoshimura at the Freer/Sackler Library; and to Cecilia Chin, Barbara Insidioso, and Patricia Lynagh at the Smithsonian's American Art/National Portrait Gallery Library. I am especially grateful to Kathryn Phillips who patiently bore the brunt of my many interlibrary loan requests. Among the registrars and art handlers, I want especially to thank Tim Kirk, Christina Popenfus, Elizabeth Duley, and Susan Kitsoulis. John Winter, Karen Sasaki, our contract frame conservator William Lewin, and especially Jane Norman each helped to confirm my hunch that many of the unusual Whistler frames at the Freer could be traced back to the 1884 exhibition. One of my greatest debts is to John Tsantes, head of the photography department, who was a pillar of strength and goodwill when it seemed that everything that could go wrong was going wrong. The faults of the book are my own, but the fact that it came out so wonderfully is due to the work of editors and designers both at the Freer/Sackler galleries and at Scala Publishers. In addition to Dennis Kois, Lynne Shaner, and Kate Lydon, I especially want to thank the managing editor Mariah Keller, the project editor Gillian Paul, the copy editor Alison Walker and the designer Misha Anikst.

Many people at the Freer and elsewhere helped with the acquisition of images. Of my many colleagues at the Freer, I especially want to thank Sharron Greene, Patricia Adams, Robert Harrell, Michael Bryant, Neil Greentree, Mia Vollkommer, and Rebecca Barker. Other friends and colleagues who helped with images include Dr. and Mrs. John E. Larkin; Jim and Gina Liautaud; the owners of *Blue and gold—The Schooner*, *The Yellow Room*, and *Convalescent*; Fred Hill at Berry-Hill Galleries, Inc. in New York, Mia Schläppi at Christie's, New York; Julie Aronson and Rebecca Herman at the Cincinnati Art Museum; Lucy Patrick at Florida State University; Susan Galassi, Diane Farynyk, and Katherine M. Gerlough at the Frick Collection; Eric W. Baumgartner at Hirschl & Adler Galleries; Pamela Robertson at the Hunterian Art Gallery at the University of Glasgow; Constance Carter at the Library of Congress; Louis Reed and Jennifer Hardin at the Museum of Fine Arts, St. Petersburg, Florida; Mikki Carpenter at the Museum of Modern Art; Franklin Kelly, Charlie Brock, Neal Turtell, and Barbara Goldstein Wood at the National Gallery of Art (Washington, D.C.); Anne Hodge and Louise Morgan at the National Gallery of Ireland; Janet Axten at the St. Ives Museum; and Niki Pollock at the Glasgow University Library. I also want to thank Iain Harrison at the Birmingham Museums and Art Gallery; Sue Grinols of the Fine Art Museums of San Francisco; Kim Orcutt, Marjorie B. Cohn, and Dorothy Davila at the Harvard University Art Museums; Carol Troyon, Lizabeth Dion, and Danielle Catera at the Museum of Fine Arts, Boston; Leo Kelly at the Terra Museum of American Art; and Julia Alexander, Tim Goodhue, and Melissa Gold Fournier at the Yale Center for British Art. Whistler's painting *The Yellow Room* (Museum of Fine Arts, St. Petersburg, FL), was photographed by Thomas U. Gessler.

Detail, T. Raffles Davison,
New Entrance Vestibule and Gallery
The Fine Art Society,
Engraving from
The British Architect,
December 16, 1881

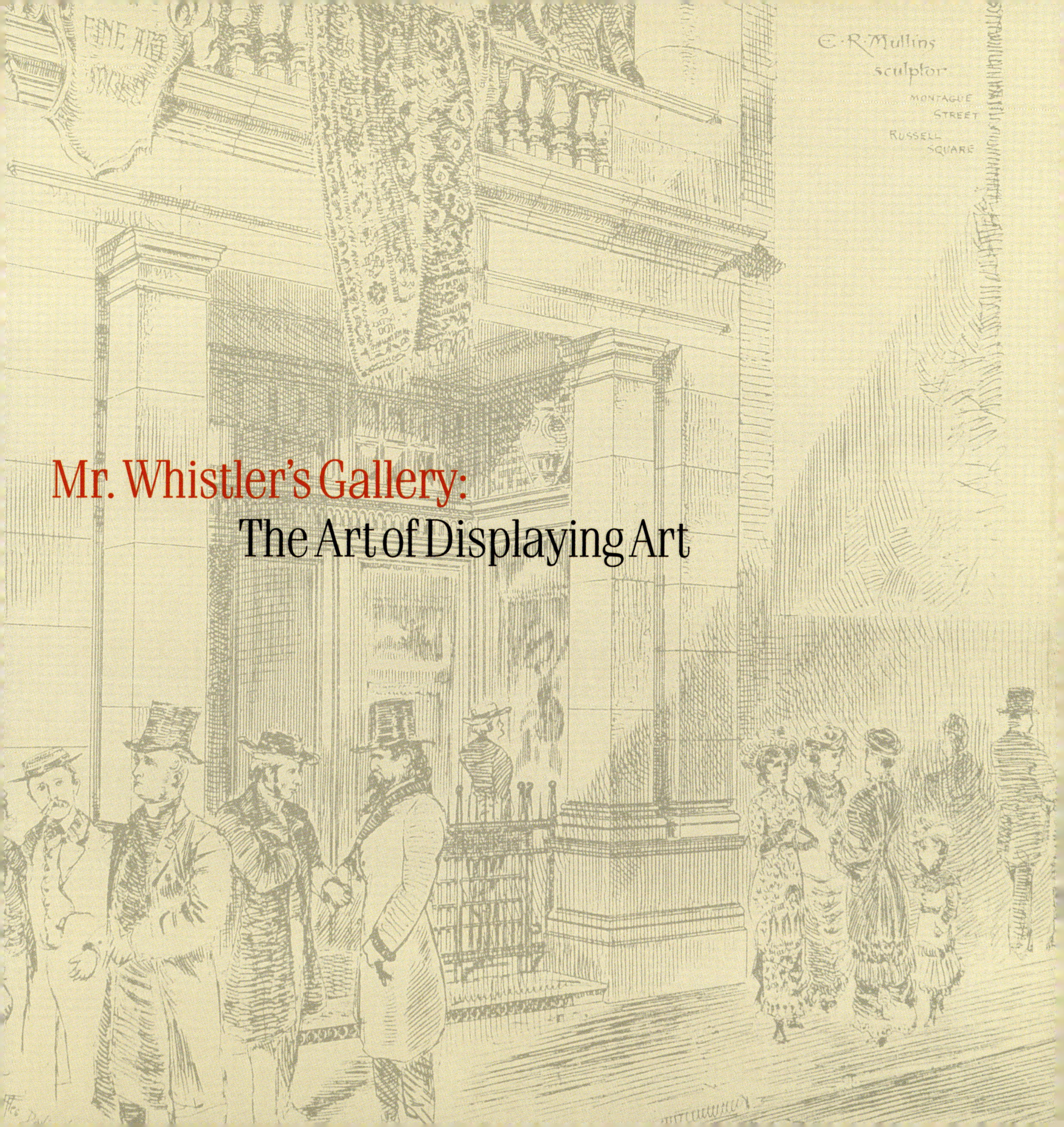

Mr. Whistler's Gallery:
The Art of Displaying Art

Figure 1.
"Notes"–"Harmonies"–"Nocturnes" (London: Dowdeswell and Dowdeswells, 1884), p.3. Freer Gallery of Art Library, Gift of Charles Lang Freer.

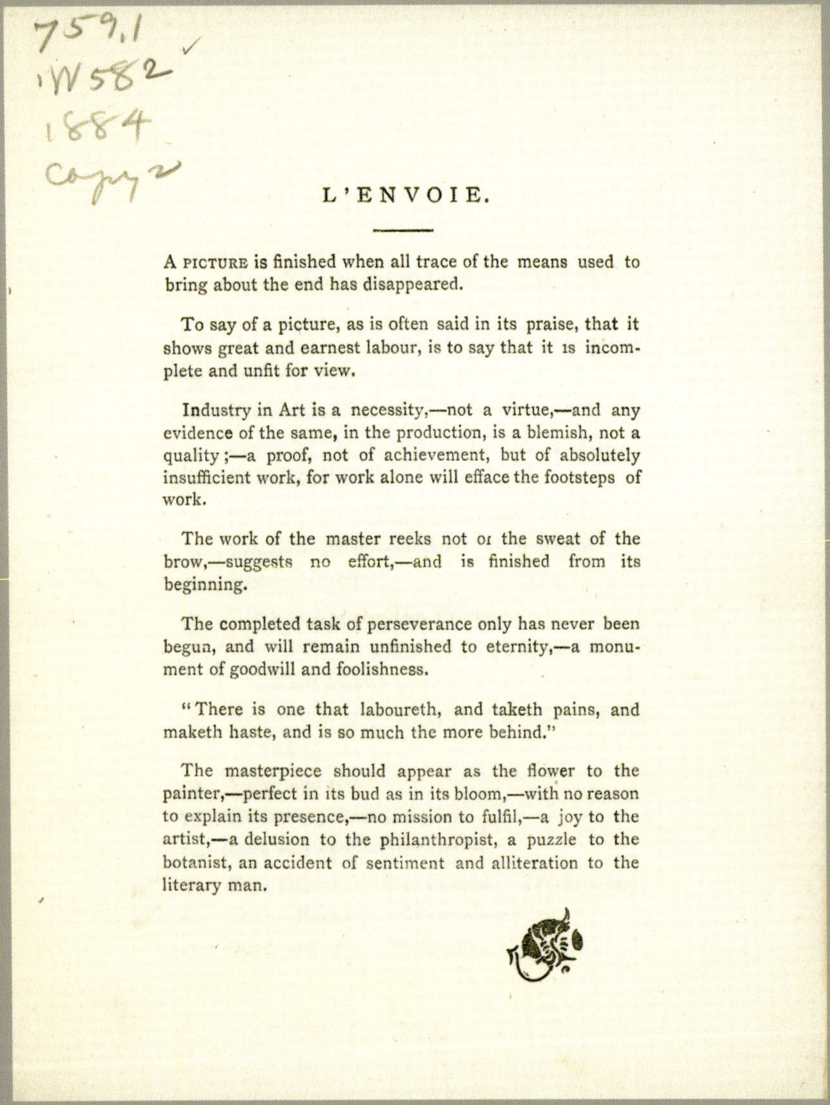

L'ENVOIE.

A PICTURE is finished when all trace of the means used to bring about the end has disappeared.

To say of a picture, as is often said in its praise, that it shows great and earnest labour, is to say that it is incomplete and unfit for view.

Industry in Art is a necessity,—not a virtue,—and any evidence of the same, in the production, is a blemish, not a quality;—a proof, not of achievement, but of absolutely insufficient work, for work alone will efface the footsteps of work.

The work of the master reeks not of the sweat of the brow,—suggests no effort,—and is finished from its beginning.

The completed task of perseverance only has never been begun, and will remain unfinished to eternity,—a monument of goodwill and foolishness.

"There is one that laboureth, and taketh pains, and maketh haste, and is so much the more behind."

The masterpiece should appear as the flower to the painter,—perfect in its bud as in its bloom,—with no reason to explain its presence,—no mission to fulfil,—a joy to the artist,—a delusion to the philanthropist, a puzzle to the botanist, an accident of sentiment and alliteration to the literary man.

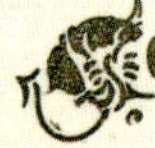

X

Although now best known as a painter and printmaker, the expatriate American artist James McNeill Whistler (1834–1903) was also an influential designer of both private and public interiors, and his work as an exhibition designer played a crucial role in the development of modernist styles of displaying art. Unfortunately, the importance of Whistler's work as an exhibition designer has been obscured by the inherently ephemeral nature of all interior decorations. Whistler began to experiment with new ways of installing art in the mid 1870s, but his most influential installations date from the 1880s when he shook up the staid art world of Victorian London by mounting a series of meticulously designed one-man shows at up-scale art galleries on New Bond Street. Whistler controlled every aspect of these installations: he designed distinctive frames for his art, painted the baseboards and crown moldings so that they harmonized with the colored fabrics he used to cover the walls, and selected carpets, furnishings, and potted plants that repeated the color harmonies established by the walls and carpeting. Whistler even designed color-coordinated outfits for the guards. As modern museum directors and gallery owners know, good design is good advertising. Whistler's installations were unlike anything that contemporary art lovers had ever seen. They promoted his work by attracting reporters, collectors, and the curious. They turned his exhibitions into widely discussed happenings.

Whistler's installations attracted attention from the press and the public but, even more importantly, they also facilitated and encouraged a more contemplative relationship between the art viewer and the art object. By the 1880s, almost all of Whistler's paintings and prints were both delicate in tone and small in scale, and therefore showed badly when displayed in the crowded confines of a typical mid-century art exhibition. The exhibition galleries that Whistler designed were comparatively empty and spare, better suited to the disinterested appreciation of the formal beauties of a work of art. Whistler designed his installations to showcase his own work, but in doing so he helped establish a style of exhibition that still influences the way we display and see art today.

Two of Whistler's installation designs were especially influential: an *Arrangement in White & Yellow* that he created for an exhibition of fifty-one of his etchings in February 1883, and an *Arrangement in Flesh Colour & Grey* that he developed for an exhibition of sixty-seven of his oil paintings, watercolors, and pastels in May 1884. Both exhibition designs were widely discussed in the contemporary press; both successfully promoted attendance and sales; and both were recreated in commercial art galleries in the United States. The 1884 exhibition was especially controversial, as the design helped to focus attention on small paintings and watercolors that challenged the widespread assumption of many mid-nineteenth century art lovers that in order to be "important" a work of art had to be both large in size and highly worked. This essay is in two parts.

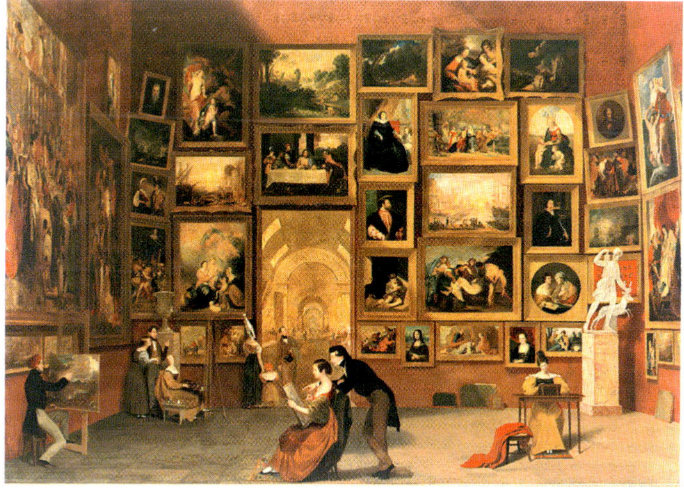

Figure 2.
Samuel F. B. Morse,
Gallery of the Louvre, 1831–33.
Courtesy of the
Daniel J. Terra Collection,
Terra Museum of American Art,
Chicago, Illinois.

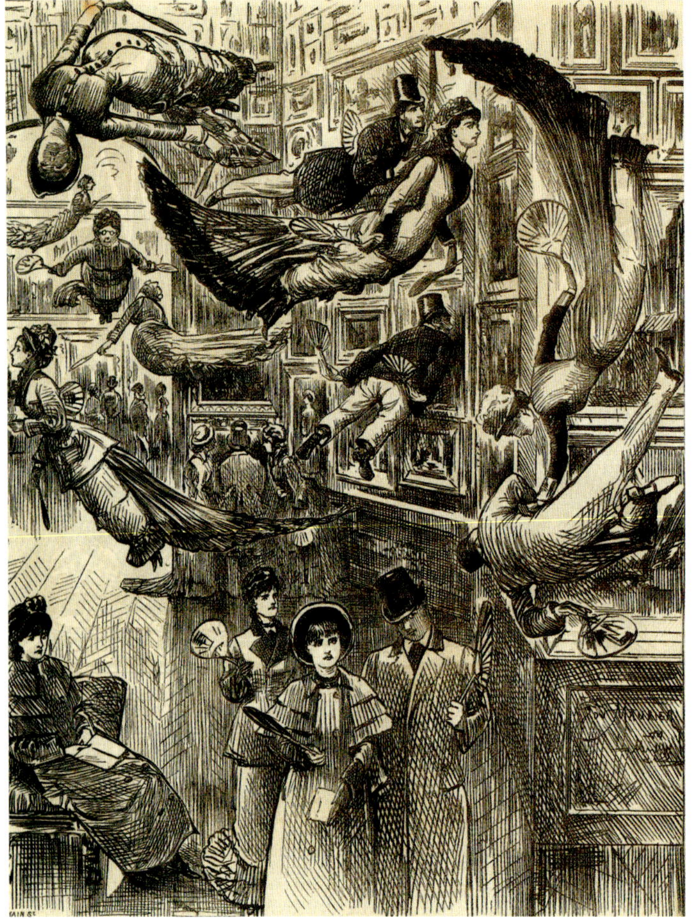

Figure 3.
George du Maurier,
Exhibition at the Royal Academy.
Cartoon in *Punch Almanack for 1879*
December 9, 1878.
Photograph courtesy of Florida State University.

The first discusses the development of Whistler's ideas about exhibition design up to the close of *Arrangement in White & Yellow* in the spring of 1883. The second focuses on *Arrangement in Flesh Colour & Grey*, exploring the genesis, short life, and subsequent impact of Whistler's path-breaking 1884 installation.

The Art of Displaying Art

Styles of art change. Indeed, general survey museums like the Louvre or the National Gallery of Art in London usually install their collections chronologically by national school, precisely so that visitors can reenact the history of western art by walking from Greek vases to early Netherlandish paintings to nineteenth-century French Impressionism. Less obviously, viewers of art change. A cubist still life by Picasso or Braque would have bewildered the most sophisticated seventeenth-century art lover. No one in the eighteenth-century would have possessed the interpretive frames of reference needed to make sense of "modern" art. But those interpretive skills are comparatively common today.

The art of displaying art also changes. From the invention of the picture gallery in the early Renaissance until the last quarter of the nineteenth century, paintings were generally displayed "salon style." As shown in Samuel F. B. Morse's *Gallery of the Louvre* and George du Maurier's *Exhibition at the Royal Academy*, gallery walls were almost completely covered with large paintings holding the center of walls, and smaller works extending to the sides, floor, and ceiling. Frames touched frames, leaving no room for labels. At best, each painting was identified by a number keyed to a checklist, which provided the artist's name and the work's title. Lighting was by skylights or, after 1860, by gaslight, but

Figure 4.
Installation view of the Museum of Modern Art's first exhibition, *Cézanne, Gauguin, Seurat, Van Gogh*, November 7–December 7, 1929.
Digital Image Copyright 2003, Museum of Modern Art, New York.

whatever the source of illumination, many works were either underlit or overlit, or dominated by bigger or more brightly colored neighbors. By the 1960s, salon-style hangs had almost completely disappeared, surviving mainly in geographically isolated museums far removed from the centers of art activities. Up-to-date museums had largely adopted the "white cube" style hang promoted by influential exhibitions at the Museum of Modern Art in New York in the 1920s and 1930s. The main features of the cube are familiar: white walls, neutral lighting, paintings centered along the best line of sight on largely empty walls, and discrete labels next to each painting. Unlike salon-style hangs which emphasize the ensemble, white cube installations focus the viewer's attention on each work of art as a self-contained aesthetic object, implicitly suggesting that each is a masterwork.[1]

There were many causes for the gradual abandonment of the salon-style hang and the emergence of the white cube. At a fundamental level, the transition in exhibition design was made possible by and promoted the development of the idea of works of art as self-contained aesthetic objects. Unlike earlier models of art appreciation, the idea of the aesthetic assumes that art objects should be valued neither for their accuracy as representations nor for their ability to teach moral lessons but solely for the success with which they organize their elements into a coherent, and therefore beautiful, whole. As leading artists, dealers, art writers, collectors, and viewers began to redefine the value of the art object, they put a new emphasis on the importance of the subjective moment when individuals experience the internal consistencies of an artwork, and discovered that it was difficult to appreciate a work of visual art in that way when it was surrounded by a crush of dissimilar works all clamoring for notice. The popularization of the aesthetic thus promoted the realization that works of visual art should be set apart — both mentally, in the mind of the viewer, and physically, on the wall.

When Whistler arrived in Europe as a young art student in 1855, the commercial art markets in Paris and London were still in their infancy. In both cities the rapid growth of the middle classes had already spurred demand for art and enabled ambitious booksellers, print-dealers, and frame-makers to sell art as a sideline, but in both cities the commercial art market was still dominated by auction houses that sold whatever kinds of goods they could make money on. Neither city boasted more than a

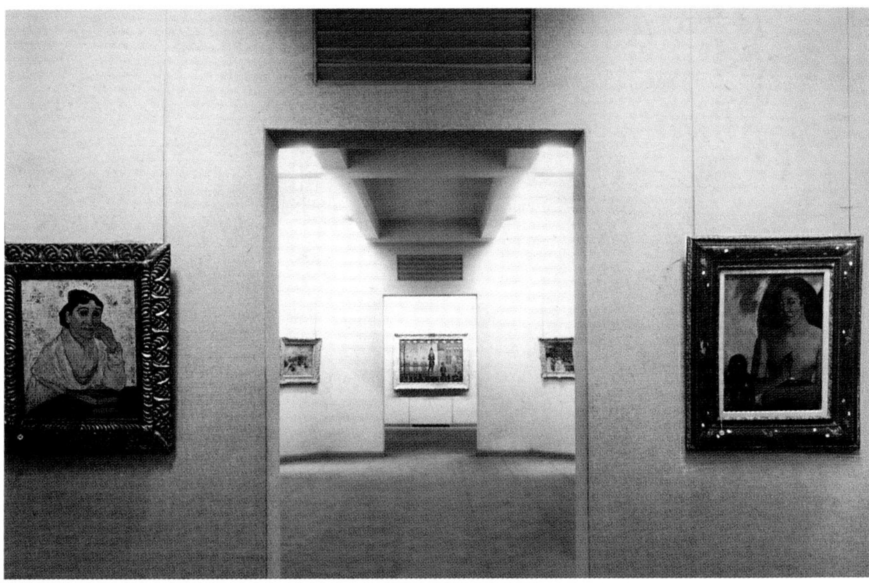

handful of full-time art dealers — and few of them were successful enough to maintain a gallery.[2] Although progressive artists chafed at the power of the governmentally supported arts organizations, the only reliable path to a successful career was by showing at the annual exhibitions at the Académie des Beaux-Arts in Paris and the Royal Academy in London. Exhibitions at both the Paris Salon and the Royal Academy were hung salon style, and although Whistler sent etchings and paintings to one or both of the academies annually from 1859 until 1865, by the early 1870s he was deeply frustrated by the aesthetic conservatism of the selecting jurors and his inability to control where or how his submissions were displayed.[3] Whistler continued to exhibit at the Paris Salon and Royal Academy intermittently from 1867 until 1872, when his now famous *Arrangement in Grey and Black: Portrait of the Painter's Mother* (Musée d'Orsay, Paris) was reluctantly accepted for exhibition at the Royal Academy only after the painter Sir William Boxall (1800–79) had threatened to resign from the Academy if it was rejected. Whistler never sent another submission to the Royal Academy, and he did not send any more work to the Paris Salon until 1882, by which time the tides of taste had begun to shift and he was confident that his submissions would be treated sympathetically.

The timing of Whistler's abandonment of the academies was no doubt influenced by his invention, in 1871, of the low-toned night landscapes that he titled "nocturnes," which are especially difficult to display and light effectively. As the influential American art critic James Jackson Jarves (1818–88) observed in a newspaper article published in 1879, a Whistler nocturne has to be displayed "precisely in the light and situation for which it was designed by the artist, [or] it seems to be as formless and void as the creative principle in a state of chaos. . . . In any unfavorable location it presents a meaningless jumble of brush strokes, guiltless of artistic form and relief."[4] In comparison to the academies, private art galleries offered Whistler much greater control over the selection, installation, and lighting of his work. Whistler painted his first nocturnes during the summer or, more probably, the autumn of 1871. That November he exhibited two of them in a group exhibition at the non-profit Dudley Gallery in London.[5] From that time on, Whistler relied on private galleries and international expositions as the primary venues for displaying and marketing his work.

After 1871, Whistler participated in numerous group exhibitions both at private galleries and at many of the most important of the late nineteenth-century expositions, but it was his one-man shows that had the greatest impact on the subsequent history of installation design.[6] Except for posthumous "memorial exhibitions," single-artist shows were still uncommon in mid-nineteenth-century Paris and London, although the Paris dealer Paul Durand-Ruel (1831–1922) gave Théodore Rousseau (1832–83) a one-man show in 1866, and both Courbet (1819–77) and Édouard Manet (1832–83) organized exhibitions of their own work in opposition to the official Paris salon in 1867. Whistler was in Paris in the spring of 1867, so he undoubtedly knew of the Courbet and Manet installations. Whether or not he saw either exhibition, Whistler's awareness of them probably contributed to his desire to commandeer a gallery for himself.

Whistler organized his first one-man exhibition in 1873, and a second, larger one in 1874. The 1873 exhibition opened in January at Durand-Ruel's gallery in Paris. Durand-Ruel was a politically conservative but aesthetically adventurous dealer, who handled a wide range of artists, including many of the independents who later became known as "impressionists." In 1874 he organized the famously disastrous auction of impressionist paintings. The following year he hosted the second impressionist exhibition.[7] Whistler's 1873 exhibition at Durand-Ruel's gallery was small, consisting of seven paintings and several drawings. The paintings included Whistler's stylistically innovative self-portrait, *Arrangement in Grey: Portrait of the Painter* (Detroit Institute of Arts), the Freer's *Variations in Flesh Colour and Green: The Balcony*, and two unidentified nocturnes.[8] Durand-Ruel does not seem to have issued a catalogue, and Whistler's work was probably installed in a secondary room. None of the surviving evidence suggests that Durand-Ruel allowed Whistler to change the décor of the space in which his work was hung, although one review suggests that Whistler was already challenging conventional exhibition practice by insisting that the gallery "put a label over each of [the paintings] showing the titles he had given them." All of Whistler's titles were musical—"arrangements," "variations," "harmonies," "nocturnes" —so the use of title labels would have implied his avant-garde belief that paintings were to be appreciated not as representations but as abstract combinations of color and line.[9]

Whistler's second single-artist show drew more attention. It opened at the Flemish Gallery in Pall Mall, London, on June 4, 1874, closing two months later at the end of July. Whistler mounted the exhibition himself, taking a year's lease on an empty space, and paying for all his renovations and improvements.[10] The exhibition included thirteen major paintings, thirty-six drawings, and fifty etchings, and introduced several of the innovations that would characterize Whistler's later installations. The walls were painted gray. The floor was covered with yellow mats. Whistler installed white blinds beneath the skylights in order to reduce glare. Couches and chairs were covered with a light maroon cloth. Flowers in blue pots were scattered about the room. The exhibition checklist was wrapped in coarse brown paper covers. Art works were spaced more generously than in a salon-style hang, although the installation was more crowded than Whistler's later one-man shows would be. Large paintings were hung high, probably at least five feet above the floor. Smaller works were hung below larger ones; in some cases large paintings were hung above medium-sized oil sketches that were placed above still smaller works. While the paintings and drawings established a strong vertical element, the etchings and drypoints were mounted above a wainscoting, forming a line at eye-level around the room. Paintings were displayed in gilded frames, many of which Whistler painted with a japonesque wave-pattern design. Prints were exhibited in plain wooden frames. As Robin Spencer was the first to explain, the installation created a "vertical/horizontal rhythm AB AB AB AB," encouraging the viewer to proceed around the room while alternately moving close to the wall in order to examine the prints and drawings, and then stepping back from the wall to look at the larger paintings that were hung high.[11]

The 1874 exhibition was an important step toward the more revolutionary and influential installations that Whistler organized in the 1880s, but it was a financial extravagance. Whistler may have sold one or two of the nocturnes that were included in the show, but he could not have sold many of the major paintings since most were borrowed from collectors and were therefore not available for sale. While Whistler's income from the exhibition must have been limited, his costs were high.

44. Fondamenta Dei Mori.

45. Bead Stringers.

46. Sunset; red and gold—The Gondolier.

47. Fishing Boats.

48. Salute—Sundown.

49. Sunset; red and gold—Salute.

50. Winter Evening.

51. Campo Sta. Martin—Winter Evening.

52. Courtyard.

53. The Brown Morning—Winter.

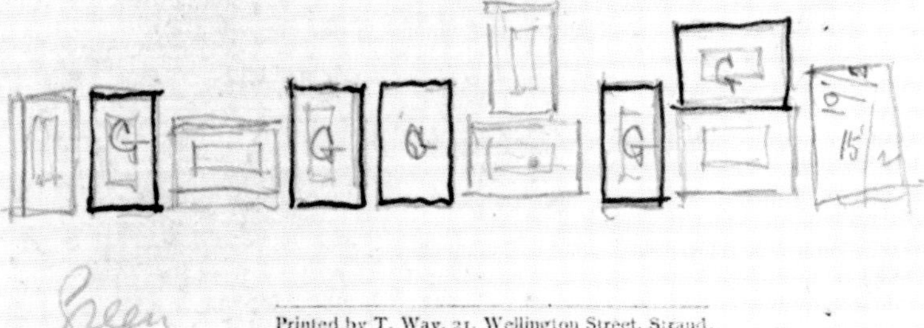

Printed by T. Way, 21, Wellington Street, Strand.

Figure 5.
Edward W. Godwin,
Annotations and sketch made in the exhibition catalogue, *Venice Pastels* (London: Fine Art Society, 1881).
Whistler Collection, Birnie Philip Bequest, Glasgow University Library.

Rent and repairs alone ran to at least 400 pounds sterling. By way of comparison, in 1874 the annual lease on Whistler's thirteen-room house and studio in Chelsea was only 80 pounds sterling.[12]

Whistler did not mount another single-artist exhibition until January 1881. The long delay can be explained in at least two complementary ways. In personal terms, Whistler's artistic interests changed and his financial situation worsened. Whistler had been able to risk the 1874 exhibition in part because he knew that he had the financial support of the Liverpool shipping magnate Frederick Leyland (1831–92), who was his most important patron. From the summer of 1876 until the spring of 1877, Whistler spent almost all of his time painting his glorious design for the dining room in Leyland's London townhouse. Creation of the Leyland dining room, which Whistler titled *Harmony in Blue and Gold: The Peacock Room*, was an artistic triumph, but led to a financially disastrous falling-out with Leyland (see figure 8). Yet despite the loss of Leyland's patronage, Whistler continued to spend money lavishly, building an architecturally innovative home and studio (the White House, which was begun in 1877 and completed in 1878), and pursuing a quixotic libel suit against the art critic John Ruskin (1819–1900) in 1878. Whistler won the Ruskin suit, but collected only a farthing in damages and by May 1879 he was forced to declare bankruptcy. Eager to escape London, he convinced the Fine Art Society to commission a series of twelve etchings of Venice, took his advance, and decamped for the Adriatic. Whistler did not return to London until late November 1880. During this period Whistler could not have afforded to mount a show of his own work if he had wanted to, but he also seems to have concluded that the responsibilities and financial risks of running his own gallery outweighed any potential rewards.

The long hiatus between Whistler's 1874 exhibition and his next single-artist show can also be explained in terms of ongoing changes in the organization of the London art market. One major reason why Whistler mounted the Pall Mall show himself was that at that time there were few substantial commercial art galleries in the city and none were willing to put his installation ideas into practice. That situation quickly changed, however, with the opening of the Fine Art Society in 1876, the Grosvenor Gallery in 1877, and the Dowdeswell and Dowdeswells Gallery in 1878. The rapid expansion of the commercial art market provided Whistler with several congenial alternatives to the Royal Academy, enabling him to market and publicize his work without having to mount his own shows.[13]

As the London art market changed, so did the nature of Whistler's work. The grand size of the exhibition spaces at the Paris Salon and the Royal Academy encouraged the production of paintings that were large enough to stand out in the visually crowded field of a salon-style hang, garner the attention of reviewers, and win the prizes that were the standard route to fame and success. Although Whistler rarely painted really big canvasses, most of the major works he produced between his 1859 move to London and his 1879 bankruptcy were large enough to command visual attention and — since art works were in part priced by size — grand enough to sell for several hundred pounds apiece. Whistler completed two medium-sized landscapes while in Venice, *Venice: Nocturne in Blue and Silver: The Lagoon, Venice* (1879/1880. Museum of Fine Arts, Boston) and *Nocturne: Blue and Gold — St Mark's, Venice* (1879/80. National Museum of Wales, Cardiff), but he spent most of his time there working on small etchings and pastels. Whistler exhibited the Venice pastels at the Fine Art Society in January 1881 and, discovering that they sold well, he apparently decided to lessen his dependence on extremely wealthy patrons such as Leyland by shifting the focus of his production to smaller and therefore more affordable works in a wide variety of media — prints, watercolors, pastels, and oils. From the Venice pastel exhibition in 1881 until his career retrospective at the Goupil Gallery in London in 1892, every one of Whistler's one-man shows was primarily or (more often) completely devoted to small works. Whistler continued to paint medium- and life-sized portraits during these years — some of friends or family that were never intended for sale, but most on commission — but after Venice he gave up painting larger landscapes almost entirely. Although now best known for his painted nocturnes, the two completed in Venice were the last large nocturnes in oil that Whistler ever painted.

As the format, scale, subject, and style of Whistler's work changed, so too did his strategies for marketing it. During the 1880s, Whistler sent large paintings — mainly recent portraits but also some figure paintings and landscapes from the 1860s or 1870s — to the international expositions, the Paris Salon, and group-shows at prestigious private galleries such as the Grosvenor where they would be reviewed by critics and seen by people of means who might commission portraits. Whistler sometimes sent smaller works to such venues, but after his return from Venice he most often showed small works in one-man shows at commercial galleries where he had great control over the viewing environment and could bundle small works into a visually striking, attention-catching whole.

Between December 1880 and February 1883, the Fine Art Society gave Whistler three one-man shows, each of which was devoted to Venetian materials. The December 1880 exhibition was small, consisting solely of the twelve Venice etchings that Whistler had selected to fulfill his commission. The show opened on December 1 in the small back room at the society. Whistler supervised the installation but did not design any special decoration. The exhibition received a good deal of attention from the press, but the prints sold slowly and the society considered the show to be a failure. Still, the exhibition effectively announced Whistler's return from Venice, and set the stage for the larger and more elaborate show of his Venice pastels that opened in the society's main room the following month.[14]

Although pastels had been a major medium for artistic expression in the eighteenth century, by the middle of the nineteenth century they had fallen from artistic favor and were widely thought of as a "feminine" medium that was best left to women artists and amateurs. Whistler had begun to use pastels in the early 1870s, but until his trip to Venice most of the pastels he had produced were working drawings that were not intended for exhibition or sale. Whistler probably had no intention of making pastels when he arrived in Venice in September 1879, but by late October a long-lasting cold front had swept through the city making it difficult for him to etch. Eager to continue working, he turned to pastels. Whistler apparently began to use pastels soon after the weather changed. By the following January, he was eager to let the head of the Fine Art Society know about the new drawings. In a letter, he bragged that the new pastels were "total[l]y new and of a brilliancy very different from the customary watercolor — and will sell — I don't see how they can help it," and suggested that the society exhibit them. Whistler completed approximately one hundred pastels before leaving Venice, most of which were drawn between the fall of 1879 and the spring of 1880.[15]

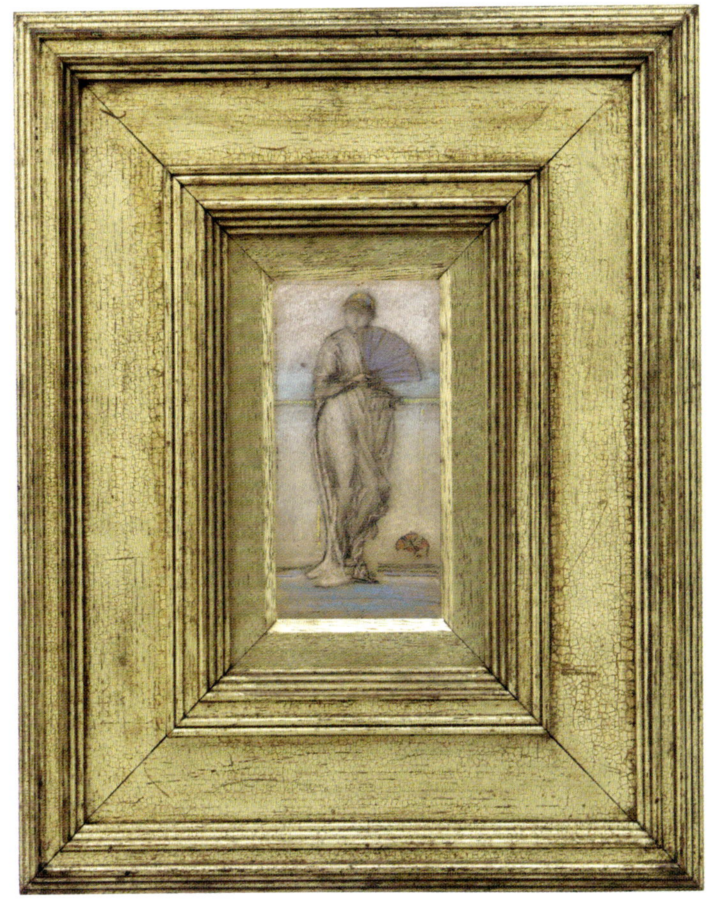

Venice Pastels opened at the Fine Art Society on January 29, 1881, and ran until the end of March. It included fifty-three of the best of the Venice pastels. The pastels varied somewhat in size, but most were small—averaging about 8 x 12 inches in size. Although the Society had agreed to mount an exhibition of Whistler's new pastels soon after Whistler suggested it, detailed planning did not start until after the artist returned to London in late November 1880. Not surprisingly, the design of the show seems to have been something of an improvisation, building on ideas that Whistler had developed in the 1870s, but not incorporating the full range of exhibition techniques and strategies that would be employed in his later installations. Unlike the 1874 Flemish Gallery installation, which had included etchings, drawings, and oil studies as well as large paintings, the 1881 exhibition was devoted solely to pastels, although the twelve Venice etchings were again hung in the back room. As he would also do in his 1883, 1884, and 1886 installation designs, Whistler divided the gallery walls into three sections. The main section was covered by a nine-foot high yellow-green cloth, topped by a green-gold crown molding. Beneath this field of yellow-green, a low skirting was painted yellow-gold. Above the crown molding, a narrow frieze was painted the same reddish brown as the ceiling.[16] The basic design, but not this specific color scheme, is suggested by Whistler's *Design for the Coloring of a Room* (see figure 7).

Most of the pastels were hung in a single row around the room, without much space between them, generally at eye-level, although some were double-hung for the sake of variety. The spacing is suggested by a drawing that Whistler's friend Edward W. Godwin (1833–66) hastily sketched on the last page of his copy of the exhibition catalogue (see figure 5). Working with the society and the framer F. H. Grau, Whistler adapted a frame that he had used for large paintings during the 1870s, creating a distinctive new frame consisting of a wide flat fillet surrounded by slim bands of reeding. Whistler was pleased with the frame, and continued to use subtly varied versions of it for small oils, watercolors, and pastels until the early 1890s.[17] The 1881 frames were all gilded, most in what one reviewer described as a "rich yellow gold," but twelve were greenish gold. In his review, Godwin explained that the green-gold frames were "dotted" about the room "with a view to decoration, and eminently successful in attaining it."[18] None of

Figure 6.
James McNeill Whistler,
Resting, ca. 1870–73.
Chalk and pastel on brown paper.
Period Dowdeswells' gallery-style
frame, 1880s, 4 5/16 in. wide molding.
Freer Gallery of Art.
Gift of Charles Lang Freer,
F1902.176.

the writers who reviewed the exhibition commented on the lighting, the floor coverings, the gallery furniture, or the dress of the guard, suggesting that Whistler limited his designing mainly to the frames, the coloring of the walls, and the placement of the pastels.

Whistler's third and final exhibition of his Venice materials at the Fine Art Society opened on February 17, 1883. It was the first of his shows to incorporate all his mature ideas about what an exhibition could and should be, and it set the pattern for all his subsequent installation designs, including the 1884 exhibition at the Dowdeswells' gallery. The 1883 exhibition consisted of fifty-one etchings — forty-five Venetian scenes and six more recent London subjects. The walls were again divided into three sections. The wood skirting around the base of the walls was painted bright yellow. Above the skirting, the walls were covered to the height of about ten feet by white felt, which was topped by a crown molding painted yellow.

The basic concept of the 1883 installation drew on the design vocabulary established by the 1881 installation, but the later plan was much more elaborate. The etchings were hung in specially designed white frames, which were ornamented with a double stripe of brown-red paint. They were probably hung singly at eye-level, although it seems likely that some would have been double hung. One reviewer commented on the unusual spacing, noting that the etchings were "hung far apart." Yellow matting covered the floor. The ceiling was hung with a yellow fabric, known as a velarium, which diffused and colored the light from the skylights in the ceiling. The fireplace surround was made of yellow tiles. The entrance to the gallery and the mantelpiece above the fireplace were adorned with yellow curtains. The couches were upholstered in yellow serge. Yellow chairs with white cane seats were scattered around the room, as were "little yellow pots," each containing "one little yellow flower." The guard was dressed in white and yellow — newspaper writers were soon describing him as the "poached-egg man." The major elements of the design, including the velarium, the wall hanging that draped over the mantelpiece, and the walls, were signed with Whistler's butterfly monogram in vivid yellow.[19]

Not only was the 1883 installation much more elaborate than the 1874 and 1881 shows, it was also much more ideologically self-conscious. Whistler's new awareness both of his ideas about art and of the ways in which he could use exhibitions to promote those ideas is most clearly suggested by his decision to name the installation, and by his innovative use of the catalogue. Before 1883, Whistler had not given any of his exhibition installations a title, although he had named the dining room that he designed for Frederick Leyland, calling it *Harmony in Blue and Gold: The Peacock Room* (1876–77). His earlier decision to name the Leyland dining room may have served as a precedent, influencing his decision to title the 1883 installation an *Arrangement in White & Yellow*. The installation title did not appear on the catalogue, but was announced on invitations to the private viewing, which were signed with Whistler's butterfly monogram — the wings being hand-painted in yellow for the occasion.[20]

In the case of both *Harmony in Blue and Gold* and *Arrangement in White & Yellow*, Whistler's decision to name his design emphasized the status of the ensemble as a complex artwork in itself, suggesting his belief that art objects should be valued not as representations *of* something, but simply as harmoniously organized arrangements of color and line. If uncomprehending reviewers would struggle to interpret Whistler's paintings as *pictures* of something, he would mock their ignorance by inviting them to an exhibition that was itself an art object. Let them try to interpret his *Arrangement in White & Yellow* as a picture of anything. As a design, it embodied its own objectivity. But even as the act of naming drew attention to the installation as being a nonrepresentational art object, it also suggested Whistler's distinctively modern recognition that no painting or art object is ever fully and finally complete in itself. The completeness, the beauty, of an art object lies less in the object itself than in the eye of the sympathetic beholder or, more precisely, in the momentary, subjective, congruence of beholder and object. Whistler's etchings, like the blue-and-white porcelains that filled Leyland's dining room, were simultaneously discrete art objects, finished and entire in themselves, and elements in the larger whole that was the "arrangement" in which they sounded their distinctive "notes."

Whistler introduced one other innovation at the 1883 exhibition. All three of Whistler's earlier one-man shows had had a catalogue. But those catalogues had been mere checklists, guides to the identification of the numbered paintings and prints hanging on the walls of the gallery. The 1883 catalogue was more ambitious. Titled *Etchings & Drypoints. Venice. Second Series*, but more pointedly subtitled *Mr. Whistler and His Critics*, it was an oddly conservative innovation, a full-throated statement of aesthetic principles in which Whistler spoke not in his own voice, but in snippets culled from unsympathetic reviews of the December 1880 and January 1881 exhibitions. In structure, it was a parody of the form that exhibition catalogues were only beginning to take, listing every object by number and providing a brief comment on each. But in this case the

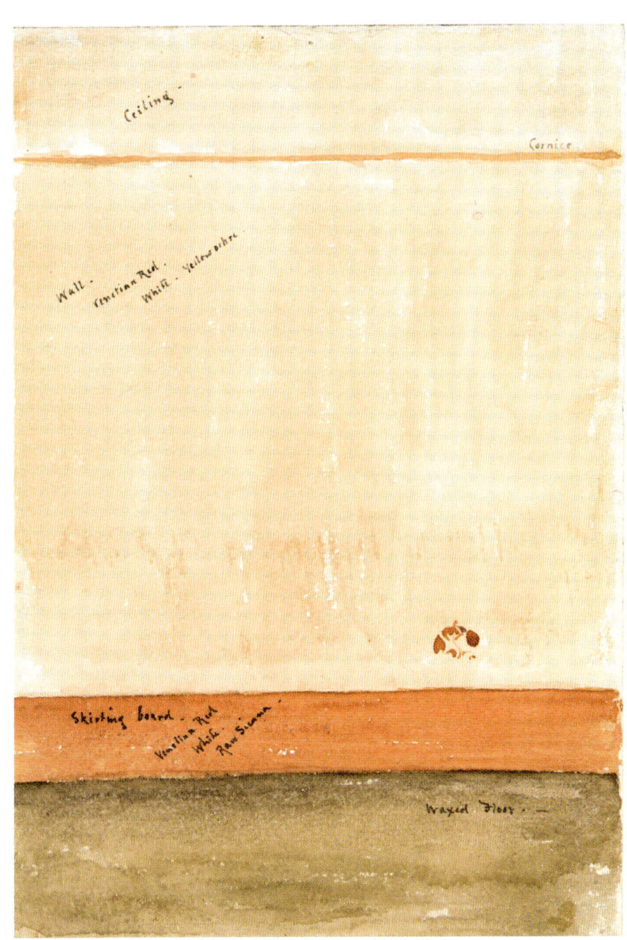

Figure 7.
James McNeill Whistler,
Design for the Coloring of a Room,
ca. 1883 or 1884.
Watercolor on wove paper.
Freer Gallery of Art,
Gift of Charles Lang Freer,
F1901.168.

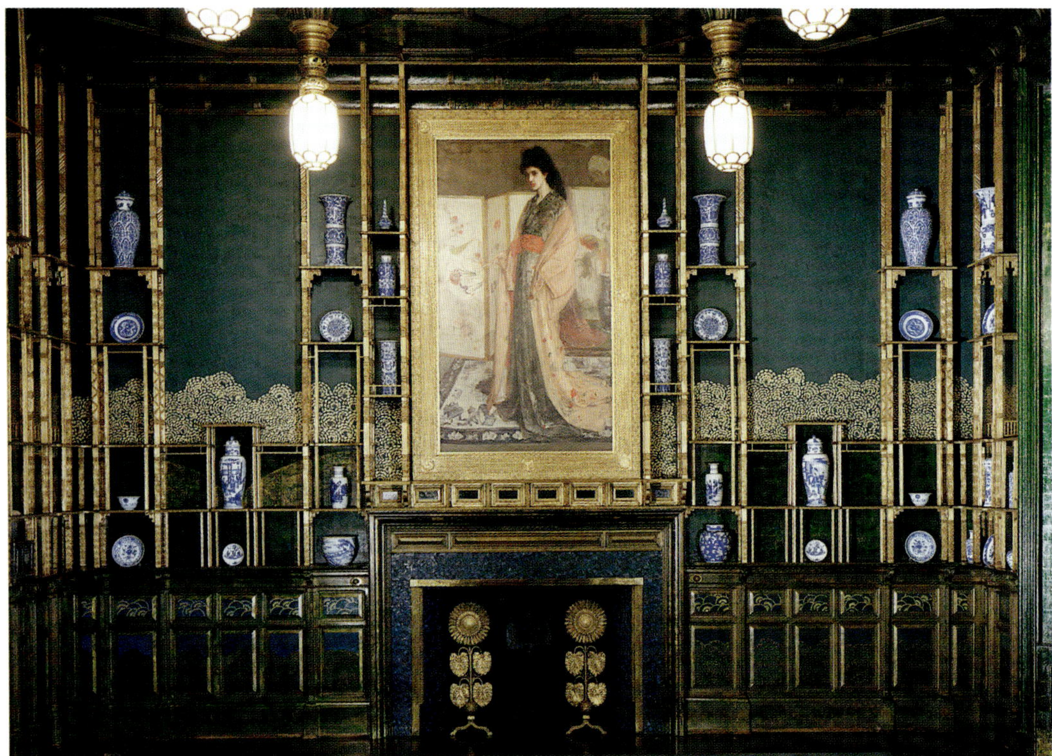

Figure 8.
James McNeill Whistler,
Harmony in Blue and Gold: The Peacock Room, 1876–77,
detail showing the north wall.
Oil paint and gold- and metal-leaf on leather, wood, and canvas.
Freer Gallery of Art.
Gift of Charles Lang Freer,
F1904.61.

comments were all barbed—quotations from negative reviews of Whistler's work, twisted so as to suggest the incomprehension and incompetence of the critic. Concerning Whistler's etching *Murano—Glass Furnace*, the reviewer for a journal with the reliable-sounding title *Knowledge* wrote, "Criticism is powerless here." So it is. As the epigraph to the catalogue put it, "Out of their own mouths shall ye judge them." Like the extravagant yellow and white interior that Whistler designed for the installation, the catalogue functioned on at least two levels. On the one hand, it attracted attention with its wit and playfulness. On the other, it indirectly advanced a serious defense of Whistler's challengingly innovative work. While Whistler was too arch to mount a structured argument, as a whole the critical snippets suggest what by 1883 were commonplace criticisms of Whistler's recent work: he was once a careful craftsman who presented finished pictures of recognizable subjects; now his work has become slap-dash, sketchy, unfit for public display as completed works of art. "His pictures do not claim to be accurate" (p. 13). "He is never literary"; that is, his pictures do not tell stories about the world (p. 10). Moreover, the etchings are "little" (p. 5). Whistler did not deign to answer these aesthetically conservative complaints directly, but instead held them up to ridicule, setting them against the sketchy coherences of his small etchings and the louder harmonies of his encompassing installation.[21]

Arrangement in Flesh Colour & Grey

Whistler's next single-artist show opened on May 17, 1884, in a gallery operated by Charles William Dowdeswell (1832–1915) and his sons Walter and Charles Dowdeswell. The Dowdeswells' gallery was located at 133 New Bond Street, London, two doors from the Grosvenor Gallery and a block up from the Fine Art Society. Unlike Whistler's shows at the Fine Art Society, which essentially stuck to one media, the 1884 Dowdeswell exhibition included watercolors and pastels as well as oil paintings. Whistler titled the exhibition "Notes" — "Harmonies" — "Nocturnes," a title he would reuse for a second one-man show at the Dowdeswells' gallery in 1886, and for an exhibition that opened at Hermann Wunderlich's gallery in New York City in 1889. The Wunderlich version of "Notes" — "Harmonies" — "Nocturnes," traveled to several other American cities after closing in New York, and was the first substantial showing of Whistler's paintings and drawings in the United States. As announced on the invitation to the private viewing, Whistler titled the 1884 Dowdeswell installation an *Arrangement in Flesh Colour & Grey*. The 1884 exhibition followed the basic design program established by the 1883 show at the Fine Art Society, but because of the shift from etchings to paintings and drawings, the impact of both the installation and the catalogue was even more overtly polemical. Indeed, the 1884 *Arrangement in Flesh Colour & Grey* was the most ideologically purposeful exhibition that Whistler ever mounted.[22]

Whistler's three exhibitions at the Fine Art Society had been limited to etchings and pastels. Critical reviewers sometimes noted the unusually small scale of these works, but scale generally remained a secondary issue because even aesthetically conservative reviewers were prepared to accept that etchings and even pastels could be comparatively small and still be artistically important. Since Whistler's choice of media in those exhibitions did not directly challenge contemporary norms of scale, unhappy reviewers tended to direct their complaints at what they took to be the incompleteness and sketchiness of the etchings and pastels. Most of the negative reviews of etchings and pastels that Whistler showed at the Fine Art Society emphasize their supposed lack of "finish." But even in the early 1880s shows, Whistler found opportunities to raise the lurking issue of scale. The most revealing of those occasions arose on December 8, 1880, when a writer for the London newspaper *The World* described the

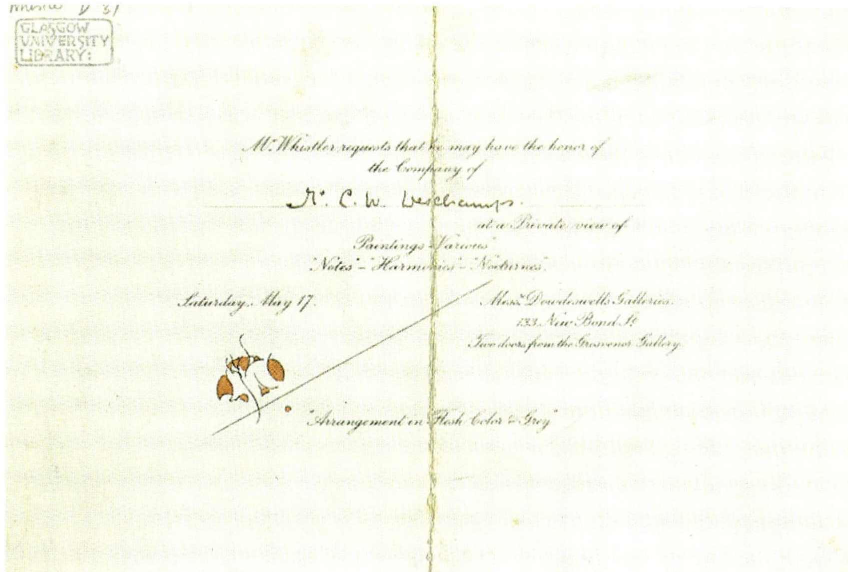

Mr. Whistler requests that he may have the honor of
the Company of
Mr. C. W. Deschamps.
at a Private view of
Paintings Various
"Notes" – "Harmonies" – "Nocturnes."
Saturday. May 17.
Mess. Dowdeswells Galleries.
133. New Bond St.
Two doors from the Grosvenor Gallery.
"Arrangement in Flesh Color & Grey"

Figure 9.
Invitation card, engraved with Whistler's butterfly monogram, colored pink, 1884. Whistler sent this invitation to the "private view" of his *Arrangement in Flesh Colour & Grey* to the London art dealer Charles W. Deschamps. Whistler Collection, Birnie Philip Bequest, Glasgow University Library.

first Fine Art Society exhibition as consisting of twelve etchings, "of unimportant dimensions, and of the slightest workmanship." Eager to go public with his rejection of the commonplace equation of size with importance, Whistler wrote a peremptory letter to the paper's proprietor and editor. Strategically ignoring the issue of finish, he magisterially announced: "an etching does not depend for its importance upon its size. 'I am not arguing with you — I am telling you.'" Eager to immortalize both the put-down and, more importantly, the point, he reprinted the exchange in his 1890 compendium of Whistlerian wit and wisdom, *The Gentle Art of Making Enemies*.[23]

The 1884 version of "Notes" — "Harmonies" — "Nocturnes" consisted of sixty-seven oils, watercolors, and pastels. The catalogue listed works by media, leaving oil paintings unmarked but identifying watercolors and pastels parenthetically. Newspaper reviews establish that some of the unmarked entries were watercolors, so an exact breakdown by media is impossible, but the exhibition was almost equally divided between oils and watercolors, with only a sprinkling of pastels.[24] Most of the works in the show were even smaller than the Venice pastels shown at the Fine Art Society in 1881. Based on the evidence of the paintings and drawings known to have been in the show, the average size was probably no more than 6 x 9 inches. Indeed, at least six of the oil paintings were even smaller: *The Pier; a grey note* (no. 1), *Note en rouge: L'Éventail (*probably in the exhibition, possibly no. 64), *Blue and gold — The Schooner* (no. 32), *Harmony in brown and gold — Old Chelsea Church* (no. 44), *Blue and grey — Unloading* (no. 56), and *Black and Emerald — Coal Mine* (no. 59) are all on wood panels that are approximately 3½ x 5¾ inches in size.[25]

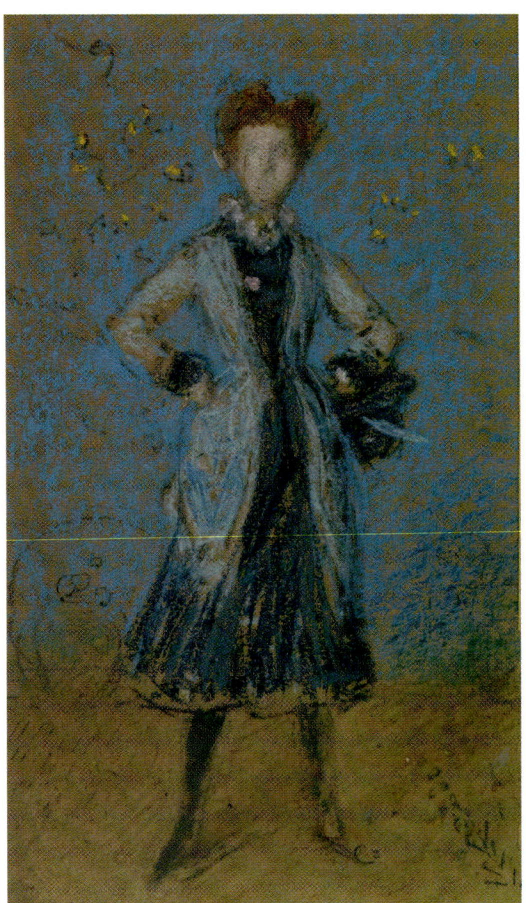

Figure 10.
James McNeill Whistler,
The Blue Girl,
ca. 1873–76.
Chalk and pastel on paper.
Freer Gallery of Art.
Gift of Charles Lang Freer,
F1905.126.

Figure 11.
James McNeill Whistler,
Scherzo in blue — The Blue Girl,
1882.
Oil on canvas, "life-size".
Presumed destroyed.
Dowdeswell 31.
Reproduced from Pennell, *Life of Whistler* (1911): 300.

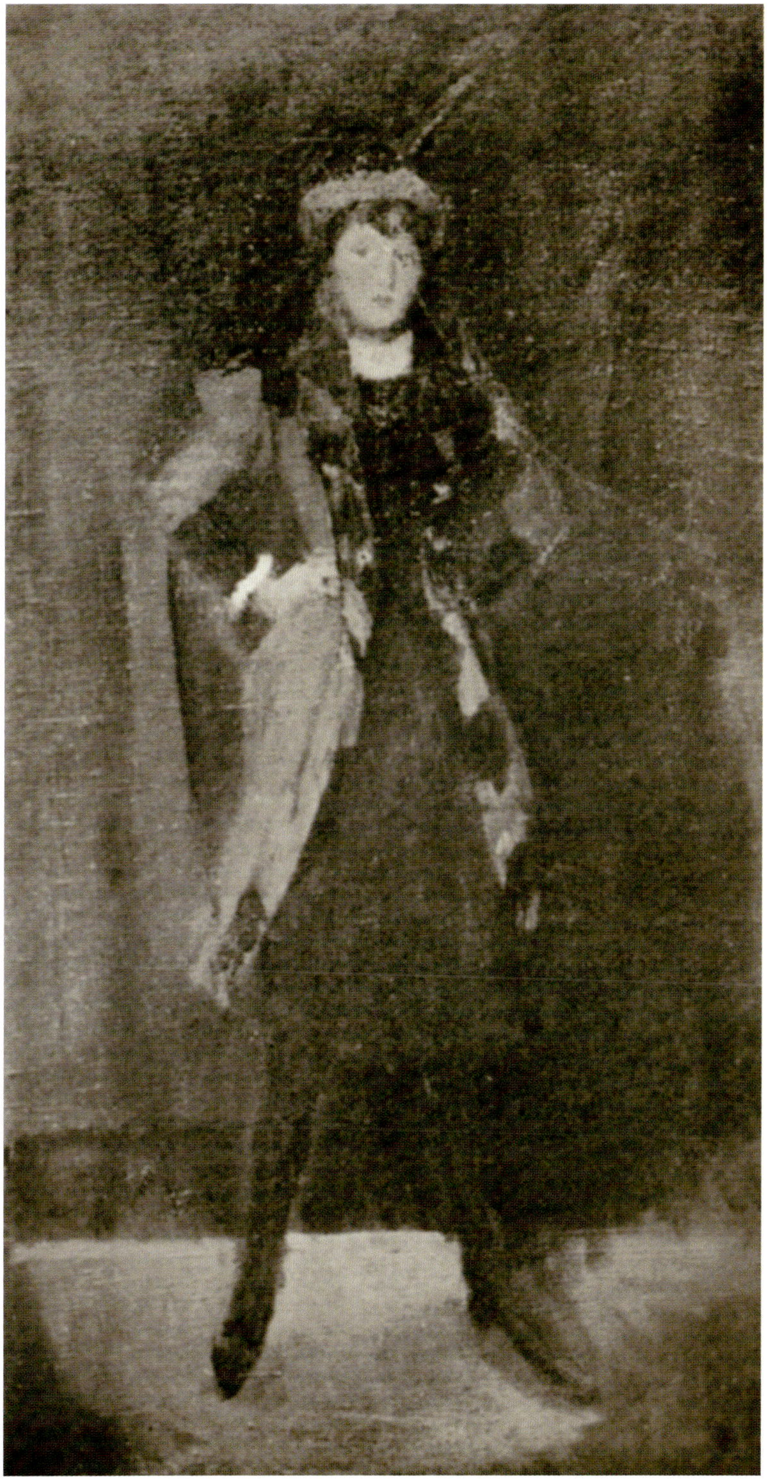

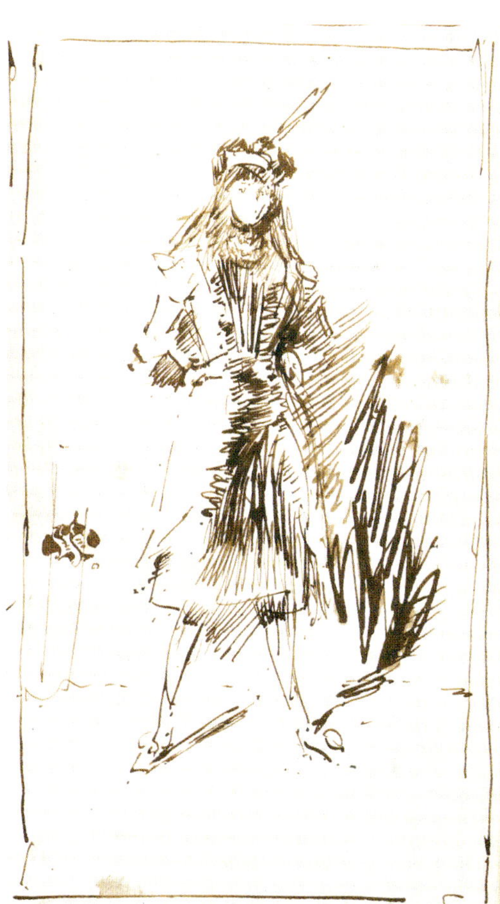

Figure 12.
James McNeill Whistler,
Study of Maud Waller for Scherzo in blue — The Blue Girl,
1881 or 1882.
Pen and ink on paper.
Dr. and Mrs. John E. Larkin, Jr.

Many of the newspaper and magazine reviews commented on the wide variety of subjects represented in the show. As the writer for the *Standard* put it:

> Mr. Whistler's work this year is unusually varied in its apparent themes. All sorts of objects are pressed into the service of his brush — Southend pier, the Cornish coast, a young woman dressed in a parasol and a red headgear, a *grisette* reading a French novel, a fog in Piccadilly, a shop in Chelsea.[26]

Although none of the contemporary accounts explicitly say so, the reviews suggest that works were to some extent grouped together by subject, style, medium — charming watercolors of young women in one section, vigorous oil paintings of the Cornish coast in another. Passing comments in the original reviews also suggest that the installation of the works generally followed the order in the catalogue. For example, after disparagingly asking whether the palette knife had not "played a heavy part" in *Green and opal — The Village*, no. 7, the reviewer for the *Kensington News* continued, "how tantalizing it is to pass on to the next work (9), *Nocturne in grey and gold — Piccadilly*." Similarly, after completing his discussion of *Petit Déjeuner; note in opal*, no. 13, the reviewer for *Artist and Journal of Home Culture* continued, "along side it hangs another water colour, striking as strong a note as 'Petit Déjeuner' strikes a sweet one," and proceeded to describe *Black and red*, no. 15.[27]

The only large painting in the exhibition was a life-size portrait of a young girl titled *Scherzo in blue — The Blue Girl* (no. 31) (see figure 11). The concept underlying the inclusion of the one large work was most clearly explained by Whistler's friend E. W. Godwin, who began his review of the show by noting that "the collection consists of sixty-six small paintings, drawings, pastels — stars of different magnitudes, grouped around a blue moon — a life-size, full-length portrait called by the artist 'Scherzo in blue — The Blue Girl.'"[28] That Godwin's metaphor expressed the artist-designer's own conception of the installation seems to be confirmed by a letter Whistler wrote the Dowdeswells shortly before the exhibition opened, requesting they send their van to his studio in order to pick up "the Blue Girl among the little ones."[29] The exhibition also included at least one and probably two medium-sized paintings: *Green and opal — The Village* (no. 7) and *Nocturne; black and gold — No. 6, Rag Shop, Chelsea* (no. 58).[30] The comparatively low and high catalogue numbers assigned to these paintings suggest that they were placed on the left and right walls, near the entrance to the room, roughly opposite each other. In his memoirs, Menpes recalled that the *Scherzo in blue* had "occupied a central position on one of the walls."[31] The catalogue number given to *Scherzo in blue*, no. 31 of 67, suggests that it was placed approximately midway around the room, so it was probably given pride of place as the focal point of the wall facing the entrance to the gallery.

Except for *Rag Shop*, which was painted about 1878, and one Venetian pastel (no. 50), it seems that every work in the show was completed after Whistler's return from Venice. Indeed, most of the works in the exhibition, probably more than fifty, were completed after *Arrangement in White & Yellow* closed, at the end of March 1883. Whistler had little choice but to include so many new works in the 1884 exhibition. He had completed a great deal of work during his fourteen months in Venice, but after three exhibitions at the Fine Art Society he had shown most of that work, including every one of the major Venice etchings, pastels, and oils except the two medium-sized nocturnes in oil. Moreover, he had spent much of 1881–82 printing the etchings and working on a few large portraits, so that while he had a few recent large paintings to send to the Grosvenor Gallery and other group venues, he did not have enough work for another one-man exhibition.[32]

Whistler probably began working toward a new single-artist show shortly after *Arrangement in White & Yellow* closed. He must have completed a significant body of new work by late October 1883, when he contacted the Fine Art Society to suggest a spring show. The Fine Art Society rebuffed Whistler's overture, but Whistler reached an understanding with the Dowdeswells by January 1884, when he began to mention an upcoming exhibition in his letters.[33]

Whistler's surviving correspondence provides some evidence as to the order in which he completed works for the show. The largest group of paintings or drawings in the exhibition was a series of seascapes done in the fishing village of St. Ives, on the Cornwall coast. St. Ives was readily accessible from London by train, and was in the early stages of becoming an important tourist destination. Whistler departed from London in late December 1883, arriving in St. Ives by December 27. Perhaps trying to recapture something of the camaraderie of the heady days in Venice, he invited his students Mortimer Menpes (1860–1938) and Walter Sickert (1860–1942) to accompany him. Whistler had taken several working trips to villages on the English coast after his return from Venice, all of which seem to have been quite brief. His correspondence makes it clear that he originally intended to stay in St. Ives for no more than a week or two, but once there he repeatedly put off his return to London, and ended up staying until the end of January. Whistler's St. Ives paintings generally ignore any signs of the nascent tourist industry, instead focusing on the narrow streets or shops in the village, fishermen tending to their boats or nets, boats in the harbor or silhouetted against the sea, and—especially—the sea itself.[34]

During the five or so weeks he spent in St. Ives, Whistler completed a major body of work, including more than twenty oil paintings and at least seven watercolors. Most of the paintings and watercolors are unusually small even for Whistler, and letters he wrote from St. Ives show both his excitement with his new work and a preoccupation with scale. The letters focus on the oils and repeatedly emphasize their small size, describing them as "little beauties," "little things," and "little games." The description of the oil paintings as "little games" seems especially revealing because it suggests that Whistler was already imagining the ruckus he expected them to stir up when they were displayed at the Dowdeswells' gallery. In a letter dated January 15, 1884, to an important patron, for example, he bragged that he had "another game 'Amazing'! coming off shortly that will be as successful as the Pastels!—and bring lots of money as that did—this time, oil paintings—little beauties—you will be delighted to know." And in a more detailed letter to the American sculptor Waldo Story (1854–1915), he explained that he had been doing "delightful things—and have a wonderful game to play soon," and concluded, "Now when my exhibition comes off I [will] have plenty of amazing little beauties—new game!—that will bring golden ducats—like the pastels" [emphasis in the original]. At least ten of the oil paintings and one of the watercolors exhibited at the Dowdeswells' were done in St. Ives, including at least three of the tiny oils (3½ x 5¾ inches) and the smallest watercolor that is definitely known to have been in the show.[35]

In his letters from St. Ives Whistler does not discuss new watercolors, so it seems likely that his decision to include watercolors in his spring 1884 show was made after his return to London. The turn to watercolors was another new departure for Whistler, who rarely used the medium before 1881, and had never previously exhibited a substantial group of them. Whistler's adoption of watercolors, like his use of pastels while in Venice, reflects his inveterate curiosity as an artist, but the choice also expresses the polemical intentions informing all his actions in the months leading up to the opening of the 1884 exhibition. Unlike pastels, which British critics and collectors generally associated with work by amateurs, women, or distressingly "advanced" French artists, the use of watercolor had a long history in England, and was closely identified with the most important English school of landscape art, the Pre-Raphaelites, and Joseph Mallord William Turner (1775–1851). Like his small oils, the watercolors Whistler showed at the Dowdeswells' gallery in 1884 were unusually small and sketchy, provocations to conventional expectations about the size and degree of finish appropriate for an exhibition watercolor.[36]

Arrangement in Flesh Colour & Grey included several watercolor seascapes (at least one of which had been done in St. Ives, no. 55), three watercolors of London scenes, and four important Amsterdam nocturnes in watercolor. But the largest group of watercolors in the show, and the group that attracted the most critical attention, was a series of drawings of young female models. The watercolors of studio models are closely connected to several small oils that also show female models in the studio, including another one of the 3½ x 5¾ inch paintings, *Note en rouge: L'Éventail* (probably in the exhibition, possibly no. 64). Since Whistler's earliest securely datable oils of this size were all painted in St Ives, it seems likely to assume that *Note en rouge: L'Éventail* and all or almost all of the related oils and watercolors were painted after his return to London. This conclusion is also suggested by the fact that the model in *Note en rouge: L'Éventail* seems to be Milly Finch, who appears in several of the studio watercolors and is mentioned in two of Whistler's May 1884 letters. As Margaret MacDonald was the first to point out, Whistler seems to have begun to draw Miss Finch at a time when his long-time model and mistress, Maud Franklin, was ill, suggesting that all or most of the Finch subjects date from the same period as a series of watercolors showing Maud in bed or convalescent. In addition to *Note en rouge: L'Éventail*, works that fit into this grouping include *Note in Pink and Purple: The Studio* (probably no. 10), *Convalescent* (probably no. 13), *Pink note — The Novelette* (no. 16), *Note in red — The Siesta* (no. 17), *Harmony in violet and amber* (no. 19), *Note in pink and purple* (probably no. 27), and *A Note in Green* (probably no. 43).[37]

As winter turned to spring, Whistler moved outside to paint or draw views of his Chelsea neighborhood. In early May, he wrote Menpes, who was helping to frame works for the approaching show, to suggest that if he could get to Chelsea early in the morning, he should "pass by the [Thames] Embankment, if quite early, I shall be at the 'shop' game — & then on to the studio" [emphasis in the original]. At about the same time he wrote Charles William Dowdeswell with even greater urgency, warning Dowdeswell not to look for him in the studio, if he came by the next day, as

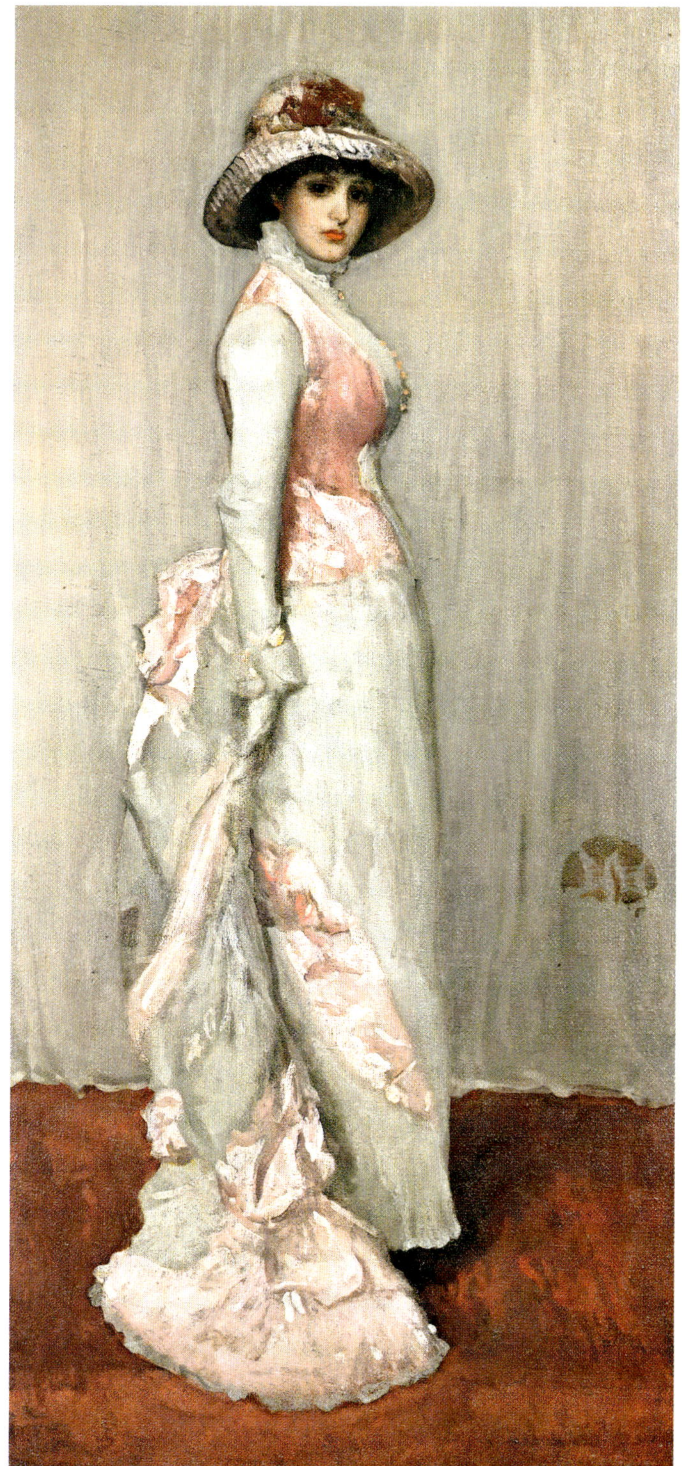

"I shall be on the Embankment painting away for dear life." These letters suggest that several of the eight Chelsea subjects in the exhibition, including *Harmony in brown and gold—Old Chelsea Church* (no. 44, another of the tiny oils), date from the spring of 1884.[38]

Whistler's *Arrangement in Flesh Colour & Grey* opened at the Dowdeswells' gallery on Saturday, May 17, 1884. The exhibition was installed in what a writer for the newspaper *Queen* described as "the somewhat circumscribed space" at the back of the gallery. The walls of the gallery were covered with a textured cloth, the color of which was variously described as "pink," "salmon," and "a delicate rose-tint." The baseboard below the cloth was painted a light gray; the wood molding above it was painted a blacker gray.[39] The color harmonies were probably similar to those found in several contemporary paintings, including the Freer's *Arrangement in Grey: Portrait of Master Stephen Manuel* (about 1885) and *Harmony in Pink and Grey: Portrait of Lady Meux* (1881–82). The upper part of the wall and the ceiling was probably painted a grayish white. Instead of using a velarium to control the natural lighting, the skylights were fitted with blinds. Early reviews report that the floor was covered with a "greenish yellow" straw matting, but it seems that this was quickly replaced with a gray carpet. The room was decorated with "magnificent azaleas in vases." Chairs were "arrangements in white and grey." The fireplace was decorated with a pale gray or "dove colour" drape, "edged with flesh-coloured cord." The corner of this drape was decorated with Whistler's monogram, "a Japanese butterfly of flesh-coloured velvet and a darker shade of grey ... appliqué in the new style of needlework." In front of the fireplace stood "a large crater of flesh-coloured earthenware containing a large plant of marguerite daisies."[40] The attendant was

Figure 13.
James McNeill Whistler,
Harmony in Pink and Grey: Portrait of Lady Meux,
1881–82.
Frick Collection,
Copyright of the Frick Collection,
New York.

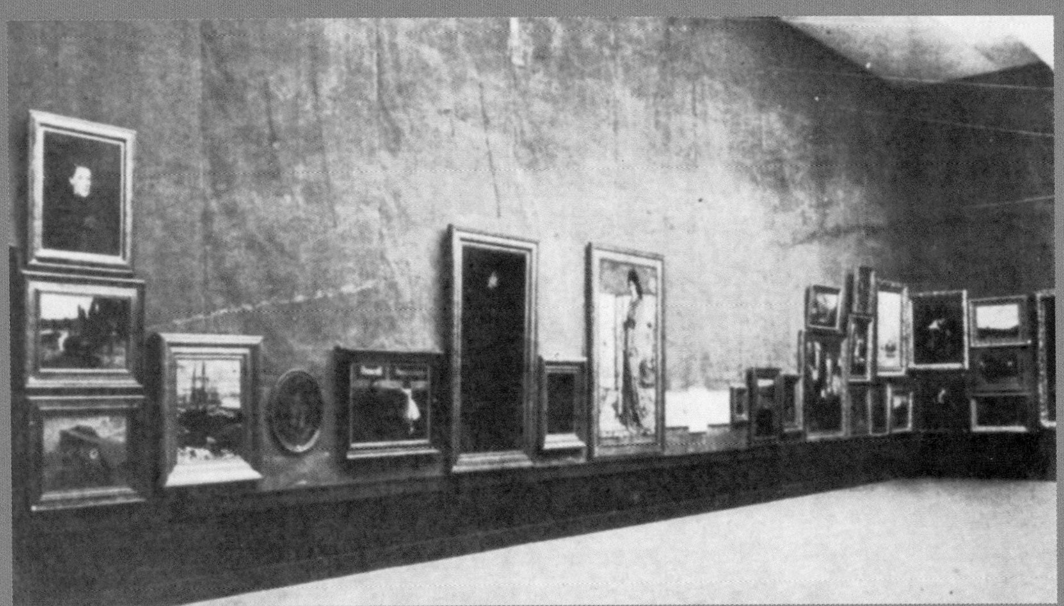

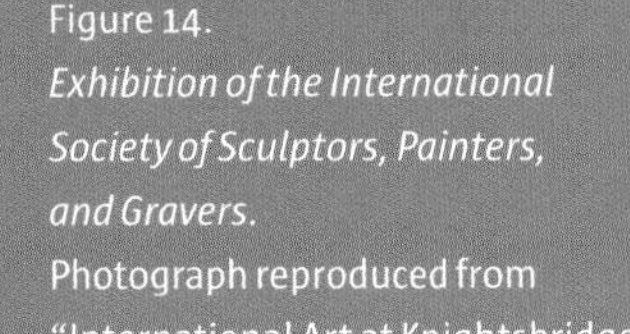

Figure 14.
Exhibition of the International Society of Sculptors, Painters, and Gravers.
Photograph reproduced from "International Art at Knightsbridge," *Art Journal* (August 1898), 249.

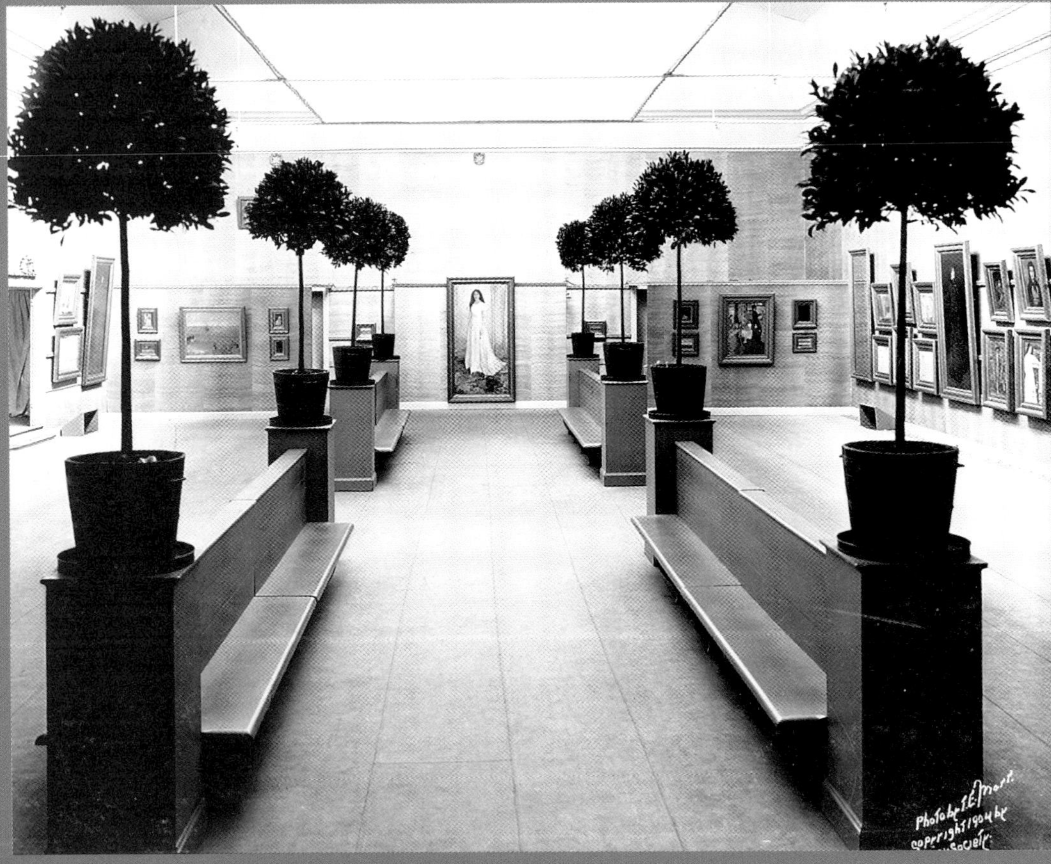

Figure 15.
South wall, *Whistler Memorial Exhibition* (1904)
Copley Society, Boston.
Photograph, courtesy of the Freer Gallery of Art Archives.

dressed "in a grey coat with flesh-coloured collar and cuffs, grey trousers, grey stockings, and fashionably cut patent leather pumps." Whistler completed the design by signing the installation with a painted butterfly high up on one of the walls.[41]

The opening on May 17, 1884, known as the "private view," was limited to invited guests and designed to attract the attention of reporters eager to document the doings of the rich and famous. The private view was much like modern gallery openings, except that it was held during the afternoon so that gaslight would not throw off the subtleties of Whistler's harmonies.[42] Guests included many painters, actors, actresses, writers, critics, and the kind of wealthy Londoners that the reviewer for *Queen* described simply as "fashionable people." The Duke of Somerset was there — "with a most aesthetic neckerchief," and Lord Justice Fry, as were Vice-Chancellor Bacon, the actress Mrs. Bernard Beere, the journalist Willie Wilde, and Whistler's good friend Oscar Wilde, accompanied by his fiancé Miss Constance Lloyd (the couple married twelve days later).[43] *Queen*, which was mainly interested in the clothes, noted that:"in the ladies' dress, the fashionable *coquelicot* was predominant, the costumes of this colour, with short shoulder capes trimmed with dark feather trimming, were generally worn. The head gear, to correspond, was either in the form of a large hat of the same colour or a small bonnet, very much cut up to show a large coil of hair, now much the mode. Grey dresses with silver trimmings, flesh-coloured lace or darker shade of feather trimming, were also to be seen — the latter trimming, however, is rather *passé* and common. Green is another of the fashionable colours represented. This colour adapts itself well to hats and bonnets trimmed with the beautiful iridescent lophophore feathers."[44]

The fact that so many fashionable women wore *coquelicot*, poppy red, was probably intentional. Whistler often asked his lady friends to dress in colors that would harmonize with his designs, and one of the most vibrant "notes" that echoed through the installation was that rung by the bright poppy reds which dominate several of the figure paintings, including *Note in red — The Siesta* (no. 17), *Red and pink — La Petite Mephisto* (no. 51), and *Note en rouge: L'Éventail* (possibly no. 64). Men generally wore tight trousers, high collars, George IV hats, and carried canes. Whistler worked the floor. The *Topical Times* described him as gliding "through the crowd like a miniature Mephistopheles," whispering "artistic diabolisms in the prettiest ears in London."[45]

There are no known drawings or photographs of the 1884 installation, although something of its design vocabulary is suggested by a photograph of the 1904 Whistler memorial exhibition at the Copley Society in Boston. As a newspaper review of this exhibition accurately noted, the Copley Society show was organized by longtime friends of Whistler's who designed it "in accordance with a plan of decoration which it is believed Mr. Whistler would have approved of." Light was diffused, the walls decorated "with a gray color scheme of generally Japanese effect," the paintings hung symmetrically along the line, in a room decorated with benches and potted plants.[46] An even more authoritative glimpse of a Whistler installation is provided by a photograph of the May 1898 exhibition of the International Society of Sculptors, Painters, and Gravers. Whistler had been elected president of the society in February 1898, and supervised the installation of the new association's first exhibition. It is therefore not surprising that the only surviving photograph of the installation focuses on Whistler's own work. The photograph appears as part of a long review in the *Art Journal*, which makes it clear that fifteen years after the Fine Art Society and Dowdeswells' gallery exhibitions, many of Whistler's design innovations were still unusual enough to merit comment. The reviewer thus explained that the paintings were hung in, " large square rooms from whence the light of glaring day is subdued by muslin blinds and white velaria, so that the tone of light is already refined before it reaches the pictures, and thus every work is made to look its very best. Each picture is hung separately and only occasionally do two frames touch, nothing is hung too high nor too near a fighting neighbor, all the modern theories of the exhibition of pictures are carried out, and in our judgment the result is both restful and stimulating: restful because the spectator is not troubled with more than one work to examine at a time, and stimulating because the variety of method of work is accentuated without the pictures, so to say, 'swearing' at one another."[47]

At the Dowdeswells' gallery in 1884, Whistler's argument against the equation of size with importance was visually suggested by the small scale of the drawings and most of the oil paintings, and verbally emphasized by the overtly polemical aphorisms with which he prefaced the catalogue (see figure 1). The visual argument made by the size of the paintings and drawings was underscored by Whistler's decision to use the oak frame developed for the 1881 exhibition of his Venice pastels to house every work in *Arrangement in Flesh Colour & Grey*. Whistler used the frames much as he had in 1881, relying on the standardization of their design to establish a consistent visual element within his installation, while varying the color of the gilding to create visual interest and to complement the color harmonies of particular paintings and drawings (see figure 16).[48] But Whistler's use of a standardized frame picked up a new polemical significance because he used the same width molding to house works in different media, implicitly challenging the conventional assumption that oil paintings were more important than watercolors or pastels. To draw attention to this implied meaning, Whistler widened his frames. At the Fine Art Society in 1881, Whistler had placed the Venice pastels in frames with a 4½ inch-wide molding. At the Dowdeswells' gallery in 1884, he put the tiny 3½ x 5¾ inch oil paintings in frames with a molding width of 4⅜ inches, but seems to have housed almost all the other paintings and watercolors in unusually wide frames with a molding width of 5⁹⁄₁₆ inches (see figures 16 and 17).[49] Though subtle, the change was noticed. In his memoirs, Menpes recalled that visitors to *Arrangement in Flesh Colour & Grey* found the frames "fantastic," and the reviewer for the *Globe* complained that the frames were "massive."[50] By widening the molding and using identical frames to house both oil paintings and works on paper, Whistler visually suggested that works of art should be valued neither by media nor size, but solely by the completeness with which they organize color and line into a harmonious and therefore beautiful whole.[51]

Aesthetic beliefs implied by the style of Whistler's art and the design of his installation were more explicitly developed in the "L'Envoie" with which he prefaced the 1884 catalogue. Unlike the 1883 catalogue, which had implied but did not develop an aesthetic argument, the "L'Envoie" directly expressed deeply held beliefs about finish, scale, and beauty that Whistler had first publicly discussed in his testimony at the Ruskin libel trial in 1878, and would further develop in the "Ten O'Clock" lecture he wrote in early 1885.

As many of the original reviewers rushed to point out, the title "L'Envoie" seems to be a mistake. In the words of the reviewer for the *Globe*:

"Determined to be original, Mr. Whistler has furnished the catalogue with a few sentences which he calls *L'Envoie*, a word that does not exist; and further to show his independence he has placed them at the beginning. *L'Envoi* in ballad poetry, the only form of literature with which the word is rightly associated, is always an addendum."[52] But if Whistler had made a mistake with his French, it was a mistake he refused to correct in the catalogue to the 1889 "Notes" — "Harmonies" — "Nocturnes" in New York, and it is more attractive to suppose that he was risking a Mallarméan play on words. For in this prefatory postscript Whistler is struggling, not altogether successfully perhaps, to establish the terms by which his work should be appreciated by setting the terms in which the work of more representational and subject-oriented artists should be criticized. Thus the "L'Envoie" does indeed serve as an addendum, announcing the anticipated death of representational and narrative-driven visual art while at the same time heralding the birth of a new visual art that would be solely concerned with the intrinsic beauty of harmoniously arranged colors and forms.

Whistler's "L'Envoie" is made up of seven aphorisms. Numbers 1, 2, 5, and 6, are essentially retrospective, rehearsing an already familiar progressive critique of academic theories of finish. "To say of a picture, as is often said in its praise, that it shows great and earnest labour, is to say that it is incomplete and unfit for view." Uncomprehending and unsympathetic reviewers took this as a defense of the slapdash, and quoted it as an unconvincing justification for Whistler's sketchy style of painting. But Whistler's point had less to do with style than with the definition of what a painting should be. If one accepts his aesthetic assumption that a work of visual art should be valued not for its accuracy as a representation or for what it reveals about the world, but simply for the effectiveness with which it combines color and line into a harmonious whole, then of course the amount of work that goes into its creation is irrelevant to the evaluation of its quality — as is its size. Indeed, if one's goal is the moment of disinterested aesthetic appreciation, then any concern with the life of the artist, or the meaning of the work of art, or its accuracy, or its size, is irrelevant. The other three aphorisms (numbers 3, 4, and 7), all attempt to clarify the point that what seems to be a critique of academic theories of proper finish is in fact indistinguishable from an avant-garde defense of 'Art for Art's Sake': "Industry in Art is a necessity, — not a virtue, — and any evidence of the same, in the production, is a blemish, not a quality; — a proof, not of achievement, but of absolutely insufficient work, for work alone will efface the footsteps of work." It is not that Whistler was opposed to artistic labor, but rather that he believed that the artist's sole goal should be to create beauty, and that in order to facilitate the viewer's experience of beauty the artist should seek to erase all distractions that might encourage viewers to think of the artist, or of themselves as centers of perception, or of the art object as an object of perception, so that they could momentarily lose themselves in an experience of beauty.

The aphorism which makes this point most successfully is the seventh: "The masterpiece should appear as the flower to the painter, — perfect in its bud as in its bloom, — with no reason to explain its presence, — no mission to fulfil, — a joy to the artist, — a delusion to the philanthropist, a puzzle to the botanist, an accident of sentiment and alliteration to the literary man." As an effort at self-explanation, Whistler was probably trying too hard to be clear. His meaning might have been less confusing if he had stopped with the simile about the bud and the flower. Whistler was not suggesting that there was only one "right" way to perceive a rosebud. Like any other object of experience, a rosebud can be objectified in many different ways. Rather, Whistler wanted to narrow the definition of art by insisting that visual artists should never be concerned with meaning, but solely with beauty. And if the value of art lies solely in the disinterested experience of beauty, then it makes no sense to suggest that a rosebud is any less perfect or beautiful than the flower it may become. A flower in bud is different than one in bloom, but the two are equally beautiful—and equally "finished." Or as Whistler's fourth aphorism put it, "The work of the master reeks not of the sweat of the brow,—suggests no effort,—and is finished from its beginning." Many of the newspaper reviewers mocked this aphorism as an unconvincing self-justification by an artist who was too lazy to bring his works to the expected degree of completeness. But Whistler was not defending his own practice, he was trying to evoke the ideal moment of aesthetic appreciation when a person is so moved by the internal harmonies of a man-made or a natural object that they momentarily forget themselves in the intensity of their experience of beauty. Like any good aesthete, Whistler believed that in such hoped-for moments of aesthetic pleasure all thoughts of why or wherefore, all questions about the maker of the object of beauty or of its purpose, would be (for the moment) forgotten.

Whistler did not doubt that beauty is intrinsic to particular objects. But neither did he doubt that beauty is a creation of the beholder. More precisely, Whistler believed that the completeness of a beautiful painting or drawing inhered in the object, and in the perceiver, and in the enlivening relationship between the two. Which brings us back to that odd terminal 'e' on "L'Envoie." If beauty can be defined both as a characteristic of certain kinds of man-made or natural objects and as a certain kind of experience of those objects, then objects that we think of as beautiful are simultaneously complete in themselves and brought to completion by their appreciators. They are thus always in transit, complete in the bud but always already becoming something else. Or as the French say, "en voie de," in process of. . . .

L'Envoi

Whistler aspired to create artworks that resisted interpretation so as to provoke merely aesthetic appreciation. As his use of musical terms in his titles was meant to suggest, he did not want his paintings to be read as representations of something else. Rather, he wanted them to be experienced as nonreferential arrangements of color and line. This way of appreciating artworks is not unusual in the early twenty-first century, but was still rare in late nineteenth-century London and Paris. Like all aesthetic pioneers, Whistler had to help uncomprehending reviewers and art lovers learn the mental skills they needed to acquire in order to appreciate his work. The installations that Whistler created for his one-man exhibitions were unusually effective teaching tools because it was in them that he most fully freed himself from the demands of representation. As a painter, Whistler never gave up his need for a subject. But as a designer he did. Unlike his paintings, drawings, and prints—unlike even the *Peacock Room*—Whistler's exhibition installations slipped the chains of representation and became mute non-referential objects of aesthetic appreciation.

Figure 16.
Frame for *Nocturne in grey and gold — Piccadilly,* 5⁹⁄₁₆ in. wide molding, with old gilding.
Manufactured for the Dowdeswells' gallery in 1884.
National Gallery of Ireland, Dublin.
Dowdeswell 9

Figure 17.
Reverse of frame for *Grey and silver — Pier, Southend,* 5⁹⁄₁₆ in. wide molding.
Manufactured for the Dowdeswells' gallery in 1884.
Freer Gallery of Art.
Gift of Charles Lang Freer, F1902.169.
Dowdeswell 62

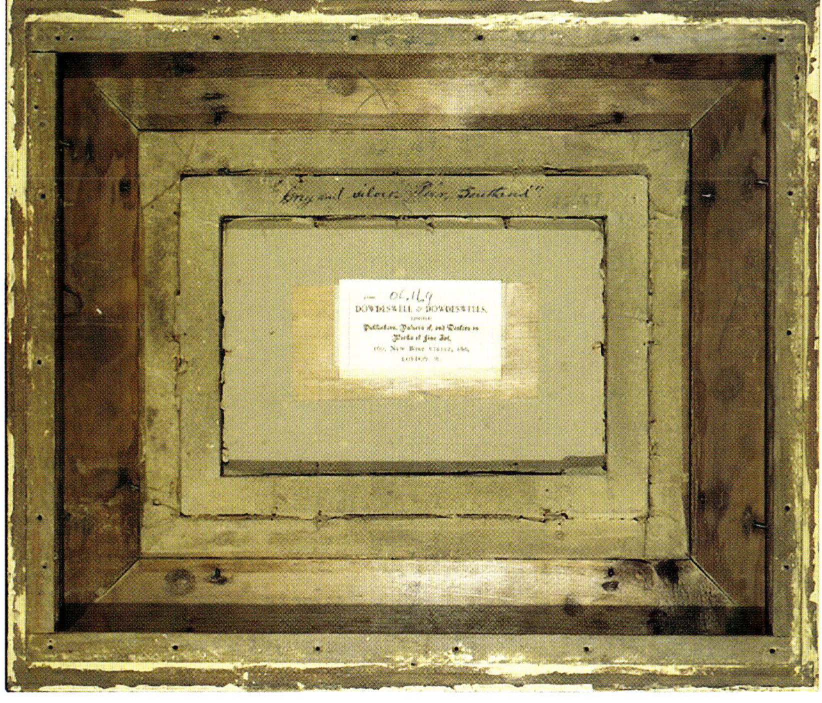

The ironies here work in many different ways. In Whistler's mature paintings, drawings, and prints, he eschewed conventional finish in order to highlight the artifice of the art object. In his paintings, he laid the paint on thinly so that the viewer could not help but notice the weave of the canvas or the grain of the board support. In his drawings, he was parsimonious with his watercolors or pastels so that the viewer had to see the paper beneath. In his etchings and lithographs, he left large areas of his plate or stone untouched. In all these media, Whistler let the support show because he wanted the viewer to remember that his works were not windows onto another world, but only arrangements of color and line on a flat support.

But as Whistler noted in a letter to Walter Dowdeswell written shortly before the opening of the 1886 installment of "Notes" — "Harmonies" — "Nocturnes," as a designer he worked very differently. Eager to spur Dowdeswell on to greater care and, no doubt, expense, Whistler reminded him that their exhibition "will be the Artistic event of the season, if we dont [sic] break our necks and spoil things by undue haste — no coming upon the Public without the usual complete perfection of finish which is the great characteristic of the Whistler shows" (emphases in original).[53] Whistler was, of course, making a joke about "finish." But from the vantage point of the early twenty-first century we can clearly see something that he probably could not — that both the sketchiness of his work and the meticulousness of his designs promoted an awareness of beauty as a nonreferential arrangement of color and line. Indeed, the decorations may have done as much or more to help prepare the way for twentieth-century nonrepresentational art as the notes, harmonies, and nocturnes did.

I want to point out one more irony. Unlike Whistler's seemingly ephemeral prints, pastels, watercolors, and small oils, which are portable and therefore surprisingly durable, the installations, like all interior decorations, were truly ephemeral. But instead of being a sign of their unimportance, this is part of what makes them seem so contemporary and powerful. E. W. Godwin caught something of this in his review of the *Arrangement in Flesh Colour & Grey*. Writing several weeks after Whistler's show had come down but before the Dowdeswells painted over the decoration, Godwin mourned the impending passing of that which still remained: "The restlessness of modern fashion, for ever changing, that cannot allow the best of things to last beyond a season, will, perchance, sweep away this decoration, and it will be counted with the other delightful harmonies Mr. Whistler has produced in Piccadilly and Bond-street, and, indeed, wherever his works have been exhibited. That these exquisitely lovely arrangements of colour should live as memories only, gives to the very nomenclature our painter had adopted a touch of pathos. The room in Piccadilly and the rooms at the Fine Arts Society have gone, as Whistlerian compositions, quite as effectually as the vibrations of the last quartette. . . ."[54]

More fully than any of Whistler's paintings, drawings, or prints, the seemingly ephemeral designs attain the longed-for status of absolute music. Heard melodies are sweet, but those unheard are sweeter.

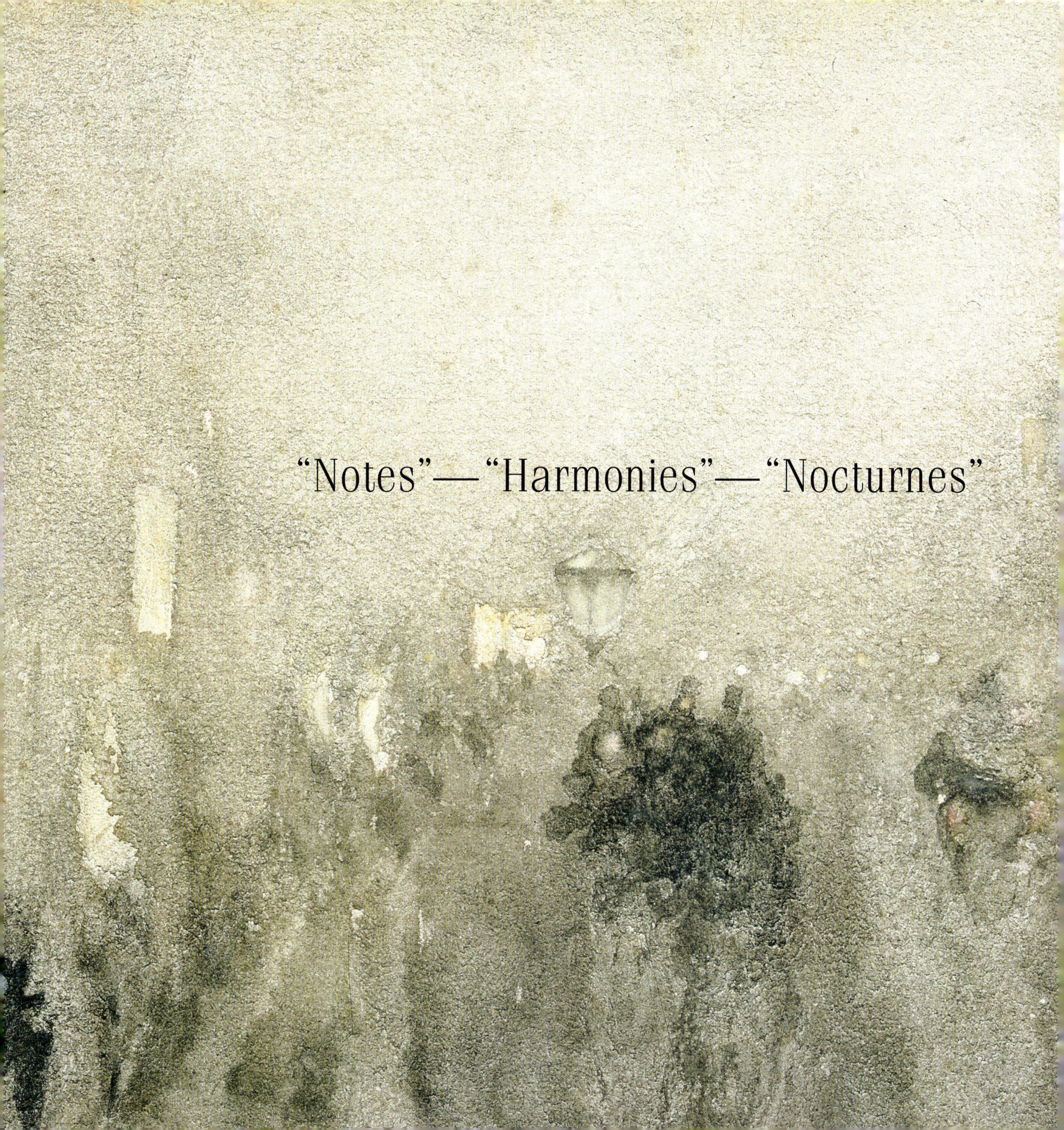

“Notes”—“Harmonies”—“Nocturnes”

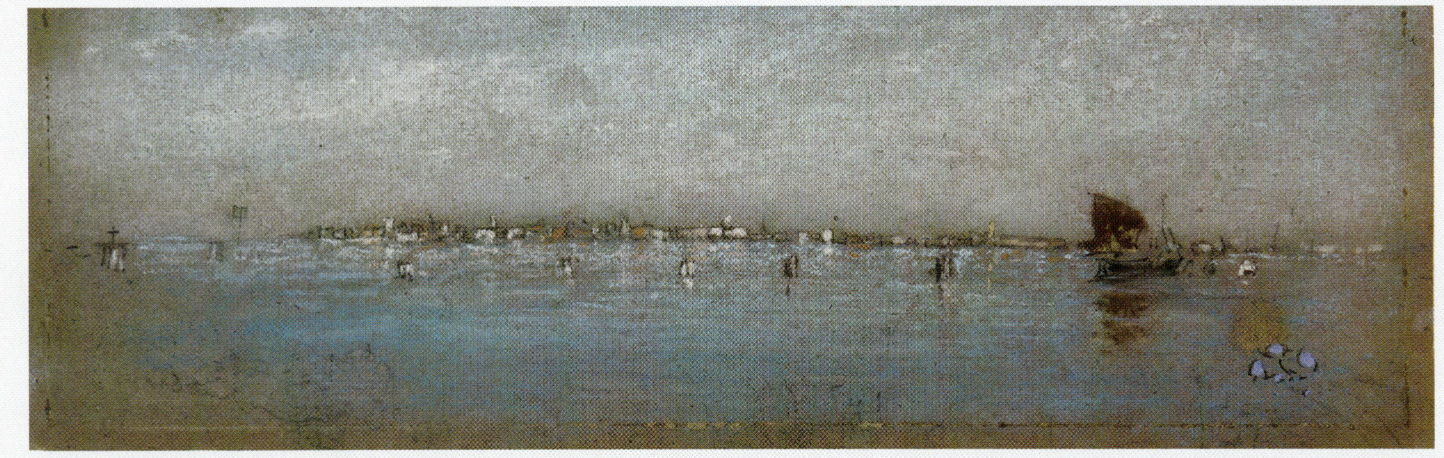

1 Blue and silver—The Islands, Venice

Blue and silver—
The Islands, Venice

1880
Chalk and pastel on brown paper,
$3^{9}/_{16} \times 11^{3}/_{16}$ in.
Freer Gallery of Art,
Washington, D.C.
Gift of Charles Lang Freer
F1905.215
Dowdeswell 50

Cliffs and Breakers

Probably December 1883 or
January 1884
Oil on wood panel,
$4^{7}/_{8} \times 8^{1}/_{2}$ in.
Huntérian Art Gallery, University of
Glasgow, Birnie Philip Bequest
Possibly Dowdeswell 37,
"The Green Headland"

Wortley; note in green

ca. 1883
Oil on wood panel,
$5^{1}/_{4} \times 9^{1}/_{4}$ in.
Freer Gallery of Art,
Washington, D.C.
Gift of Charles Lang Freer
F1902.155
Dowdeswell 34

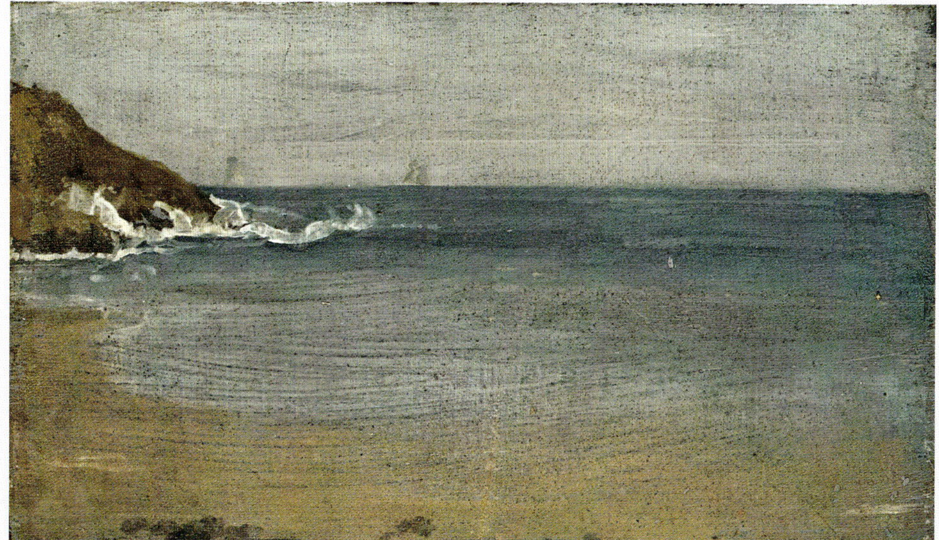

2 **Cliffs and Breakers**

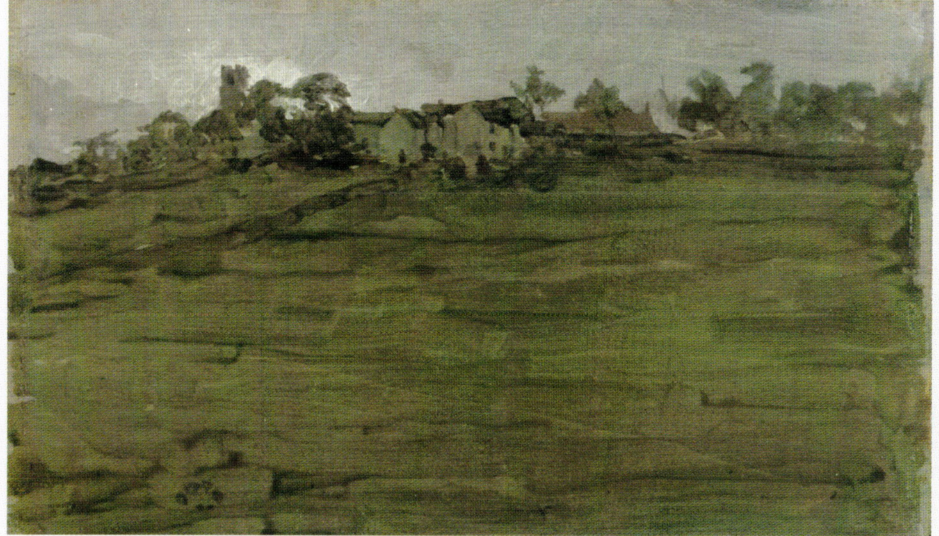

3 **Wortley; note in green**

The Angry Sea

December 1883 or January 1884
Oil on wood panel,
$4\frac{7}{8} \times 8\frac{1}{2}$ in.
Freer Gallery of Art,
Washington, D.C.
Gift of Charles Lang Freer
F1904.76
Dowdeswell 2

The Sea and Sand

Probably December 1883 or
January 1884
Oil on wood panel,
$5\frac{1}{4} \times 9\frac{1}{4}$ in.
Freer Gallery of Art,
Washington, D.C.
Gift of Charles Lang Freer
F1902.151
Probably Dowdeswell 36,
"Sea and Storm; grey and green"

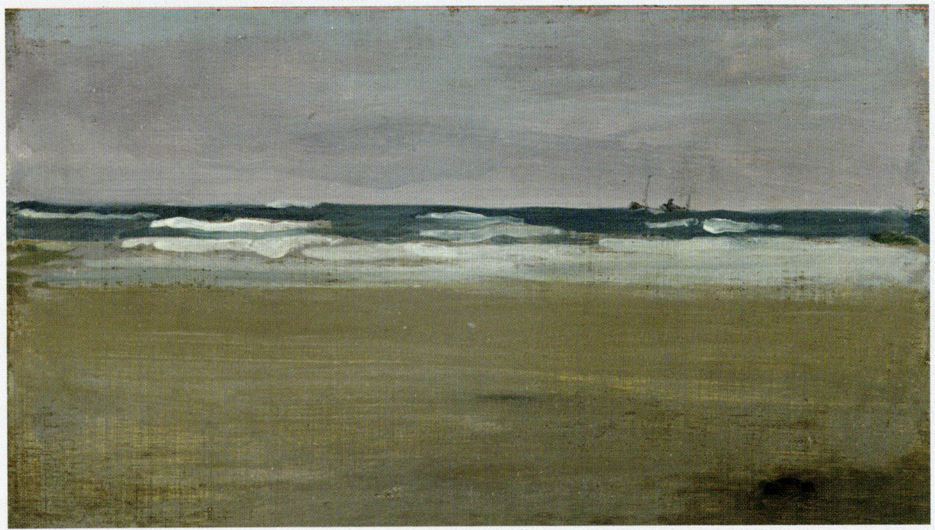

4 The Angry Sea

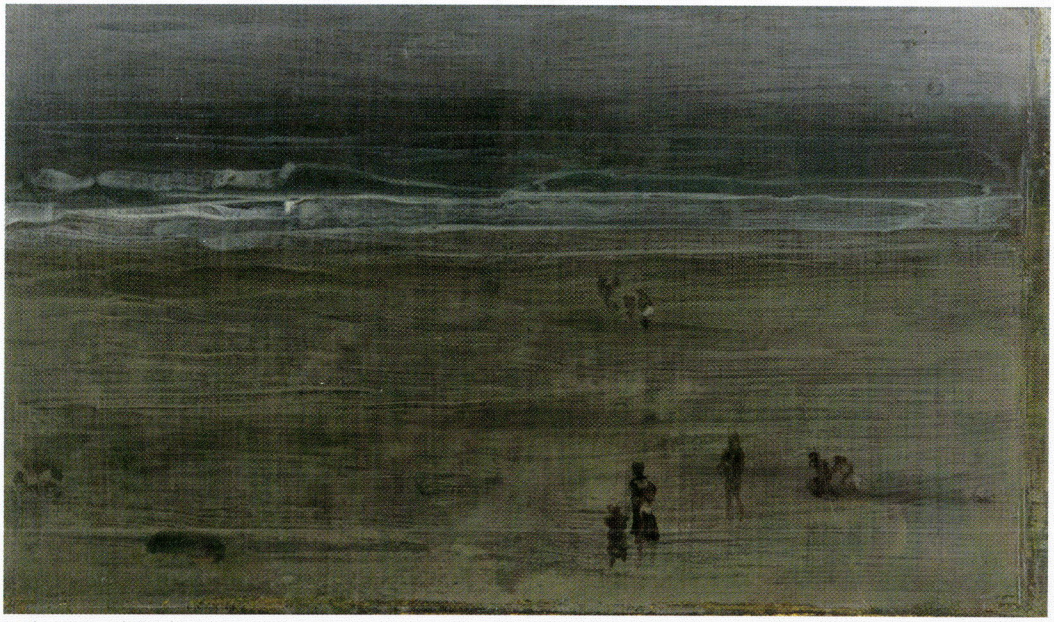

5 The Sea and Sand

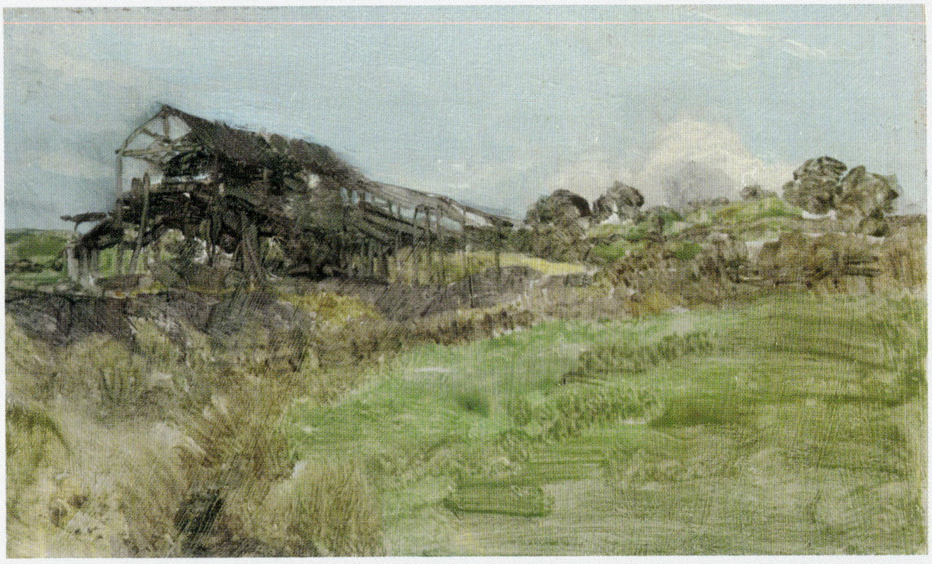

6 **Black and Emerald—Coal Mine**

Black and Emerald— Coal Mine
Probably December 1883 or January 1884
Oil on wood panel,
$3\frac{1}{2} \times 5\frac{7}{8}$ in.
Freer Gallery of Art, Washington, D.C.
Gift of Charles Lang Freer
F1902.153
Dowdeswell 59

The Pier; a grey note
December 1883 or January 1884
Oil on wood panel,
$3\frac{1}{2} \times 5\frac{3}{4}$ in.
Fine Arts Museums of San Francisco, Museum purchase, Alletta Morris McBean Bequest Fund and gifts in her honor, 1988.6
Dowdeswell 1

Blue and gold—The Schooner
December 1883 or January 1884
Oil on wood panel,
$3\frac{1}{2} \times 5\frac{7}{8}$ in.
Private Collection
Dowdeswell 32

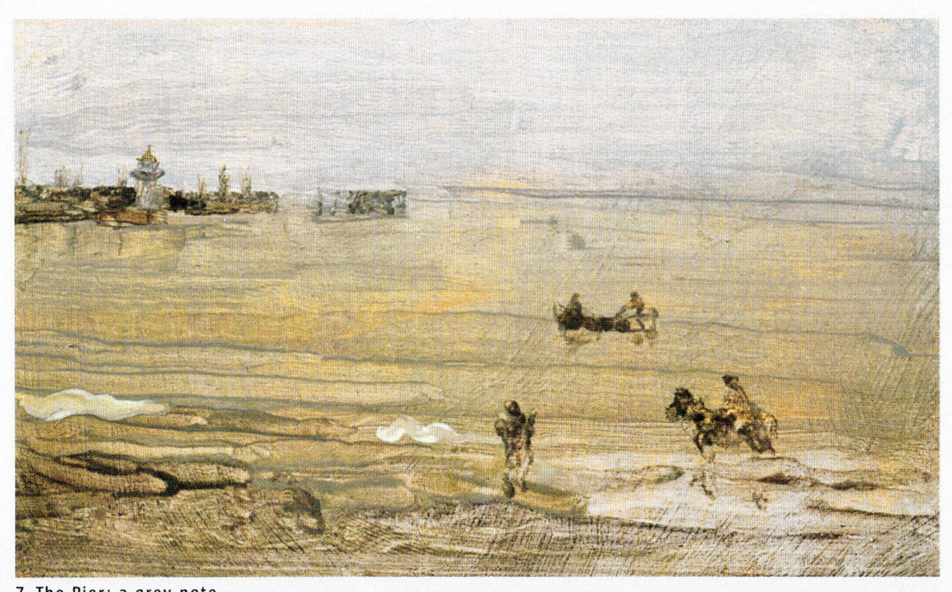
7 The Pier; a grey note

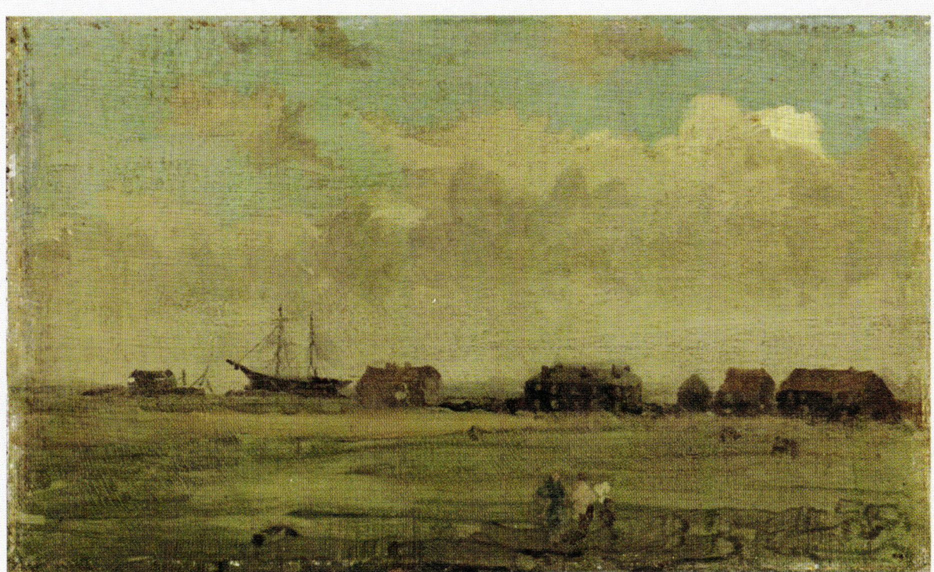
8 Blue and gold—The Schooner

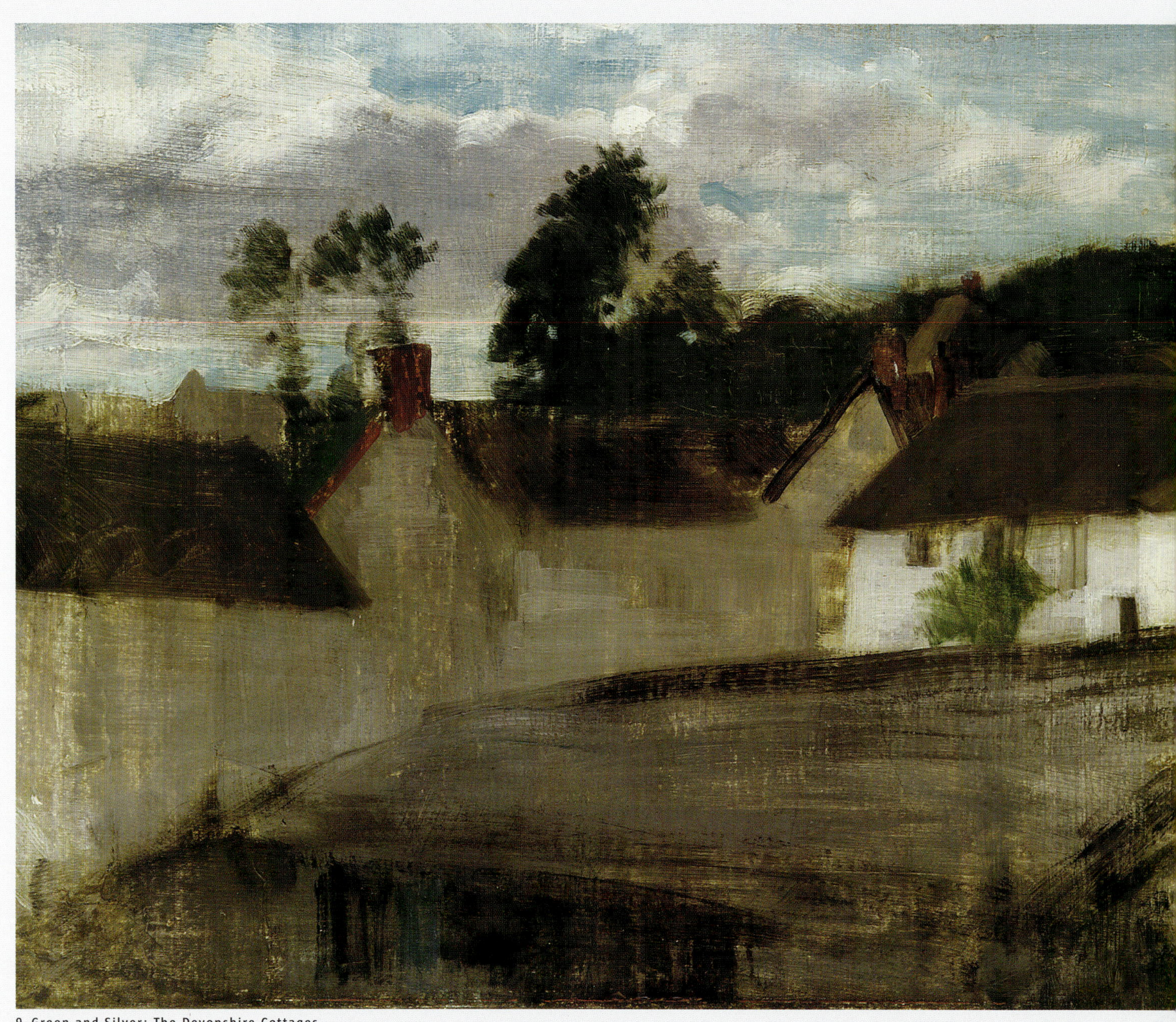

9 Green and Silver: The Devonshire Cottages

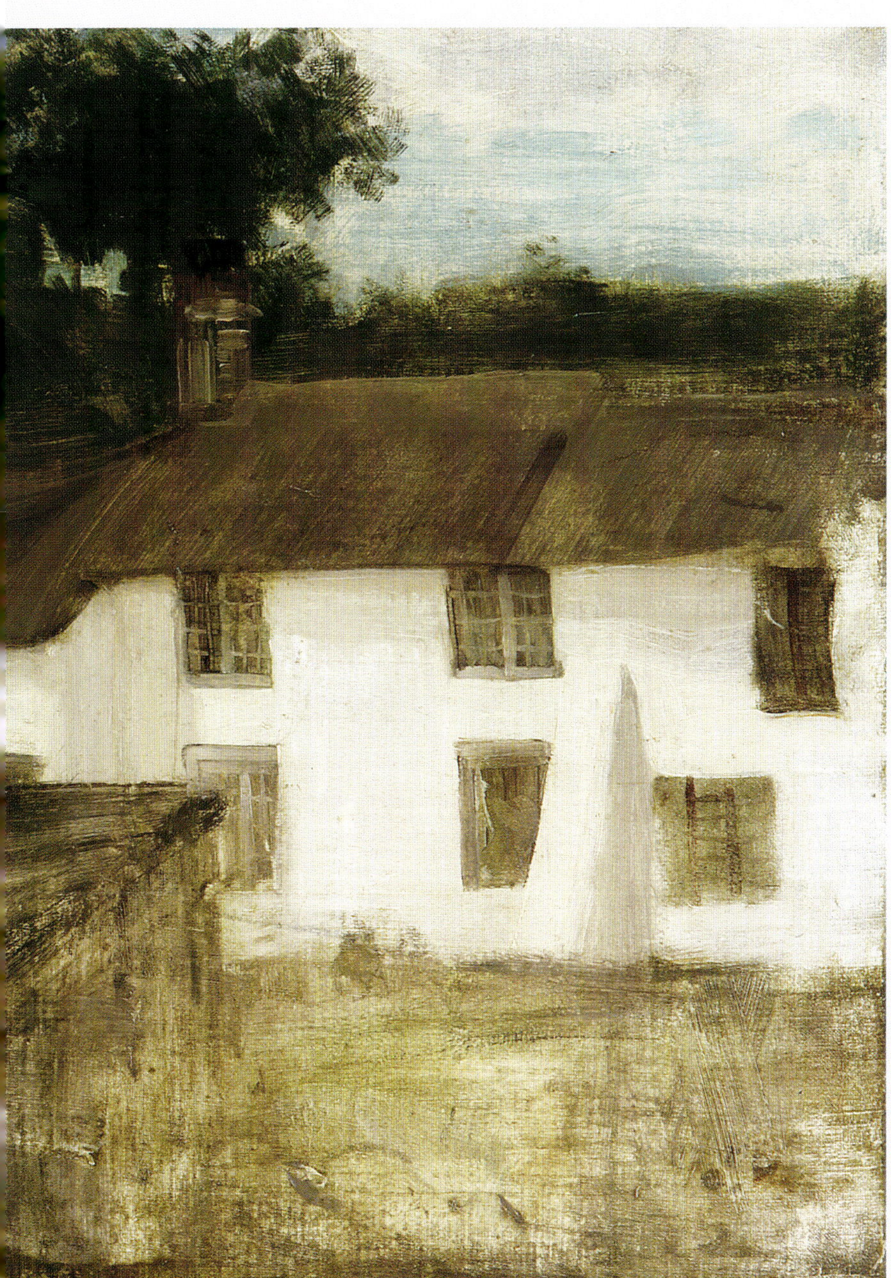

**Green and Silver:
The Devonshire Cottages**

1883 or 1884
Oil on canvas,
$12\frac{5}{8} \times 24\frac{3}{4}$ in.
Freer Gallery of Art, Washington, D.C.
Gift of Charles Lang Freer
F1906.227
Possibly Dowdeswell 7,
"Green and opal — The Village"

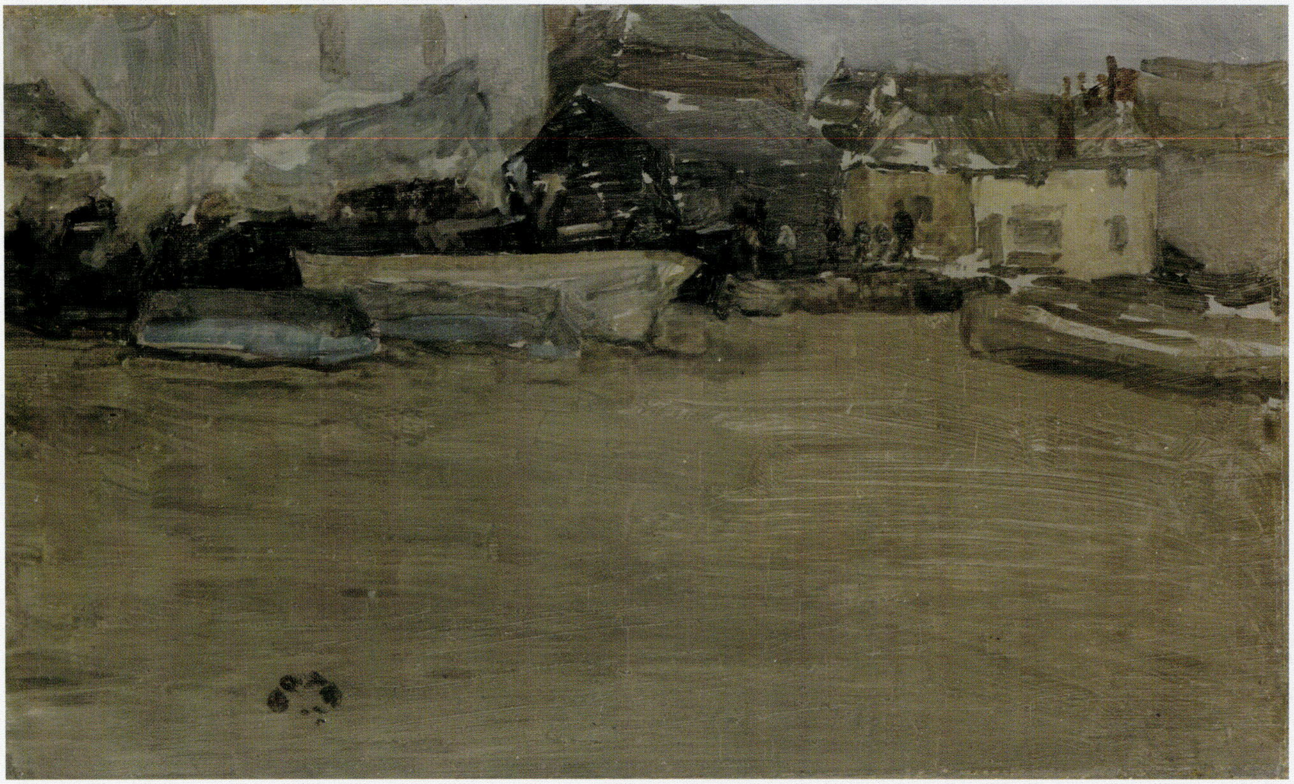

10 Low Tide

Low Tide
Probably December 1883 or January 1884
Oil on wood panel,
$5^{3}/_{8} \times 9^{1}/_{4}$ in.
Freer Gallery of Art, Washington, D.C.
Gift of Charles Lang Freer
F1902.156
Probably Dowdeswell 45, "Sands; blue note"

Grey and silver Mist—Life Boat
Probably December 1883 or January 1884
Oil on wood panel,
$4^{7}/_{8} \times 8^{1}/_{2}$ in.
Freer Gallery of Art, Washington, D.C.
Gift of Charles Lang Freer
F1914.1
Dowdeswell 54

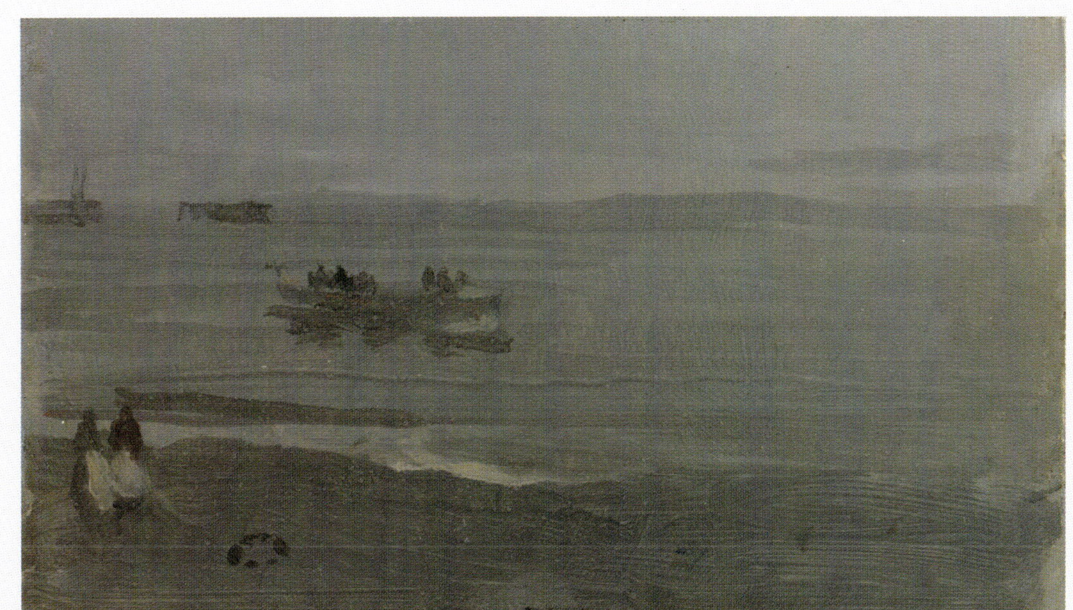

11 Grey and silver Mist—Life Boat

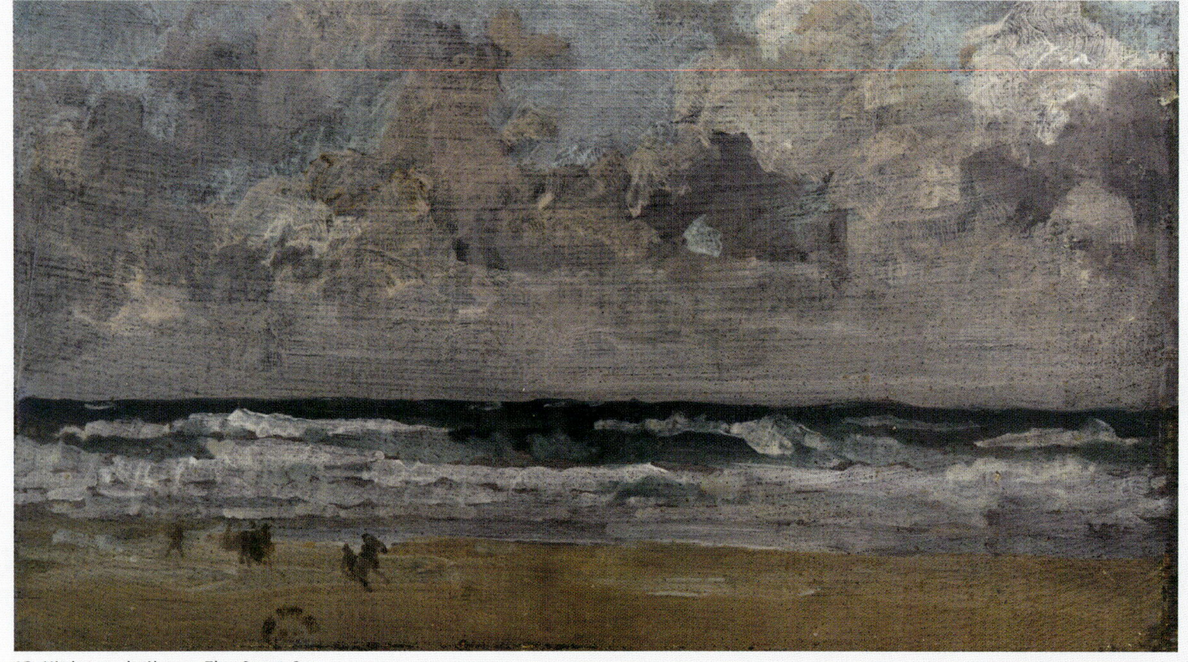

12 Violet and silver—The Great Sea

Violet and silver—
The Great Sea
ca. 1884
Oil on wood panel,
$5\frac{3}{8} \times 9\frac{1}{4}$ in.
Freer Gallery of Art,
Washington, D.C.
Gift of Charles Lang Freer
F1902.148
Dowdeswell 33

Note in blue and opal—
The Sun Cloud
Probably December 1883 or
January 1884
Oil on wood panel,
$4\frac{7}{8} \times 8\frac{1}{2}$ in.
Freer Gallery of Art,
Washington, D.C.
Gift of Charles Lang Freer
F1904.314
Dowdeswell 52

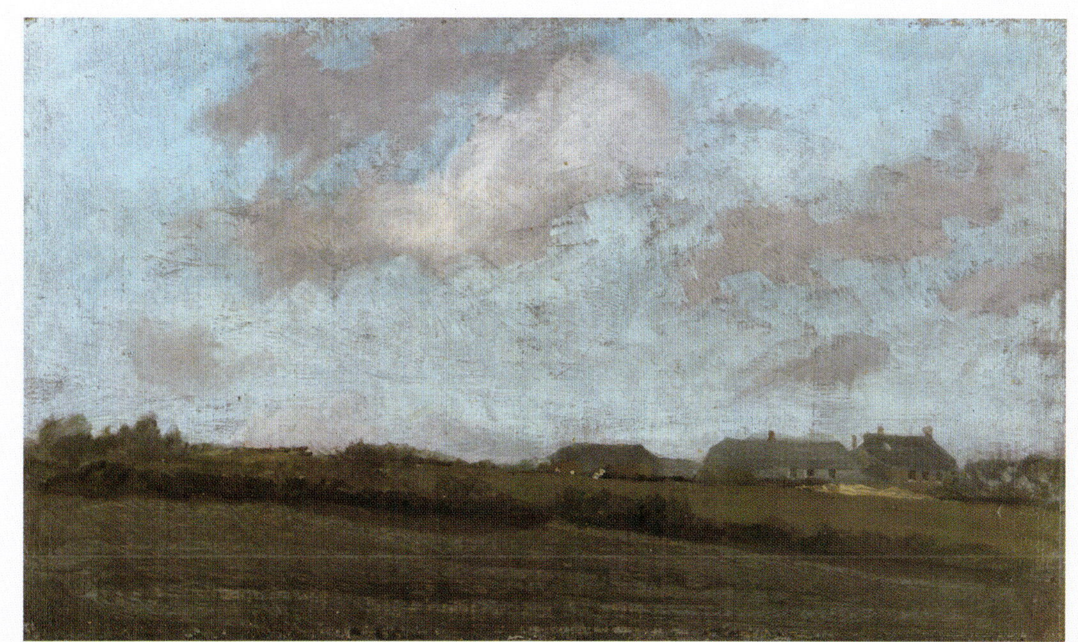

13 Note in blue and opal—The Sun Cloud

14 Blue and grey—Unloading

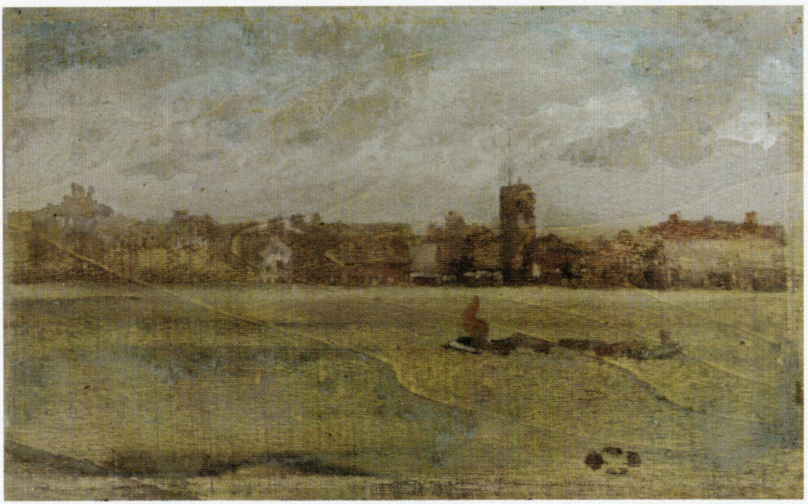

15 Harmony in brown and gold—Old Chelsea Church

Blue and grey—Unloading

Probably December 1883 or January 1884
Oil on wood panel, $3\frac{1}{2} \times 5\frac{7}{8}$ in.
Freer Gallery of Art, Washington, D.C.
Gift of Charles Lang Freer
F1902.150
Dowdeswell 56

Harmony in brown and gold—Old Chelsea Church

Probably 1884
Oil on wood panel, $3\frac{1}{2} \times 5\frac{3}{4}$ in.
Freer Gallery of Art, Washington, D.C.
Gift of Charles Lang Freer
F1902.152
Dowdeswell 44

Red and blue—Lindsey Houses

ca. 1882–84
Oil on wood panel, $5\frac{1}{4} \times 9\frac{1}{4}$ in.
Freer Gallery of Art, Washington, D.C.
Gift of Charles Lang Freer
F1902.157
Dowdeswell 4

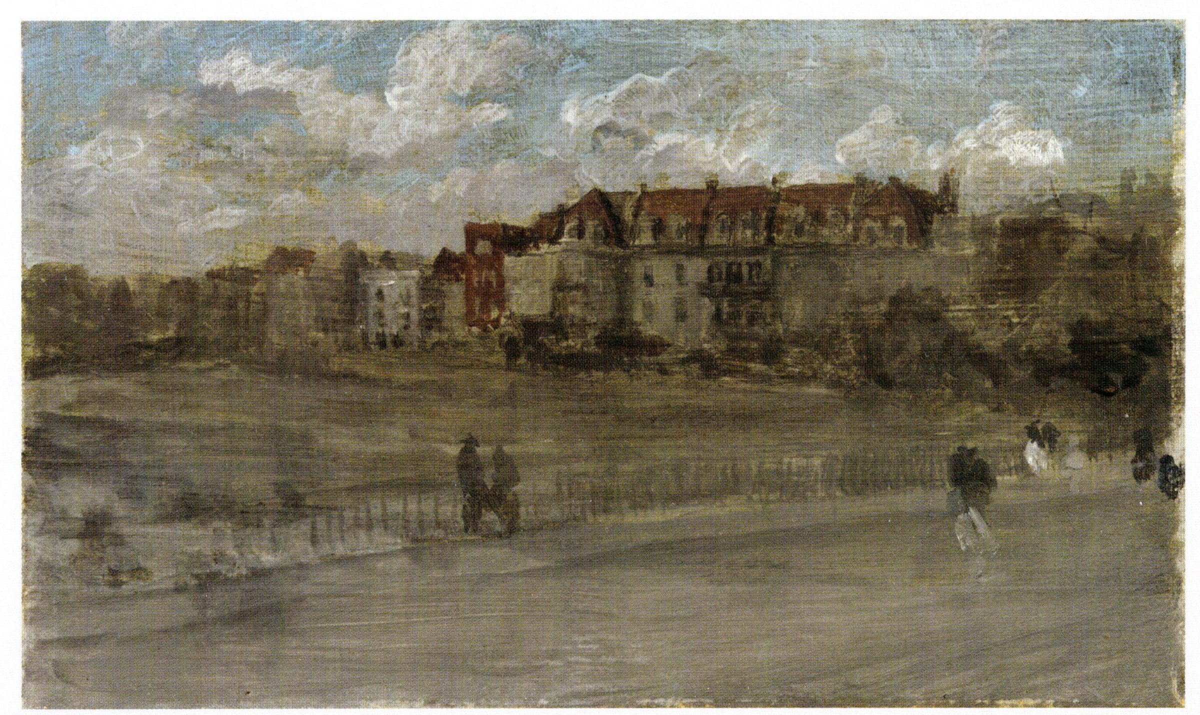

16 Red and blue — Lindsey Houses

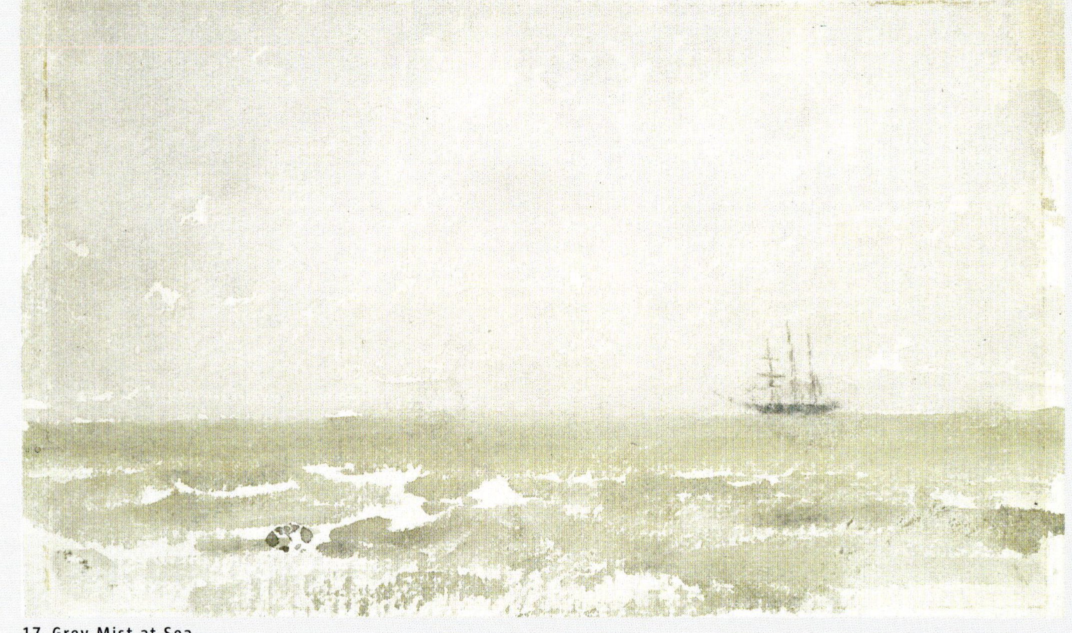

17 Grey Mist at Sea

Grey Mist at Sea

1883 or 1884
Watercolor on white wove paper,
$5^{9}/_{16} \times 9^{7}/_{16}$ in.
Birmingham Museums and
Art Gallery
Dowdeswell 22

Sunrise; gold and grey

Probably December 1883 or
January 1884
Watercolor on white wove paper,
$6^{7}/_{8} \times 4^{15}/_{16}$ in.
Courtesy of the National Gallery of
Ireland
Probably Dowdeswell 55,
"Sunrise; gold and grey;" or,
possibly, Dowdeswell 47, "Twilight;
gold and grey"

18 Sunrise; gold and grey

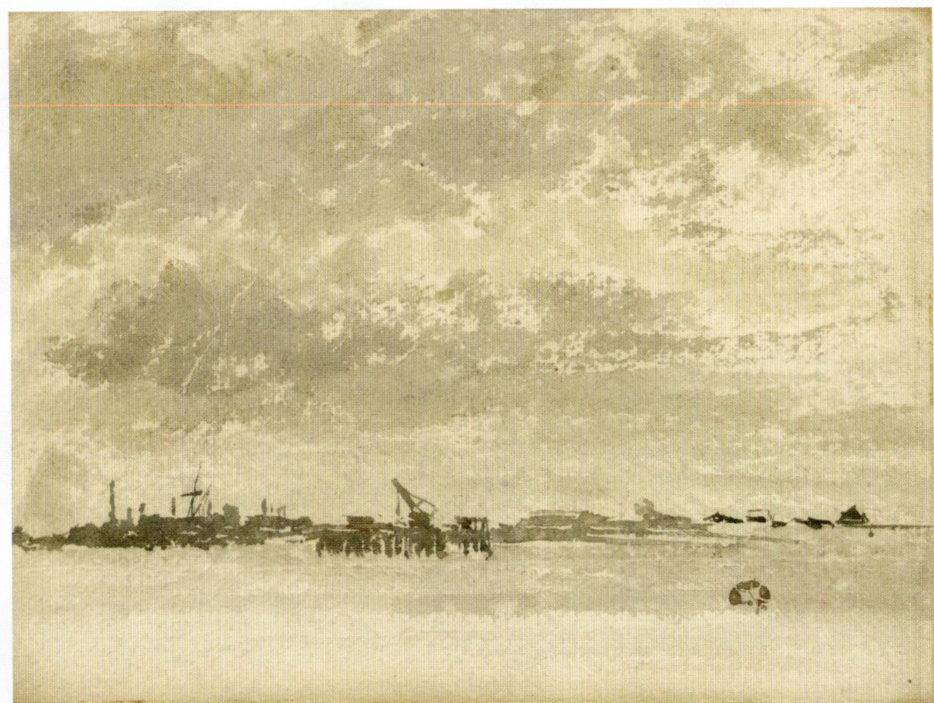

19 **Grey and silver — Purfleet**

Grey and silver — Purfleet
1883 or 1884
Watercolor on beige paper, laid down on card, 6 5/16 × 8 3/4 in.
Freer Gallery of Art, Washington, D.C.
Gift of Charles Lang Freer
F1902.117
Dowdeswell 5

Erith — Evening
1883 or 1884
Watercolor on beige paper, laid down on card, 5 11/16 × 9 7/16 in.
Freer Gallery of Art, Washington, D.C.
Gift of Charles Lang Freer
F1902.168
Dowdeswell 14

Page 46

Nocturne; black and red — Back Canal, Holland
1883 or 1884
Watercolor on cream wove paper, 8 5/8 × 11 1/8 in.
Freer Gallery of Art, Washington, D.C.
Gift of Charles Lang Freer
F1902.159
Dowdeswell 53

Page 47

Amsterdam in Winter
December 1882
Watercolor on cream paper, laid down on card, 8 × 10 7/8 in.
Freer Gallery of Art, Washington, D.C.
Gift of Charles Lang Freer
F1904.81
Probably Dowdeswell 49, "Nocturne, black and gold — Winter; Amsterdam"

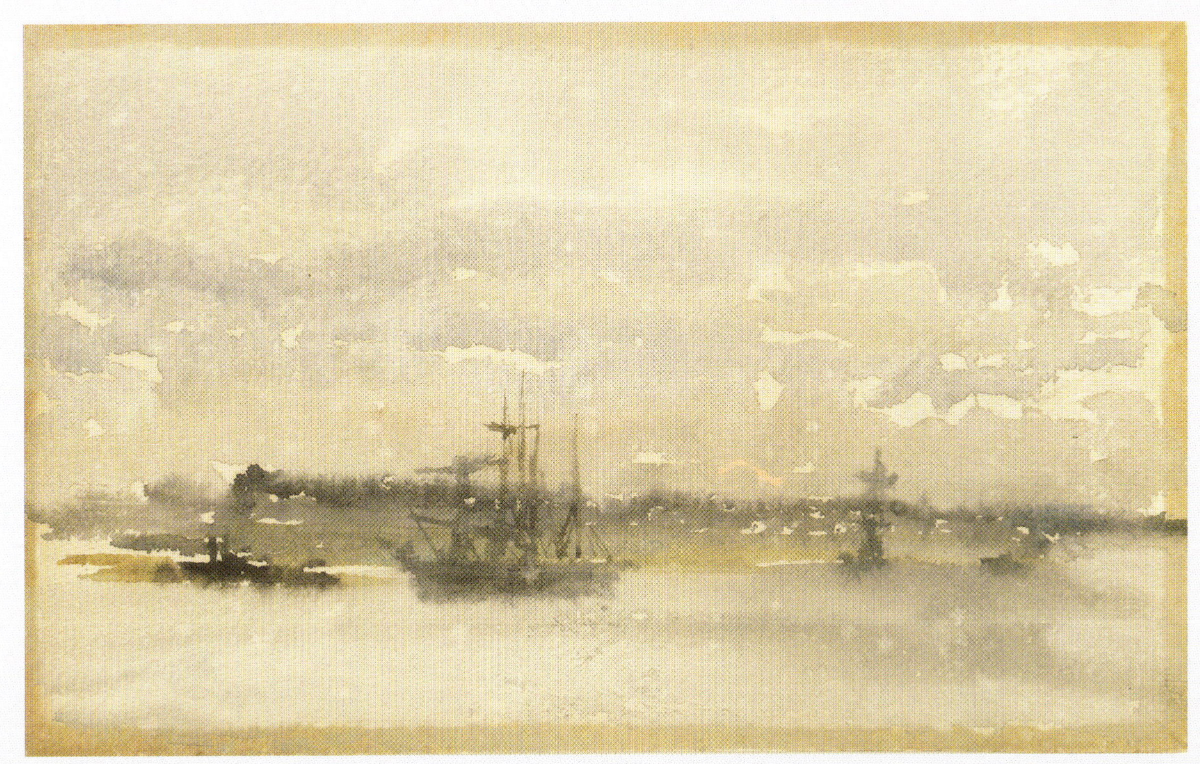

20 Erith—Evening

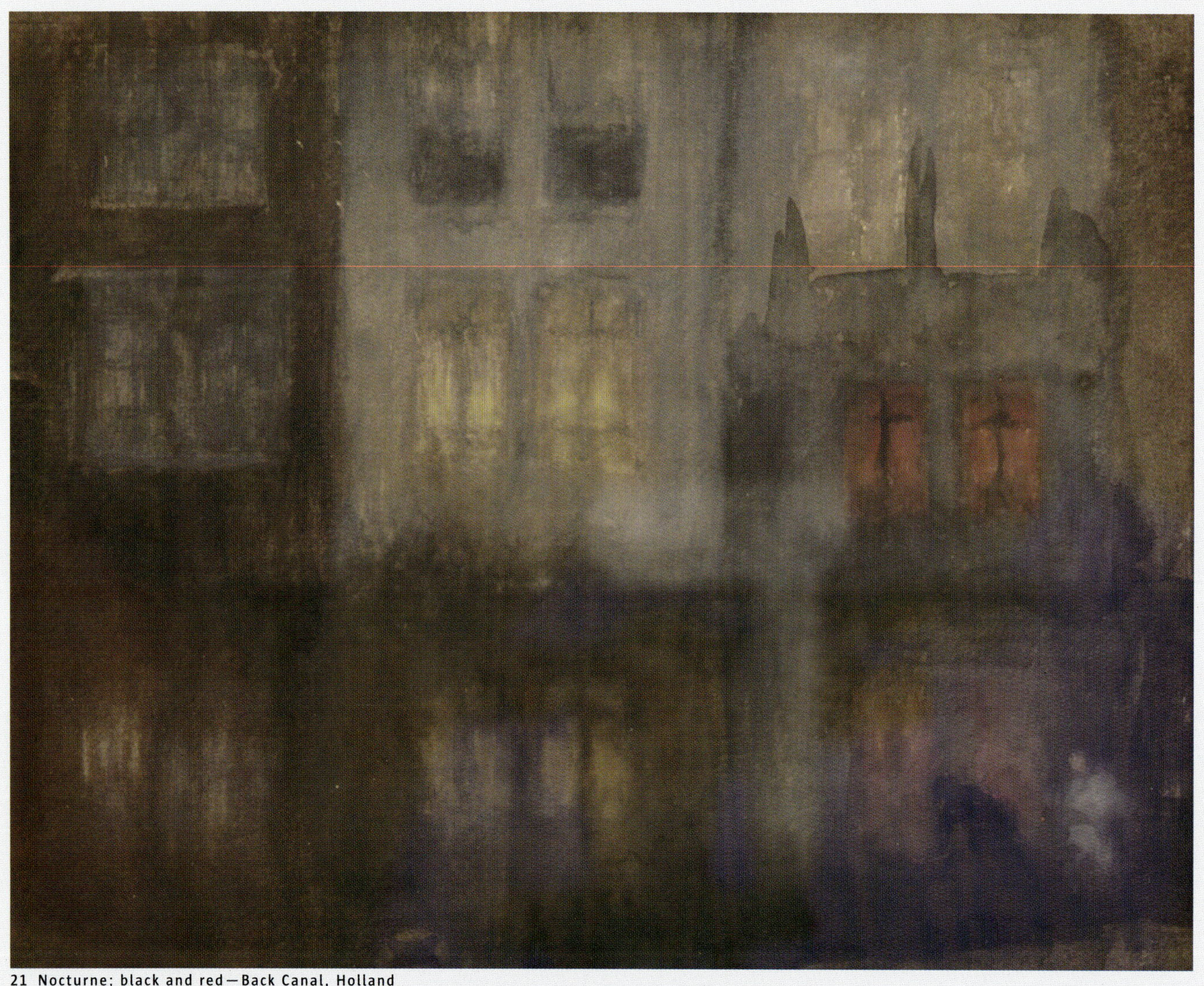

21 Nocturne; black and red — Back Canal, Holland

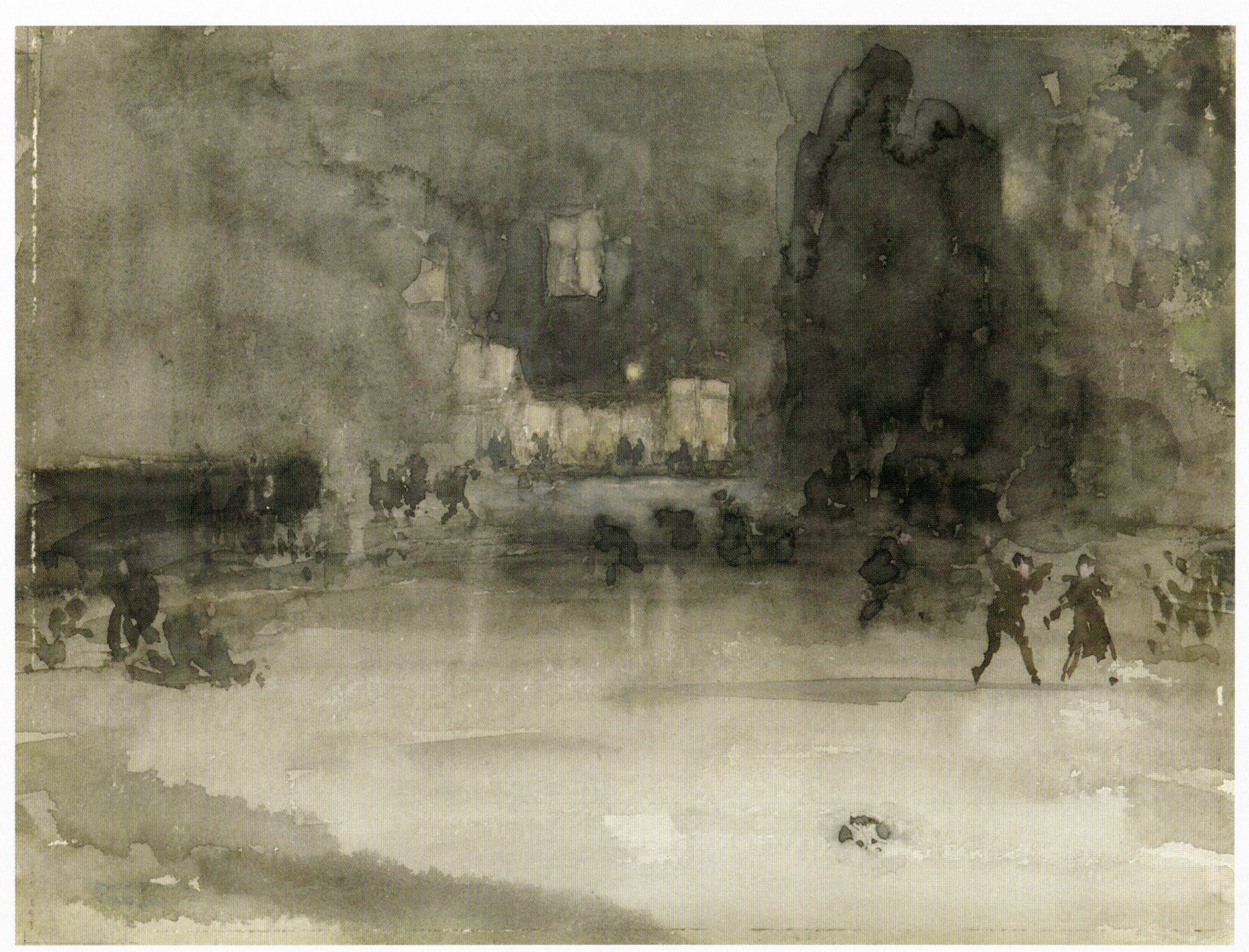

22 Amsterdam in Winter

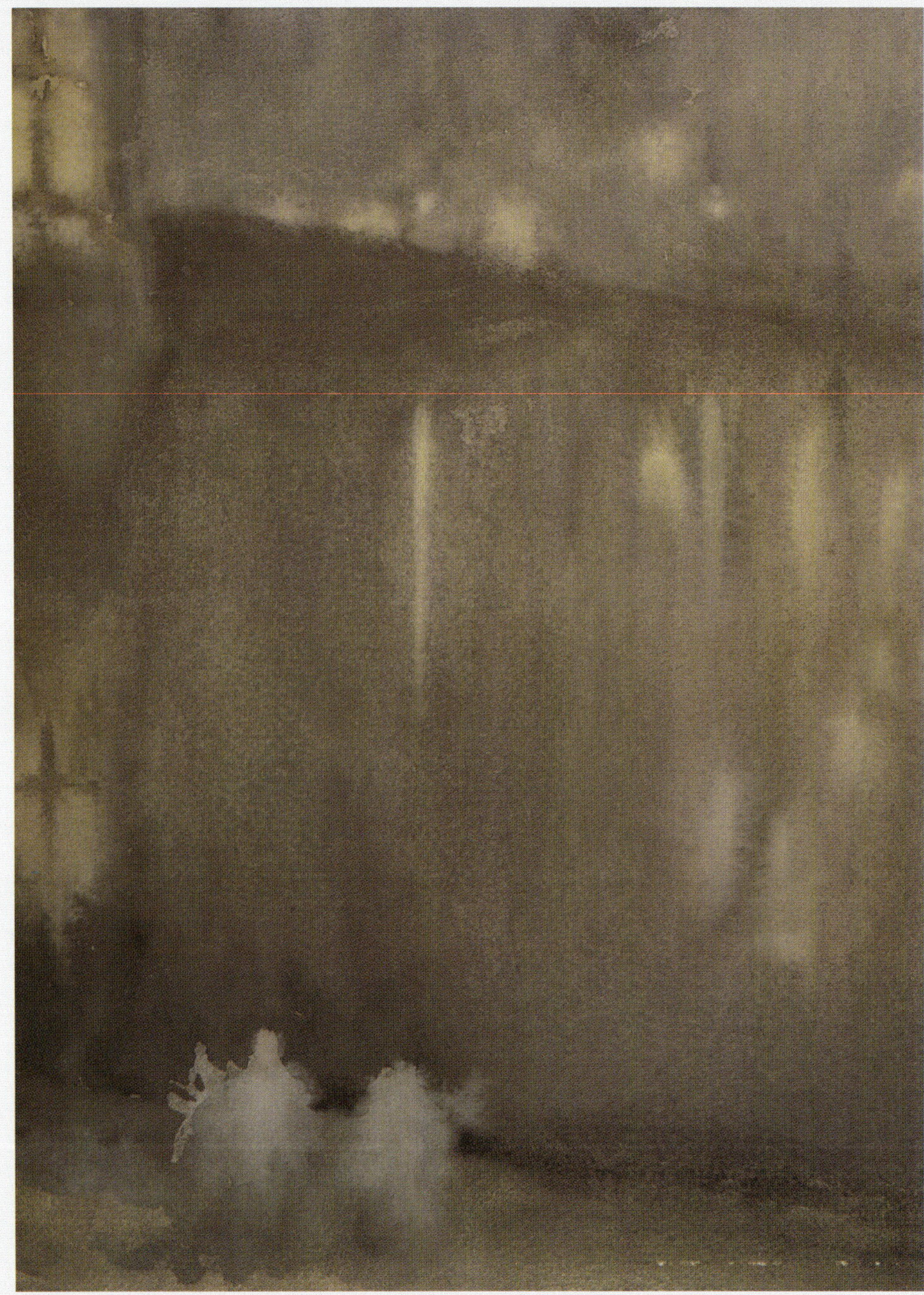

23 Nocturne; grey and gold—Canal; Holland

Nocturne; grey and gold—Canal; Holland

1883 or 1884

Watercolor on cream wove paper, $11\frac{7}{16} \times 9\frac{1}{16}$ in.

Freer Gallery of Art, Washington, D.C.

Gift of Charles Lang Freer

F1902.160

Dowdeswell 3

Grand Canal, Amsterdam; nocturne

1883 or 1884

Watercolor on cream wove paper, $8\frac{7}{8} \times 11\frac{3}{16}$ in.

Freer Gallery of Art, Washington, D.C.

Gift of Charles Lang Freer

F1902.161

Dowdeswell 18

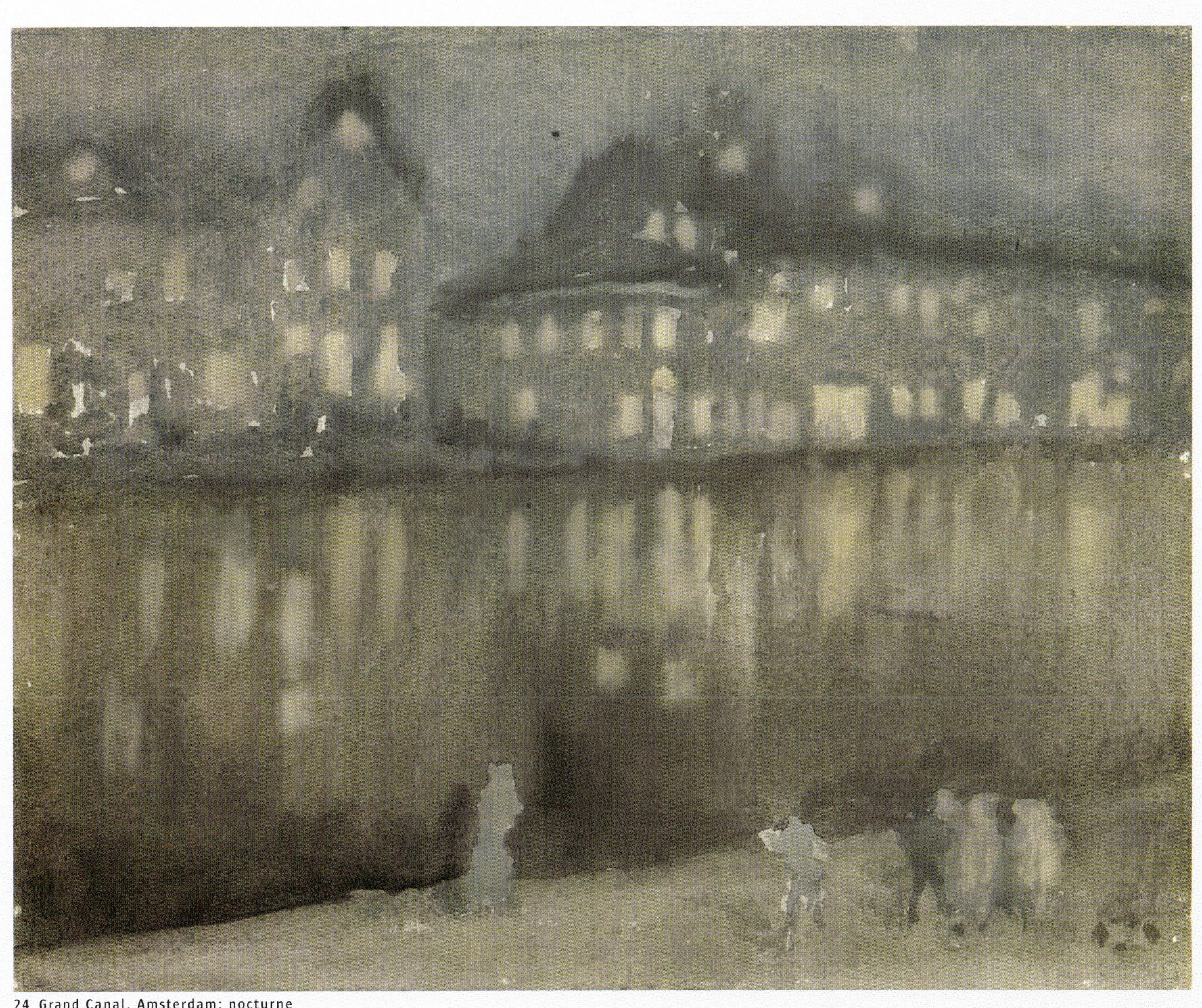
24 Grand Canal, Amsterdam; nocturne

Opal Beach

1883 or 1884
Watercolor on cream paper, laid down on card,
$6^{15}/_{16} \times 9^{15}/_{16}$ in.
Freer Gallery of Art,
Washington, D.C.
Gift of Charles Lang Freer
F1902.170
Dowdeswell 67

Grey and silver — Pier, Southend

1883 or 1884
Watercolor on cream paper, laid down on card, $6^{1}/_{4} \times 9^{11}/_{16}$ in.
Freer Gallery of Art,
Washington, D.C.
Gift of Charles Lang Freer
F1902.169
Dowdeswell 62

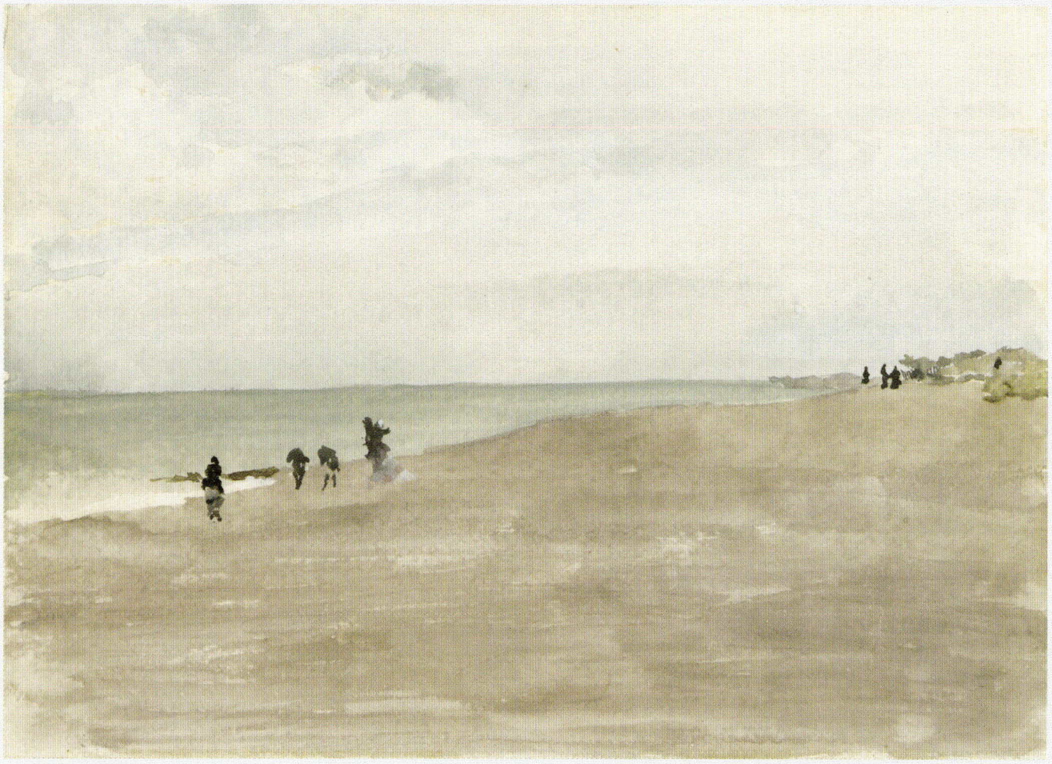

25 Opal Beach

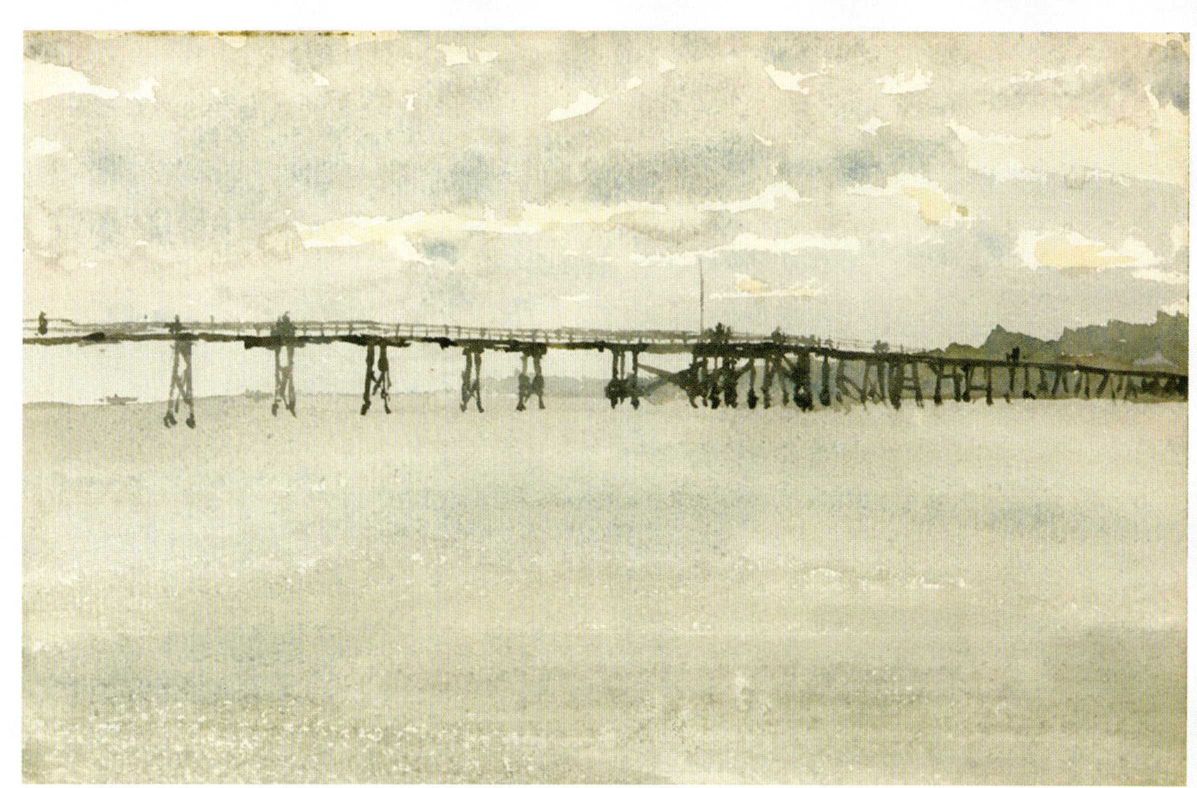

26 Grey and silver — Pier, Southend

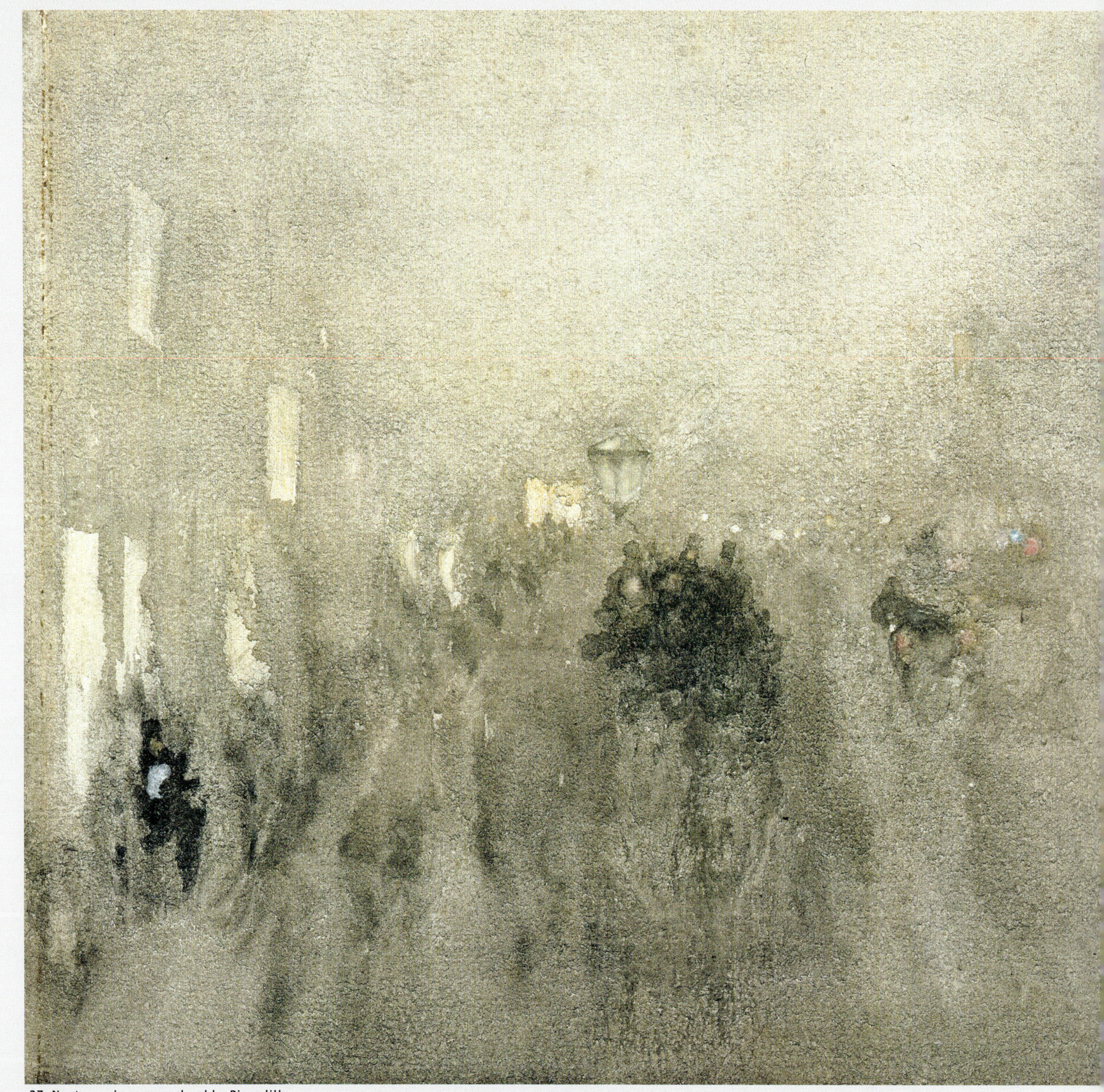

27 Nocturne in grey and gold—Piccadilly

Nocturne in grey and gold—Piccadilly

1881–83

Watercolor on white wove paper, $8^{3}/_{4} \times 11^{1}/_{2}$ in.

Courtesy of the National Gallery of Ireland

Dowdeswell 9

Nocturne; silver and opal—Chelsea

ca. 1880–84
Oil on wood panel, 8 × 10⅛ in.
Freer Gallery of Art,
Washington, D.C.
Gift of Charles Lang Freer
F1902.146
Dowdeswell 25

28 Nocturne; silver and opal—Chelsea

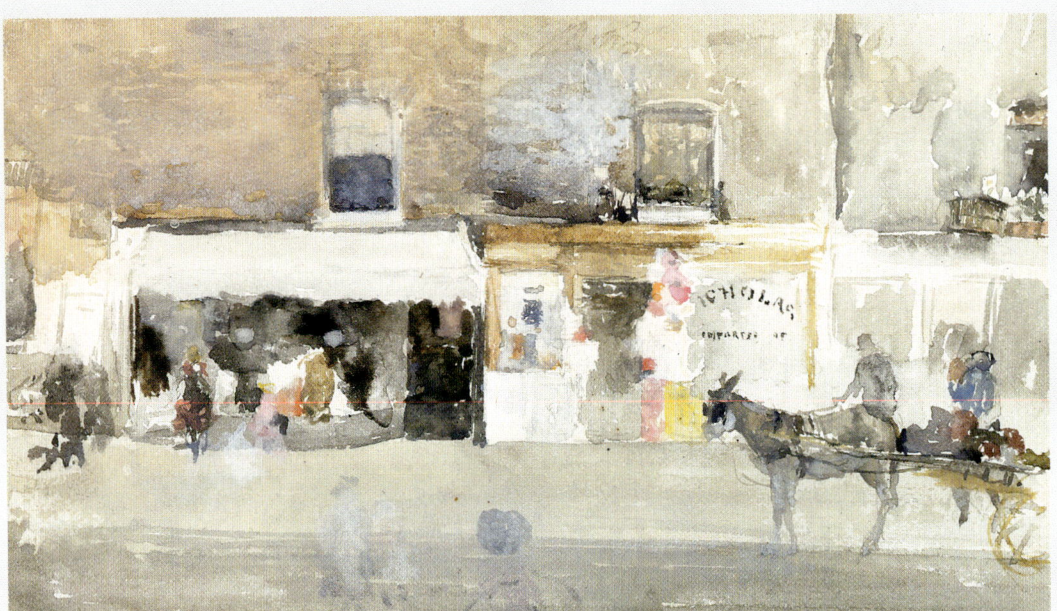

29 A Chelsea Street

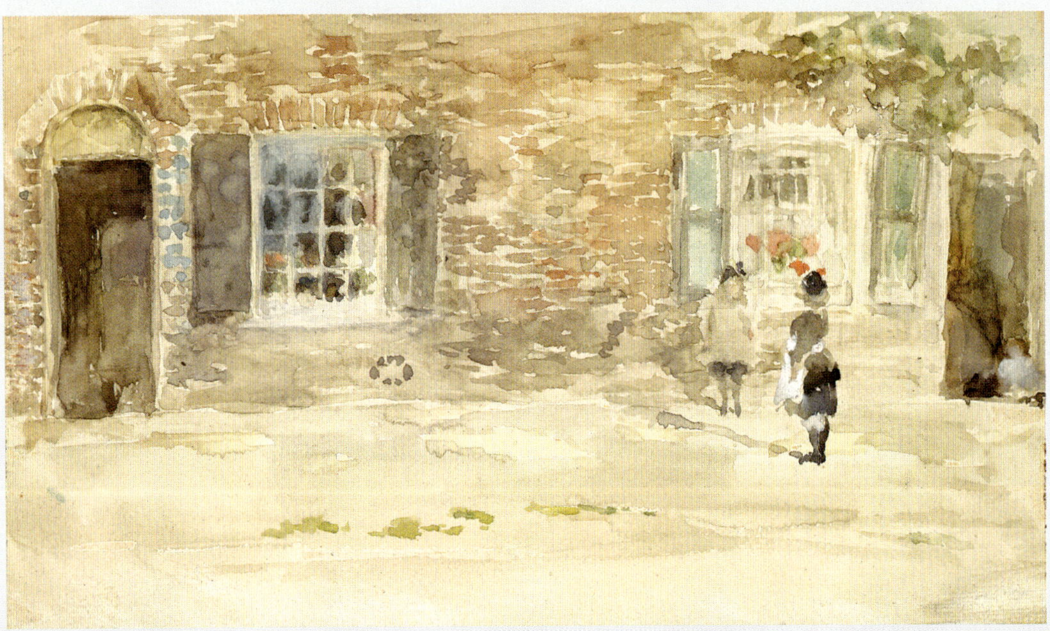

30 Village Shops, Chelsea

A Chelsea Street
Probably 1883 or 1884
Watercolor on white paper,
$4^{15}/_{16} \times 8^{9}/_{16}$ in.
Yale Center For British Art,
Paul Mellon Collection
Probably Dowdeswell 8,
"The Little Grocery, Chelsea; grey and red"

Village Shops, Chelsea
1883 or 1884
Watercolor on off-white paper, laid down on card, $5 \times 8^{1}/_{2}$ in.
National Gallery of Art,
Washington, D.C.
Gift of Mr. and Mrs. Paul Mellon
Possibly Dowdeswell 63,
"Old Shop, Chelsea; pink and grey"

Street in Old Chelsea
Early 1880s
Oil on wood panel,
$5^{1}/_{4} \times 9^{1}/_{8}$ in.
Museum of Fine Arts, Boston
Denman Waldo Ross Collection
Probably Dowdeswell 11,
"Chelsea; yellow and grey"

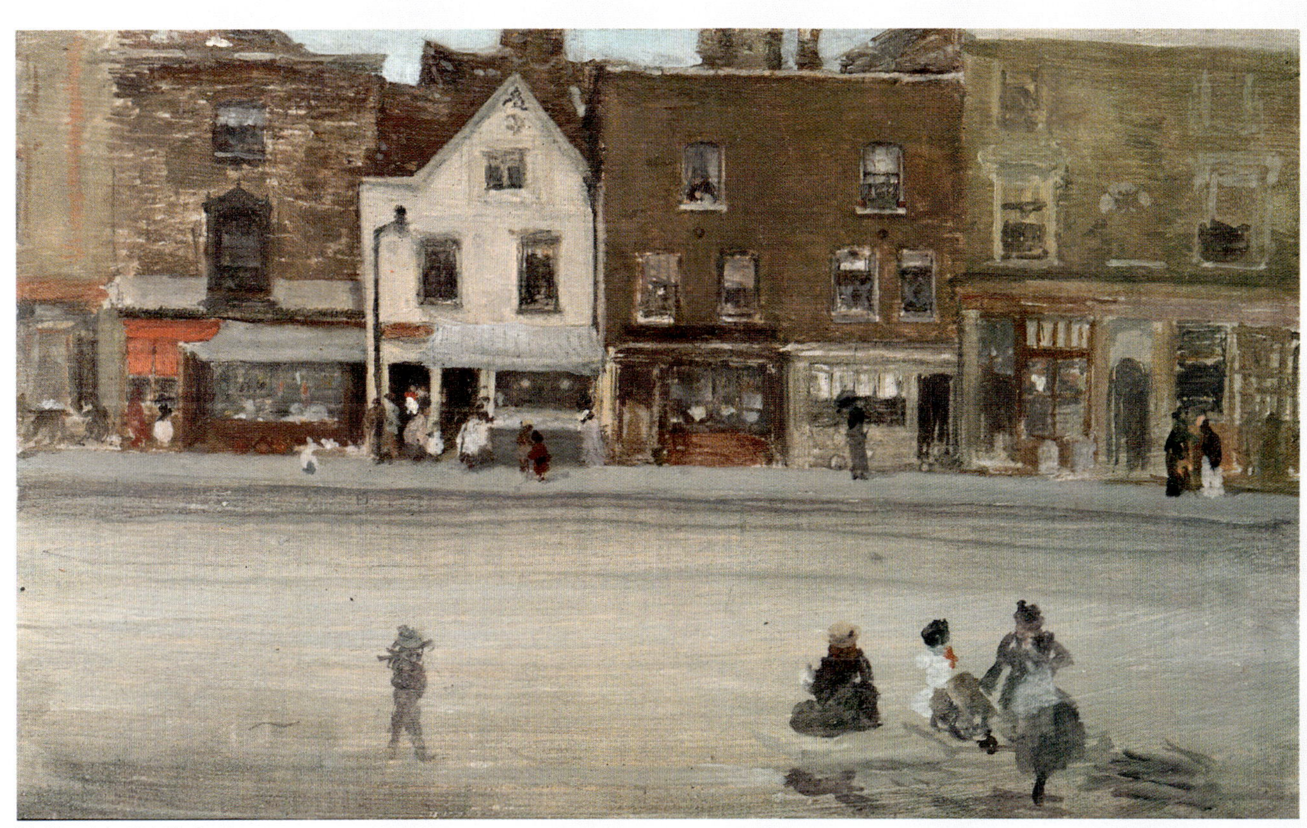

31 Street in Old Chelsea

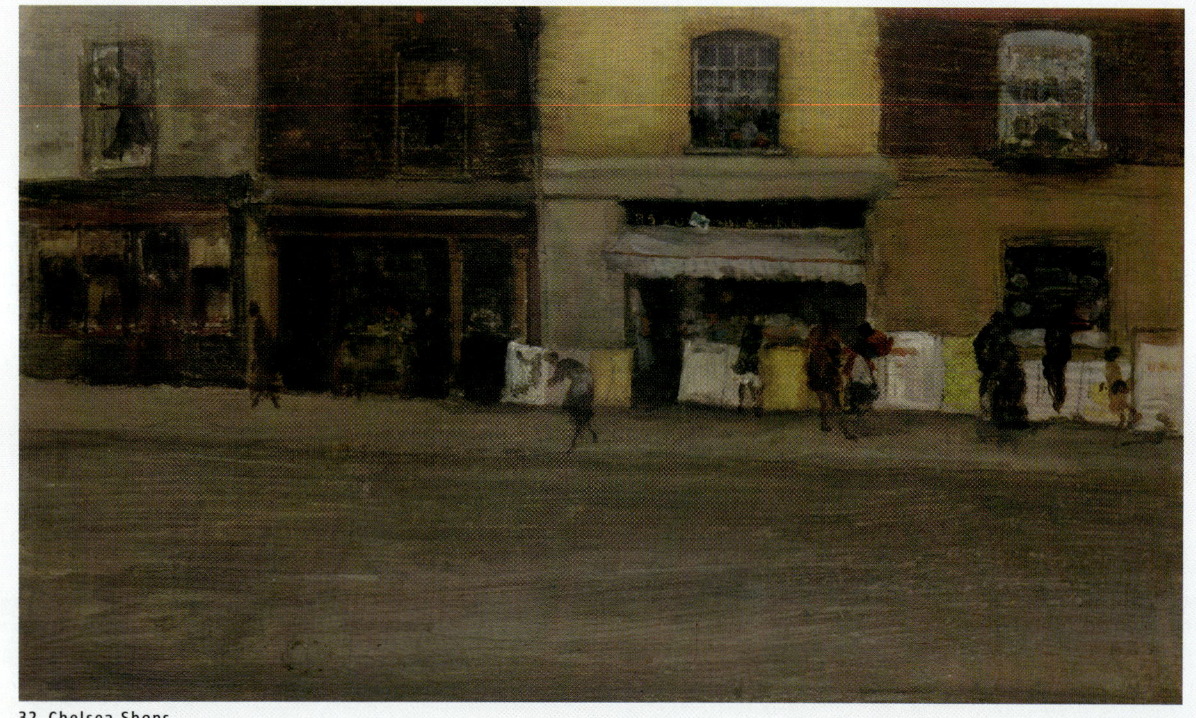

32 Chelsea Shops

Chelsea Shops

Early 1880s
Oil on wood panel,
$5^{1}/_{4} \times 9^{1}/_{4}$ in.
Freer Gallery of Art,
Washington, D.C.
Gift of Charles Lang Freer
F1902.149
Probably Dowdeswell 23, "Pink note—Chelsea;" or Dowdeswell 42, "Harmony in yellow and brown—Sunday"

An orange note—Sweet Shop

December 1883 or January 1884
Oil on wood panel,
$4^{3}/_{4} \times 8^{1}/_{2}$ in.
Freer Gallery of Art,
Washington, D.C.
Gift of Charles Lang Freer
F1904.315
Dowdeswell 38

A Grey Note: Village Street

Probably December 1883 or January 1884
Oil on wood panel,
$4^{7}/_{8} \times 8^{1}/_{2}$ in.
Hunterian Museum and Art Gallery,
University of Glasgow, Birnie Philip Gift
Possibly Dowdeswell 41,
"Little Shop; grey note"

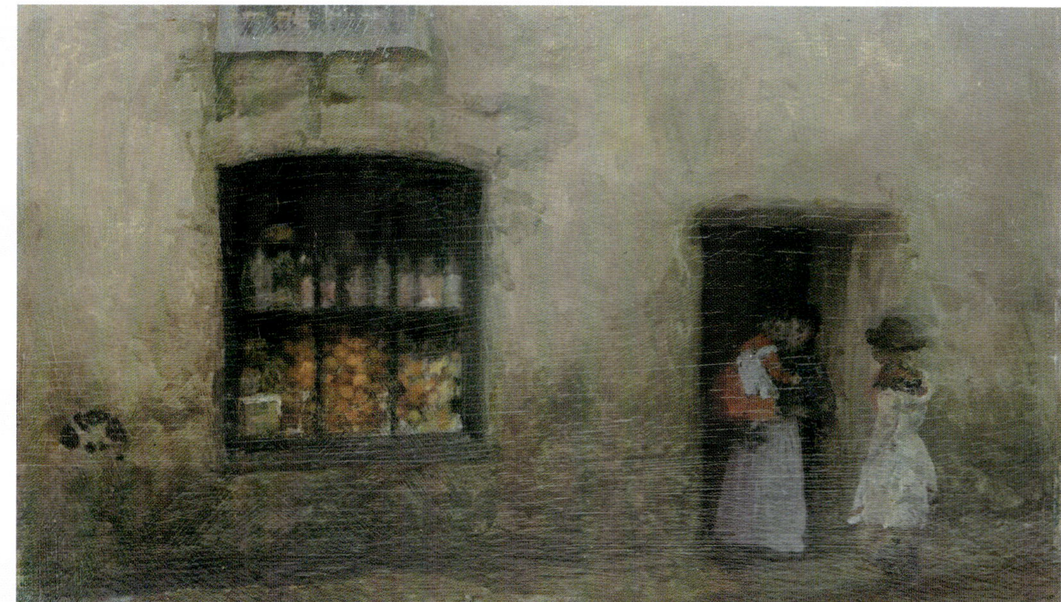

33 An orange note—Sweet Shop

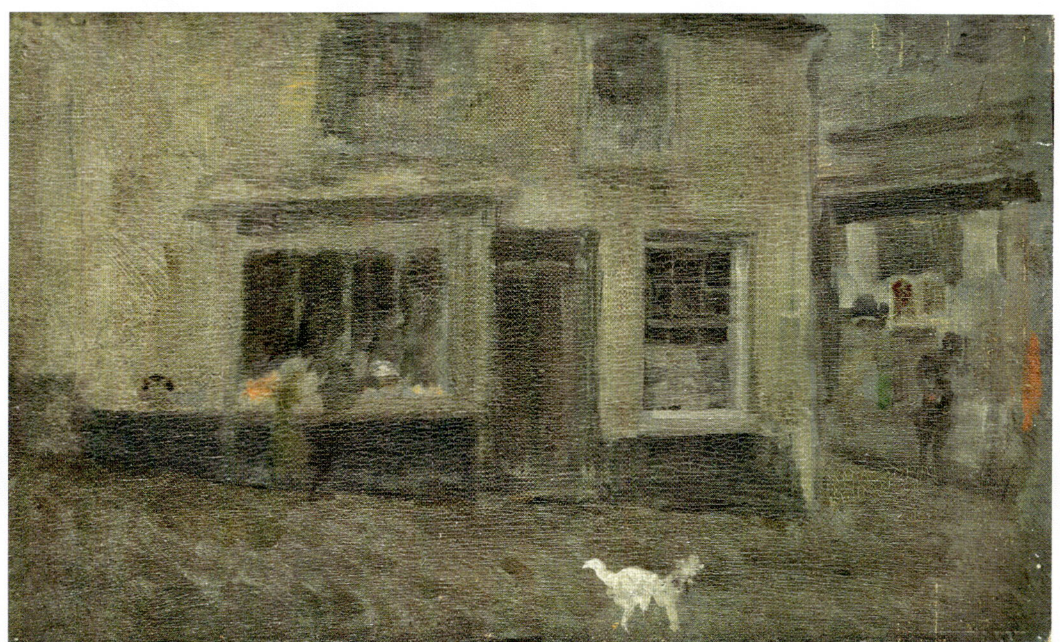

34 A Grey Note: Village Street

35 Nocturne; black and gold—No. 6, Rag Shop, Chelsea

Nocturne; black and gold— No. 6, Rag Shop, Chelsea
ca. 1878
Oil on canvas,
$14^1/_4 \times 20$ in.
Courtesy of the Fogg Art Museum, Harvard University Art Museums, Bequest of Grenville L. Winthrop
Dowdeswell 58

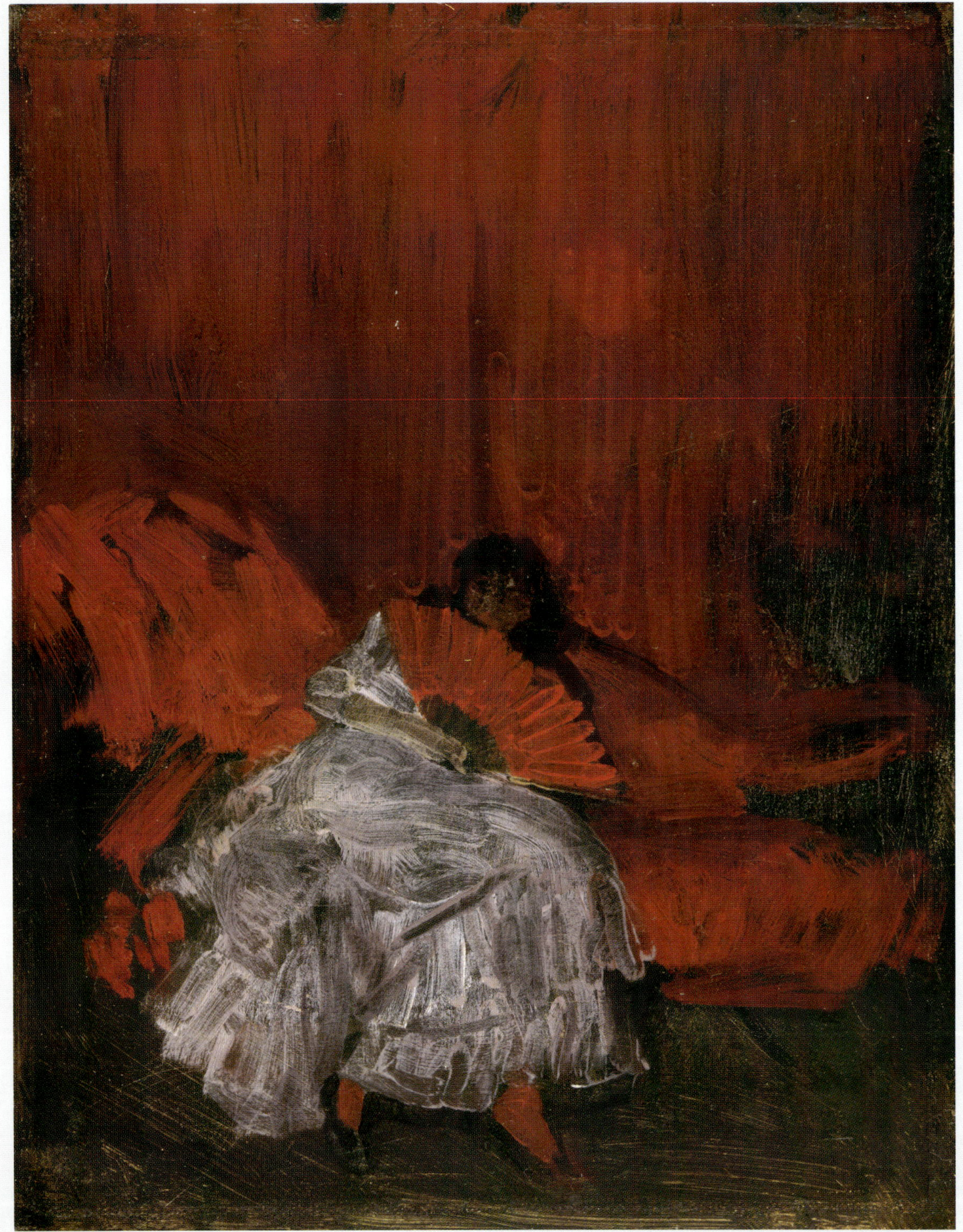

36 Red and pink—La Petite Mephisto

Red and pink—
La Petite Mephisto
Probably 1884
Oil on wood panel,
10 × 8 in.
Freer Gallery of Art,
Washington, D.C.
Gift of Charles Lang Freer
F1902.147
Dowdeswell 51

Note en rouge: L'Éventail
Probably 1884
Oil on wood,
3½ × 5¾ in.
Freer Gallery of Art
Washington, D.C.
Gift of Charles Lang Freer
F1913.91
Possibly Dowdeswell 64,
"Caprice in red"

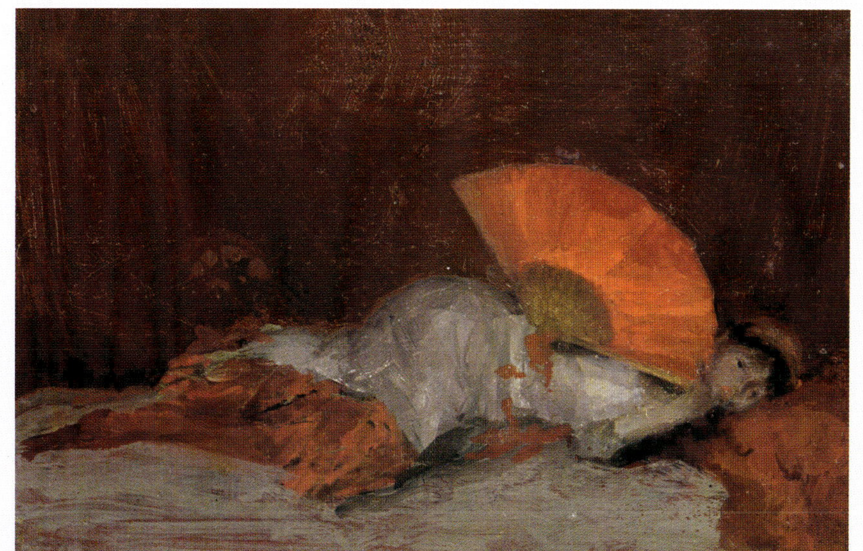
37 Note en rouge: L'Éventail

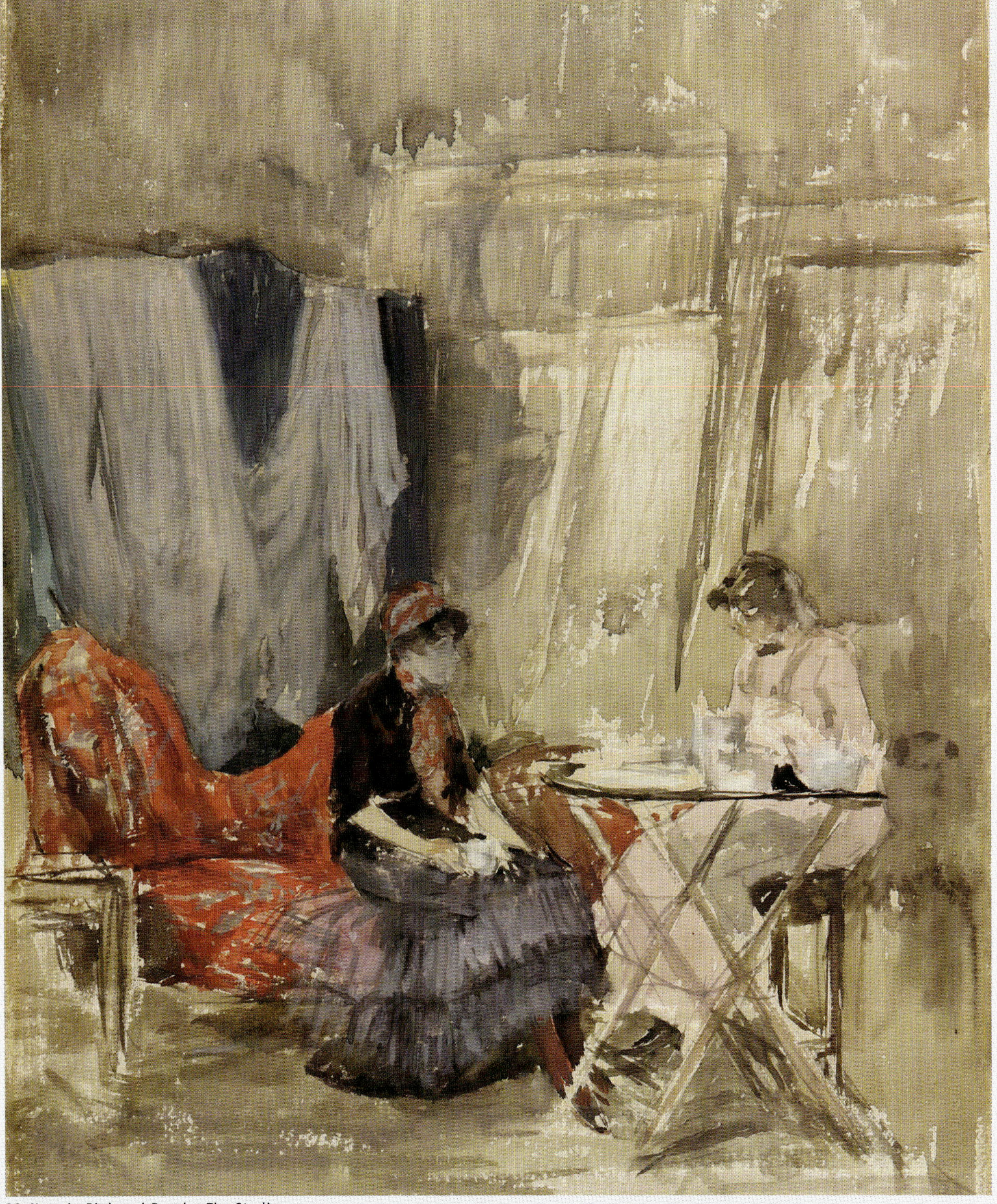

38 Note in Pink and Purple: The Studio

Note in Pink and Purple: The Studio
1883 or 1884
Watercolor on cream wove paper,
$11^{15}/_{16} \times 8^{7}/_{8}$ in.
Freer Gallery of Art,
Washington, D.C.
Gift of Charles Lang Freer
F1902.163
Probably Dowdeswell 10 or 6,
both titled
"Violet and red"

Note in Opal: Breakfast
1883 or 1884
Watercolor on cream paper,
laid down on card,
$9^{7}/_{8} \times 6^{7}/_{8}$ in.
Freer Gallery of Art,
Washington, D.C.
Gift of Charles Lang Freer
F1902.162
Probably Dowdeswell 35,
"Violet and amber—Tea"

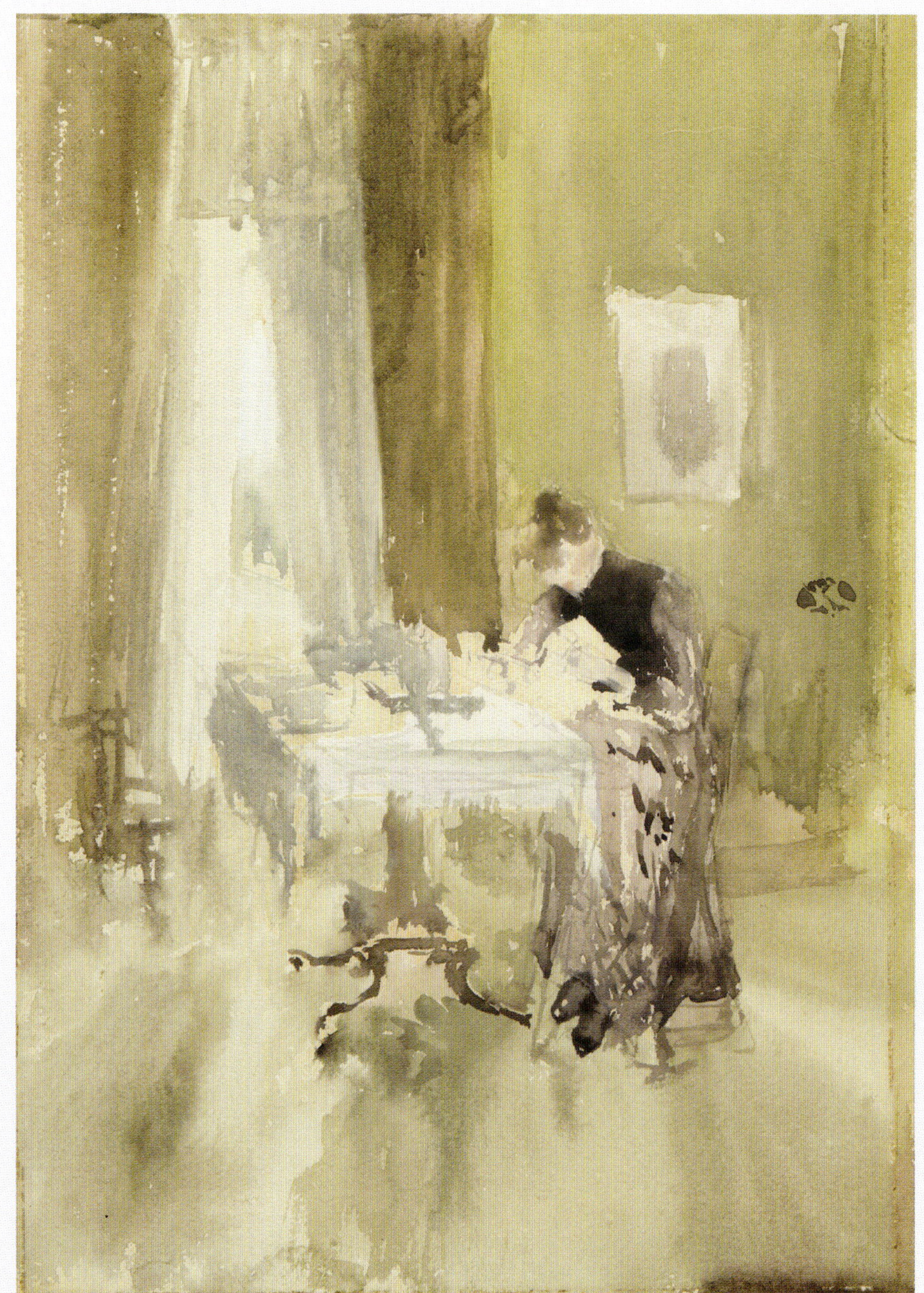

39 Note in Opal: Breakfast

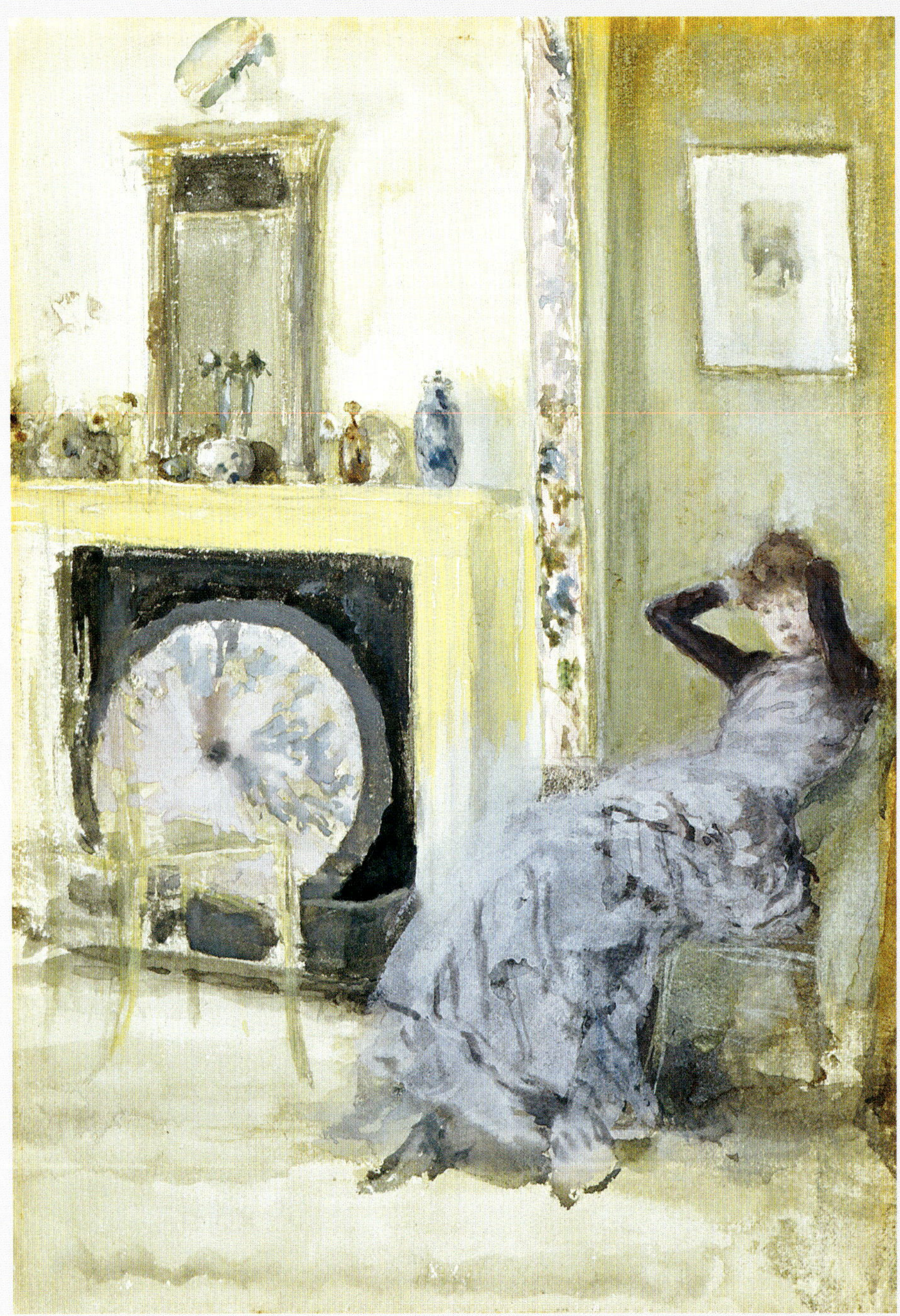

40 The Yellow Room

The Yellow Room

1883 or 1884
Watercolor on off-white paper,
$9^{13}/_{16} \times 7$ in.
Museum of Fine Arts, St. Petersburg, Florida. Extended anonymous loan.
TR 4386.1.
Possibly Dowdeswell 21,
"Harmony in violet and yellow"

Convalescent

1883 or 1884
Watercolor on off-white paper,
$9^{5}/_{8} \times 6^{3}/_{4}$ in.
Private Collection
Probably Dowdeswell 13,
"Petit Déjeuner; note in opal"

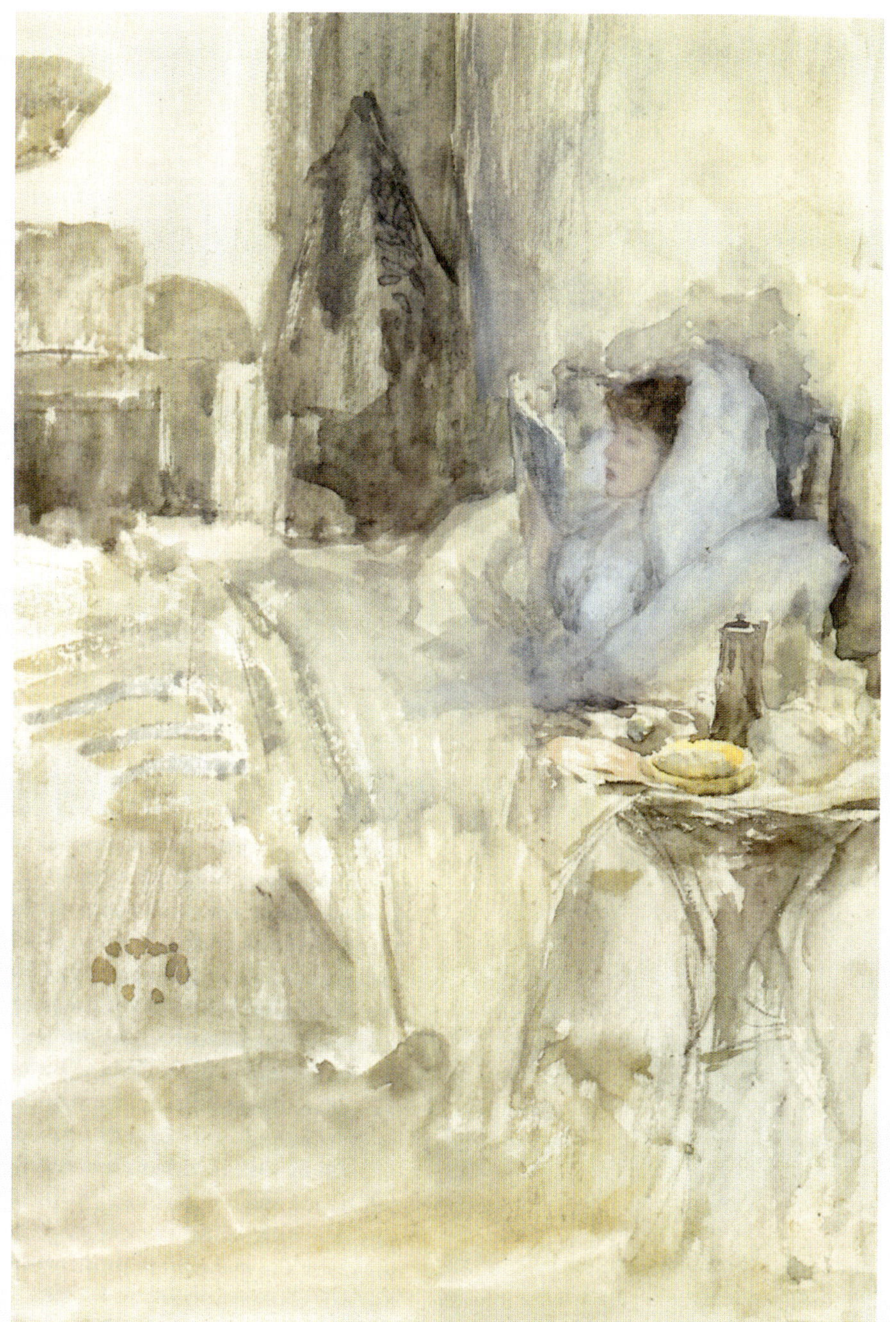

41 Convalescent

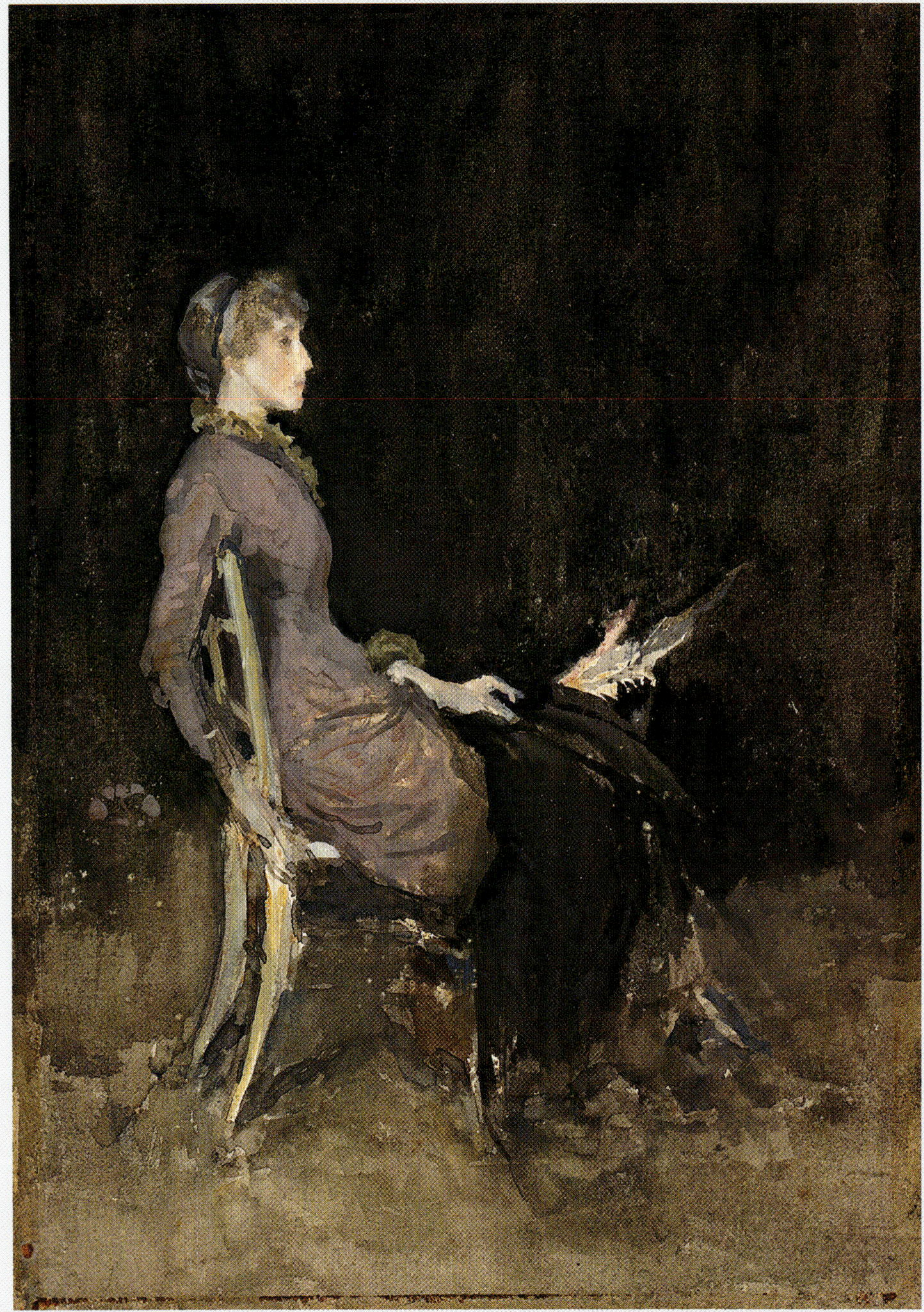

42 Black and red

Black and red

1883 or 1884
Watercolor on white laid paper,
$9 \times 6^1/_4$ in.
National Gallery of Art,
Washington, D.C.,
Gift of Mr. and Mrs. Paul Mellon
Dowdeswell 15

Harmony in violet and amber

1883 or 1884
Watercolor on cream paper,
laid down on card,
$9^{13}/_{16} \times 6^7/_{16}$ in.
Freer Gallery of Art,
Washington, D.C.
Gift of Charles Lang Freer
F1902.164
Dowdeswell 19

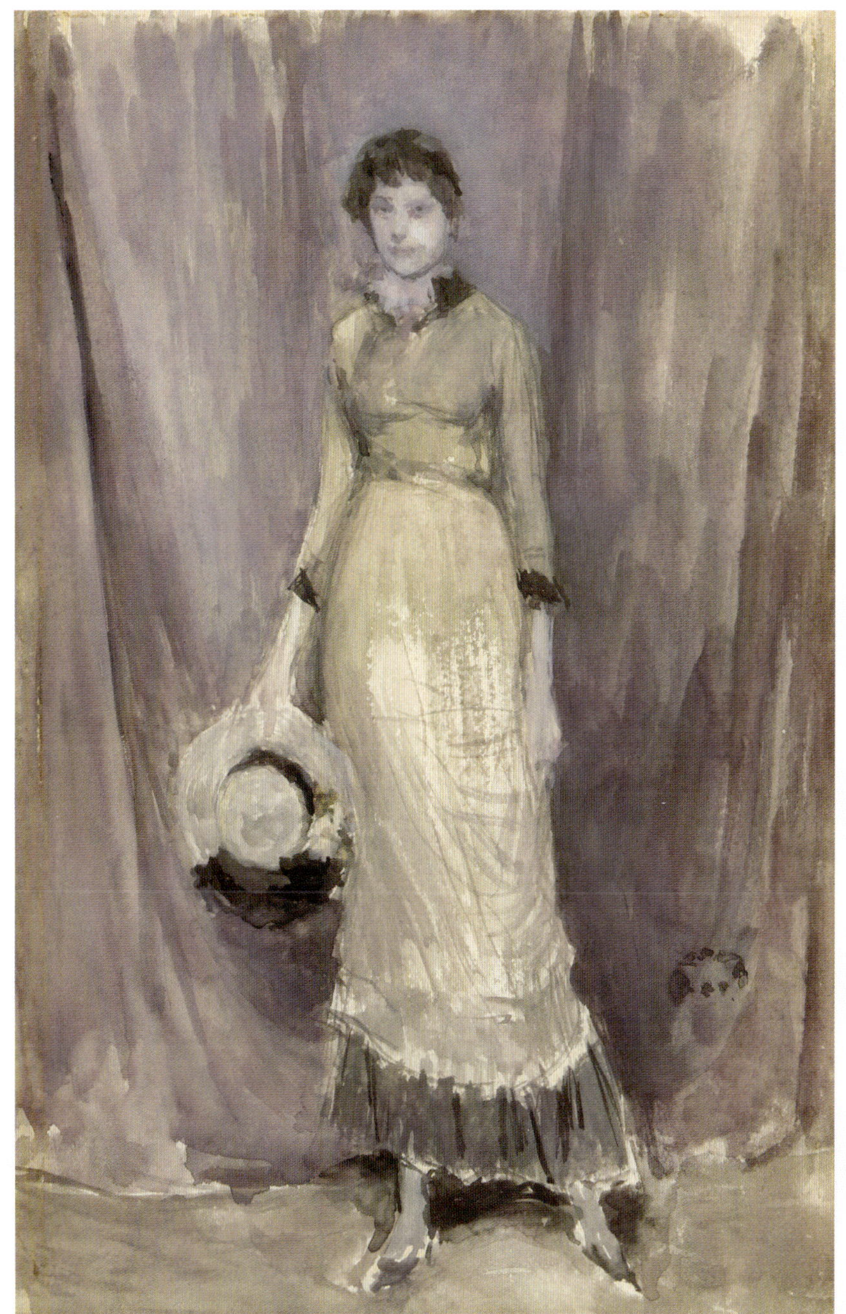

43 Harmony in violet and amber

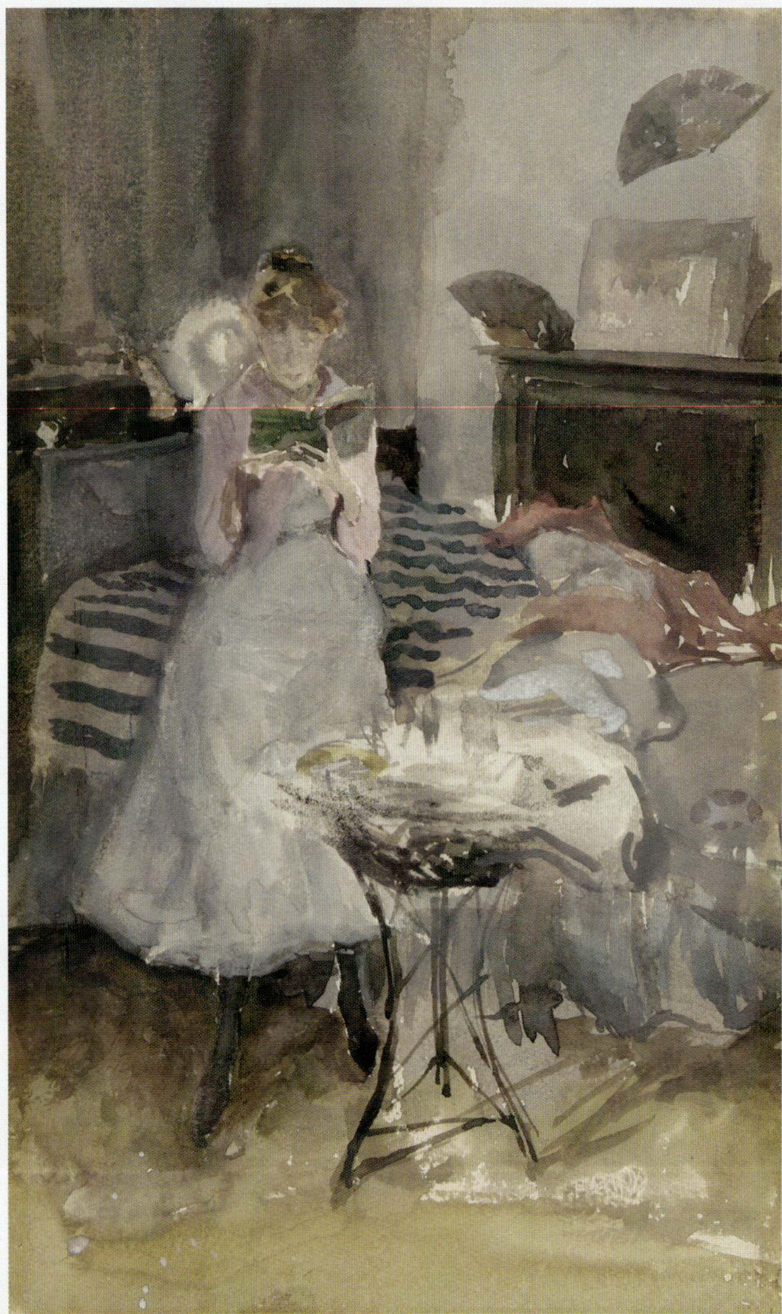

44 Pink note—The Novelette

Pink note — The Novelette

1883 or 1884

Watercolor on white wove paper,

$9^{15}/_{16} \times 6^{1}/_{16}$ in.

Freer Gallery of Art,

Washington, D.C.

Gift of Charles Lang Freer

F1902.158

Dowdeswell 16

Pink note — Shelling Peas

1883 or 1884

Watercolor on cream wove paper,

$9^{1}/_{2} \times 5^{5}/_{8}$ in.

Freer Gallery of Art,

Washington, D.C.

Gift of Charles Lang Freer

F1902.166

Dowdeswell 20

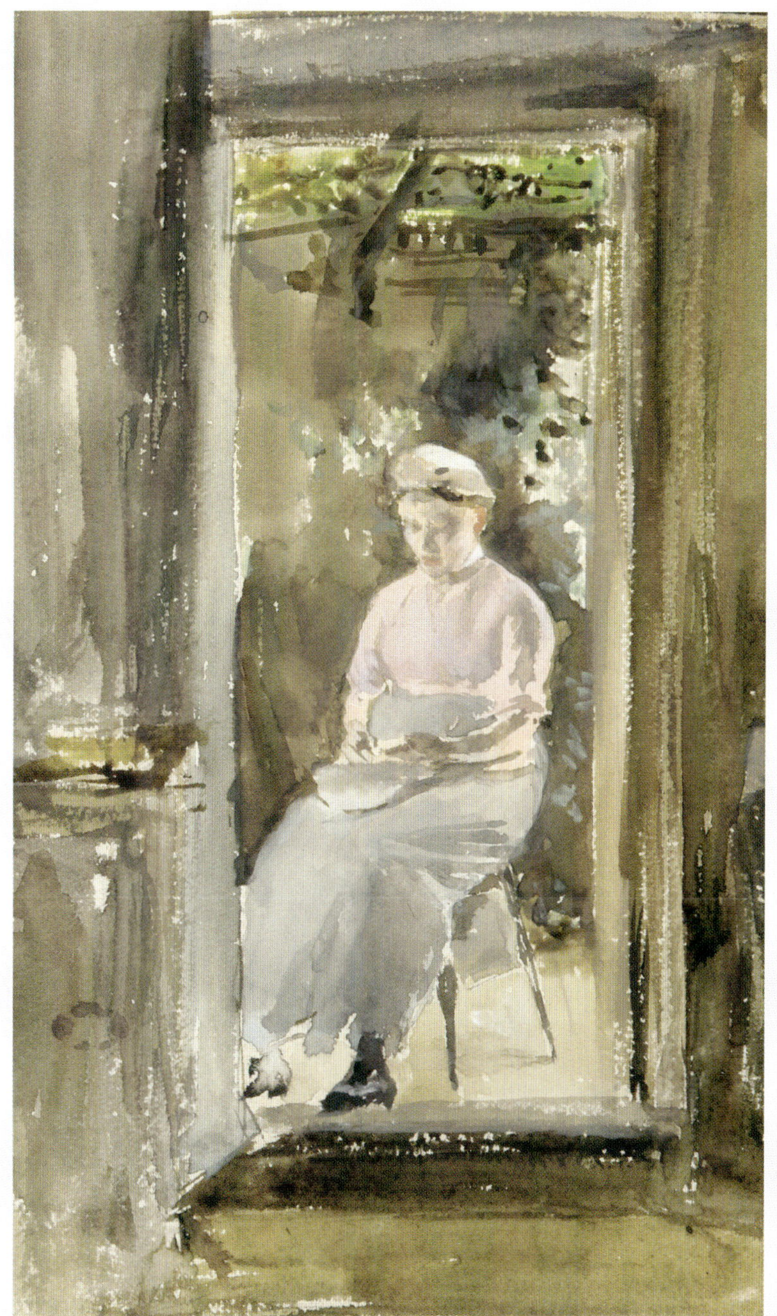

45 Pink note — Shelling Peas

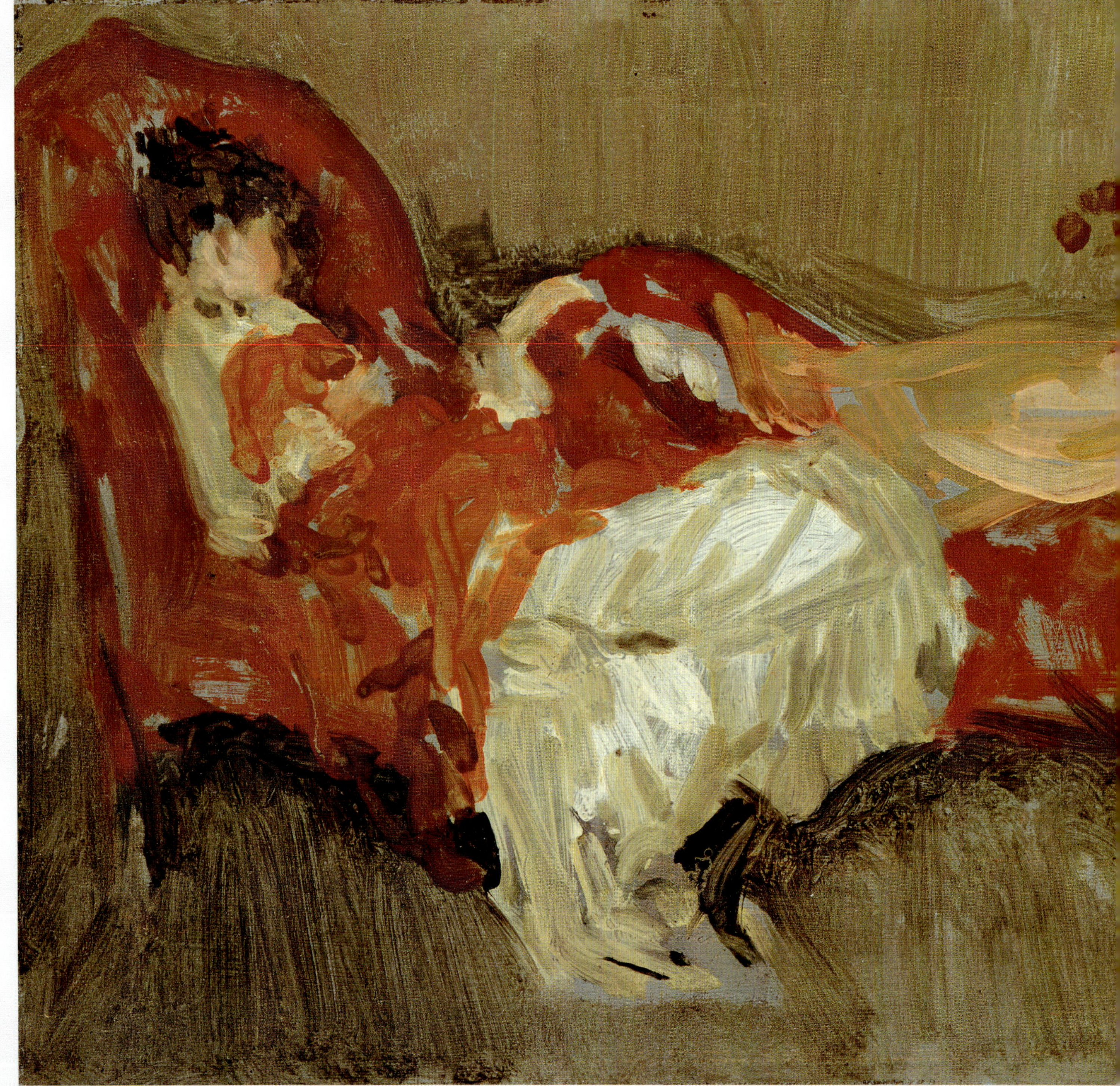

46 Note in red — The Siesta

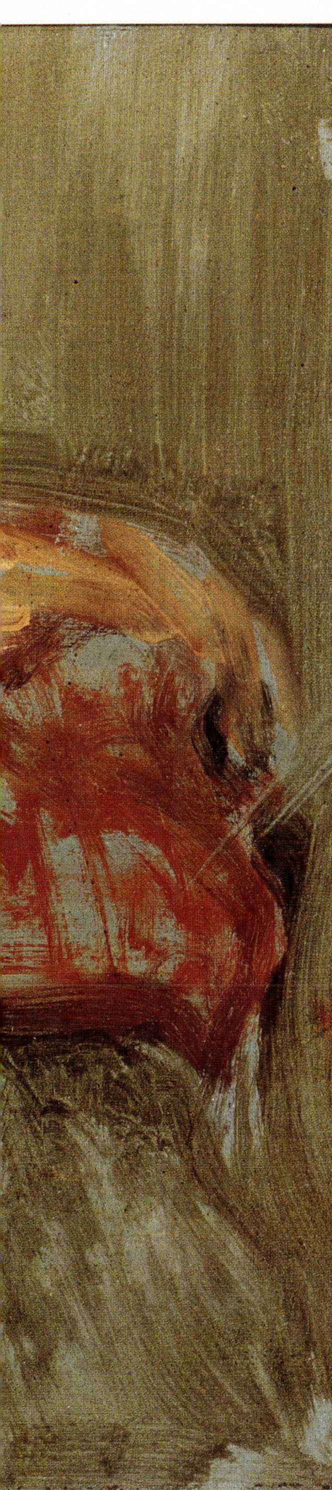

Note in red — The Siesta

Probably 1883 or 1884

Oil on wood panel,

$8^1/_2 \times 12$ in.

Terra Museum of American Art,

Chicago

Dowdeswell 17

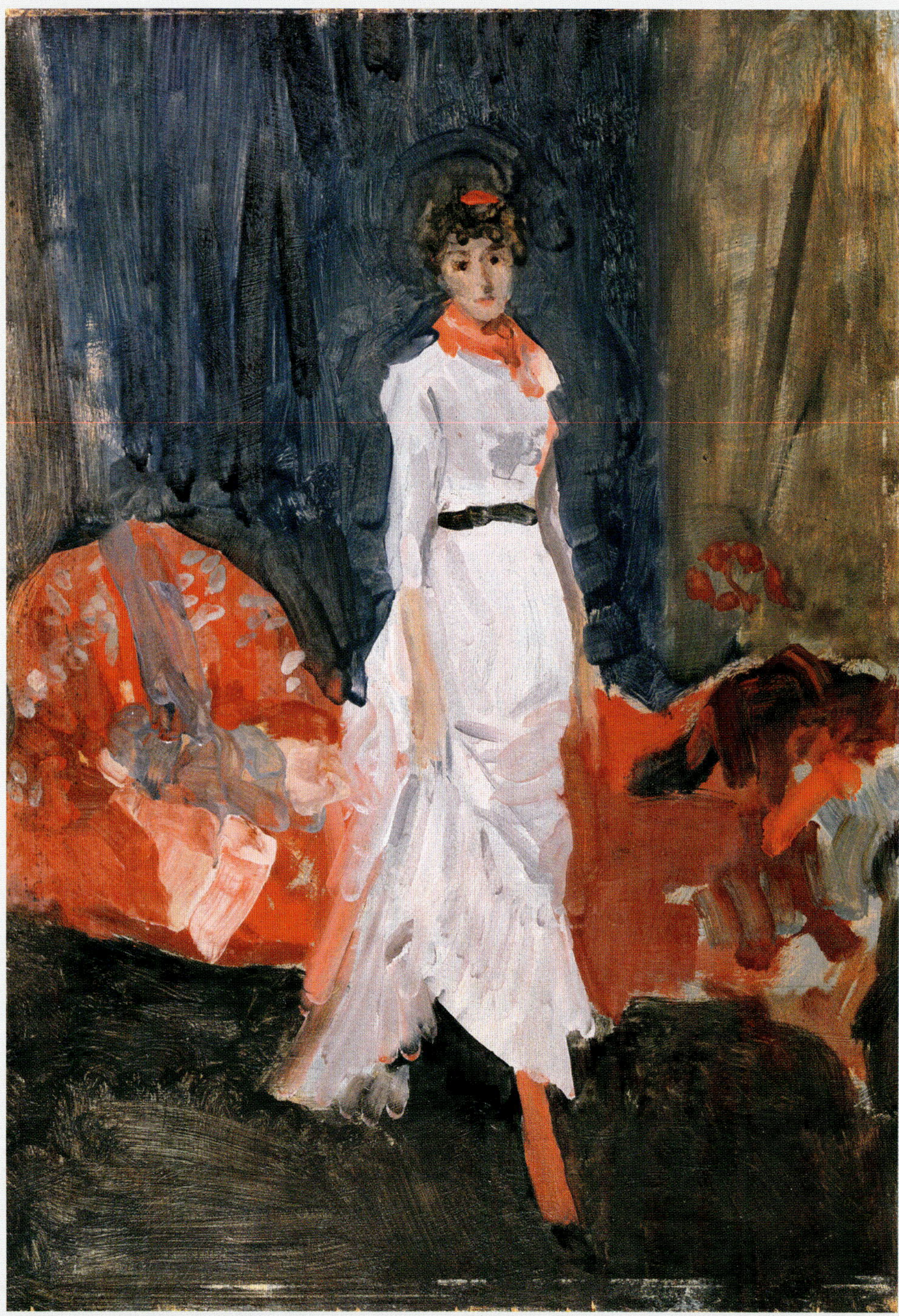

47 Arrangement in Pink, Red and Purple

Arrangement in Pink, Red and Purple
Probably 1884
Oil on wood, 12 × 9 in.
Cincinnati Art Museum
Probably Dowdeswell 6 or 10, both titled "Violet and red"
Cincinnati Art Museum, John J. Emery Fund

Note in pink and purple
1883 or 1884
Watercolor on white laid paper, $9^{3}/_{4} \times 6^{1}/_{4}$ in.
Cincinnati Art Museum
Probably Dowdeswell 27

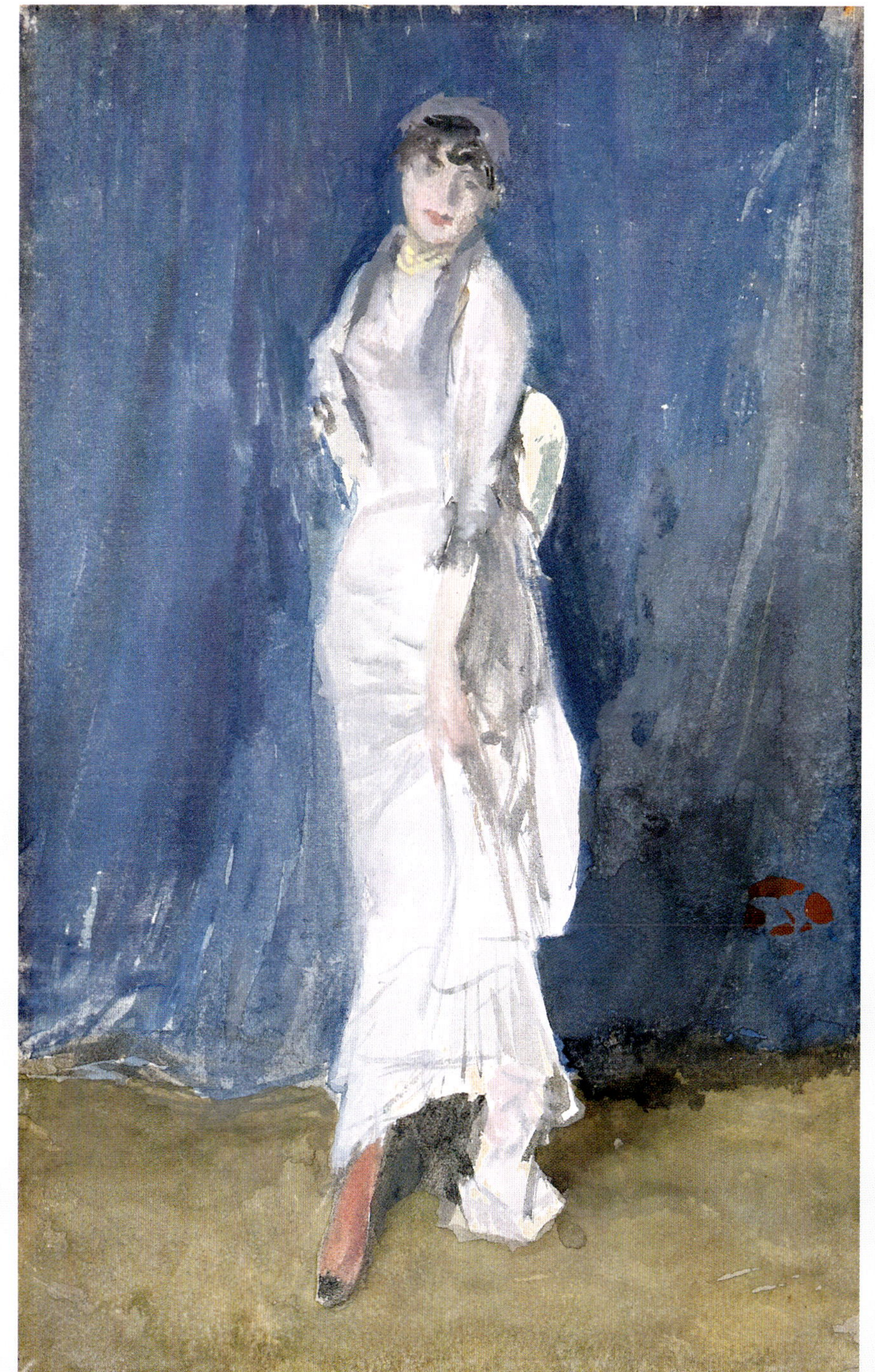
48 Note in pink and purple

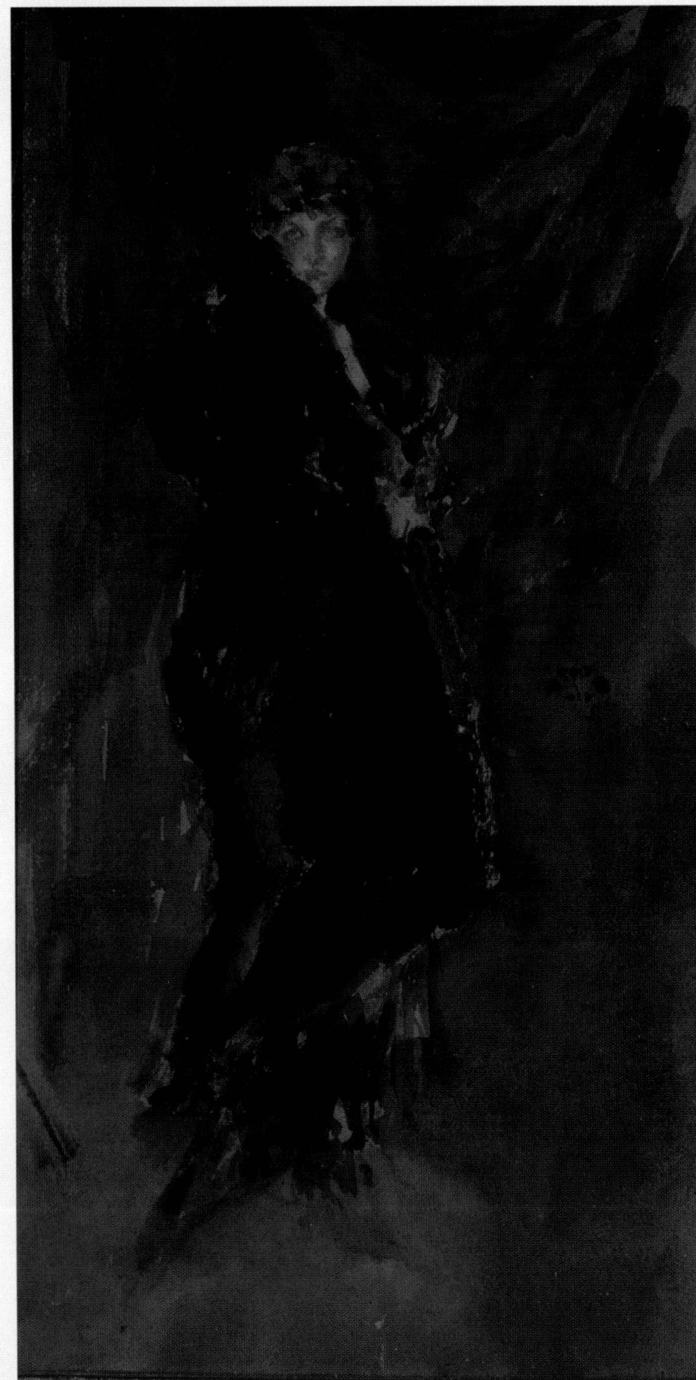
49 Red and black

Red and black

1883 or 1884

Watercolor on brown paper,

$9\frac{3}{16} \times 5\frac{1}{8}$ in.

Courtesy of the Fogg Art Museum,

Harvard University Art Museums,

Bequest of Grenville L. Winthrop

Dowdeswell 61

Yellow and grey

1883 or 1884

Watercolor on cream wove paper,

$9\frac{13}{16} \times 6\frac{7}{8}$ in.

Freer Gallery of Art,

Washington, D.C.

Gift of Charles Lang Freer

F1902.165

Dowdeswell 43

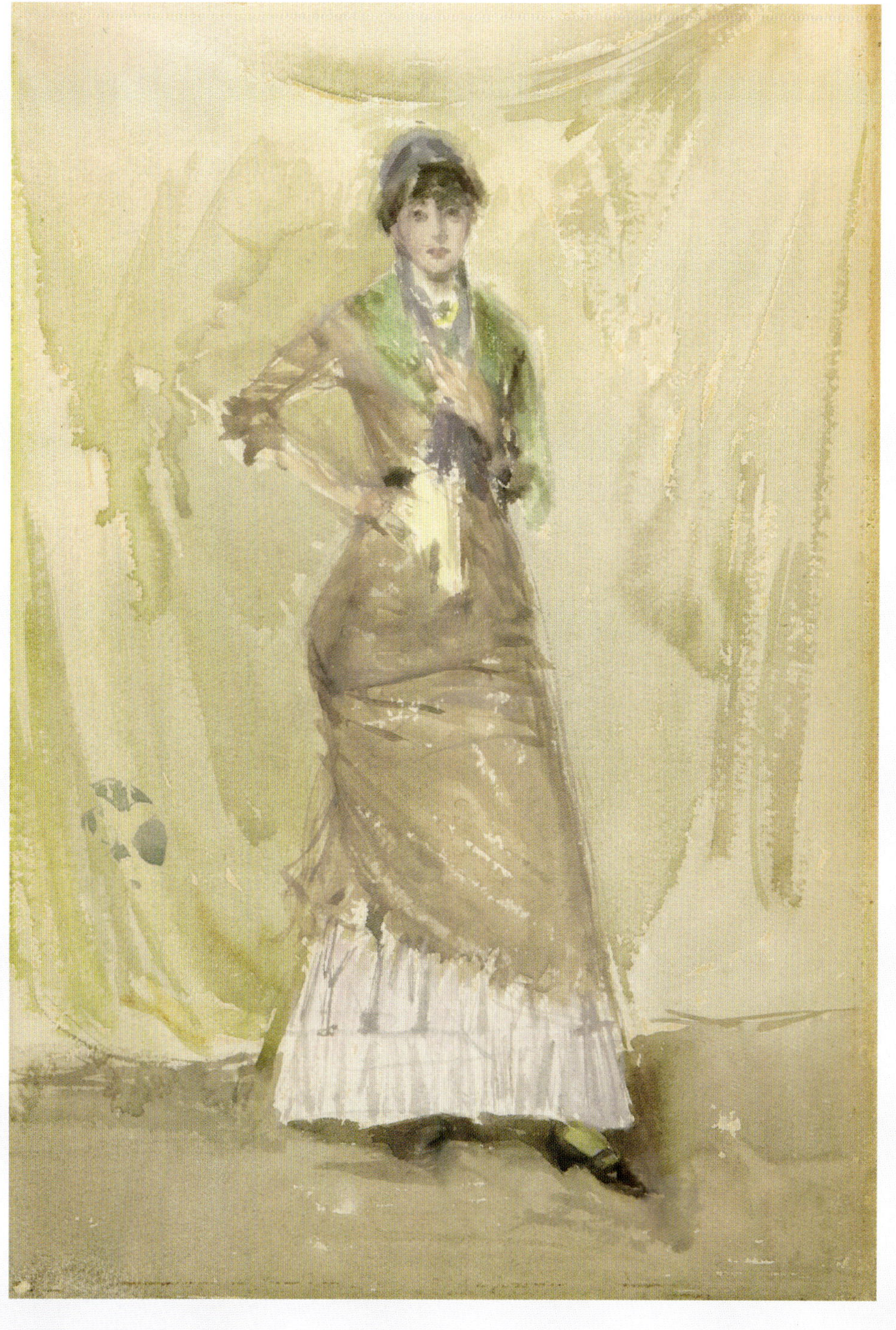

50 Yellow and grey

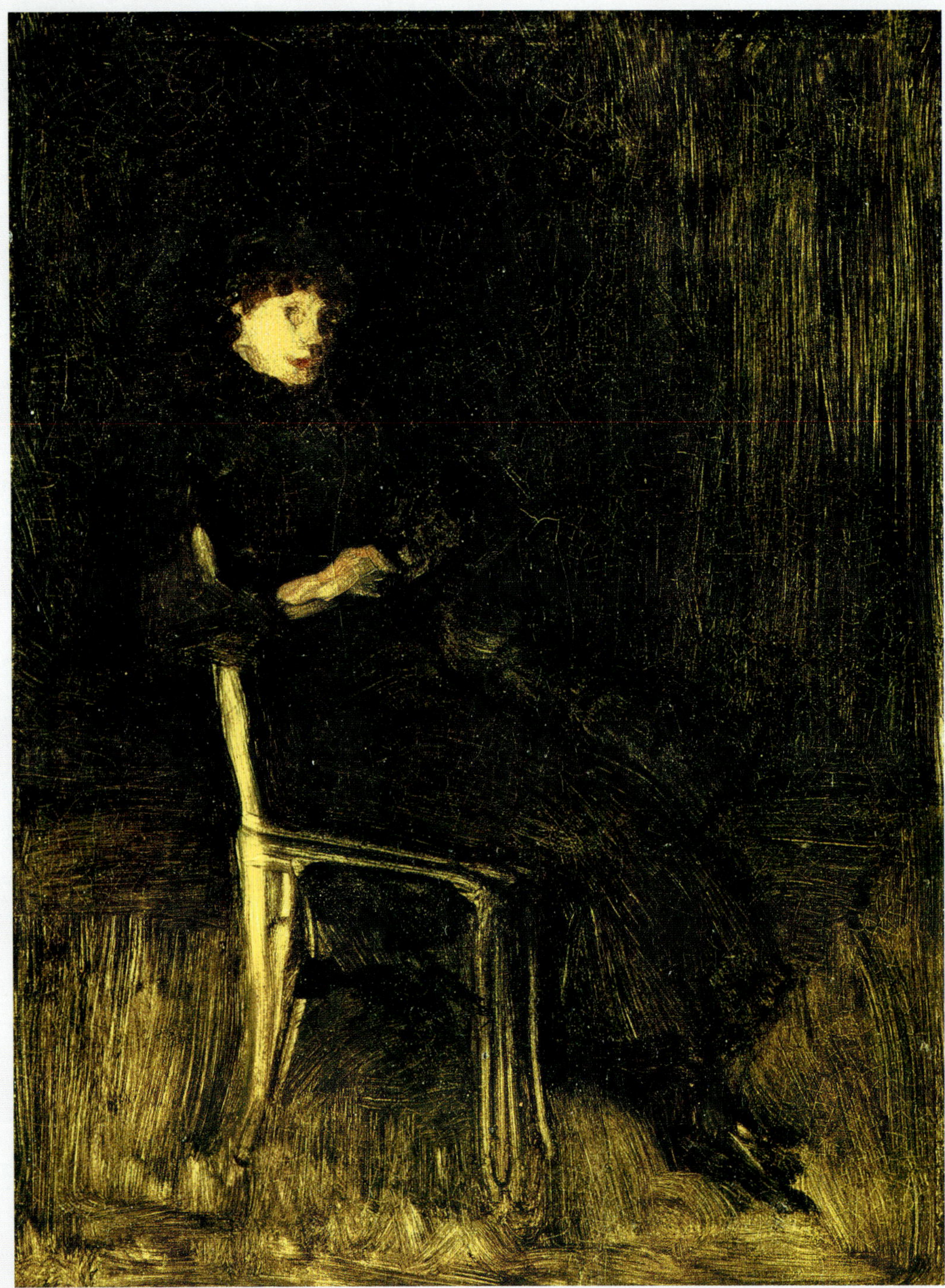

51 Arrangement in black— Reading

Arrangement in black—Reading

Early 1880s

Oil on wood panel,

$9^3/_4 \times 7^1/_2$ in.

Jim and Gina Liautaud

Dowdeswell 26

Bravura in brown

1883 or 1884

Watercolor on cream wove paper,

$8^9/_{16} \times 6^{15}/_{16}$ in.

Freer Gallery of Art,

Washington, D.C.

Gift of Charles Lang Freer

F1902.167

Possibly Dowdeswell 66,

"Bravura in brown"

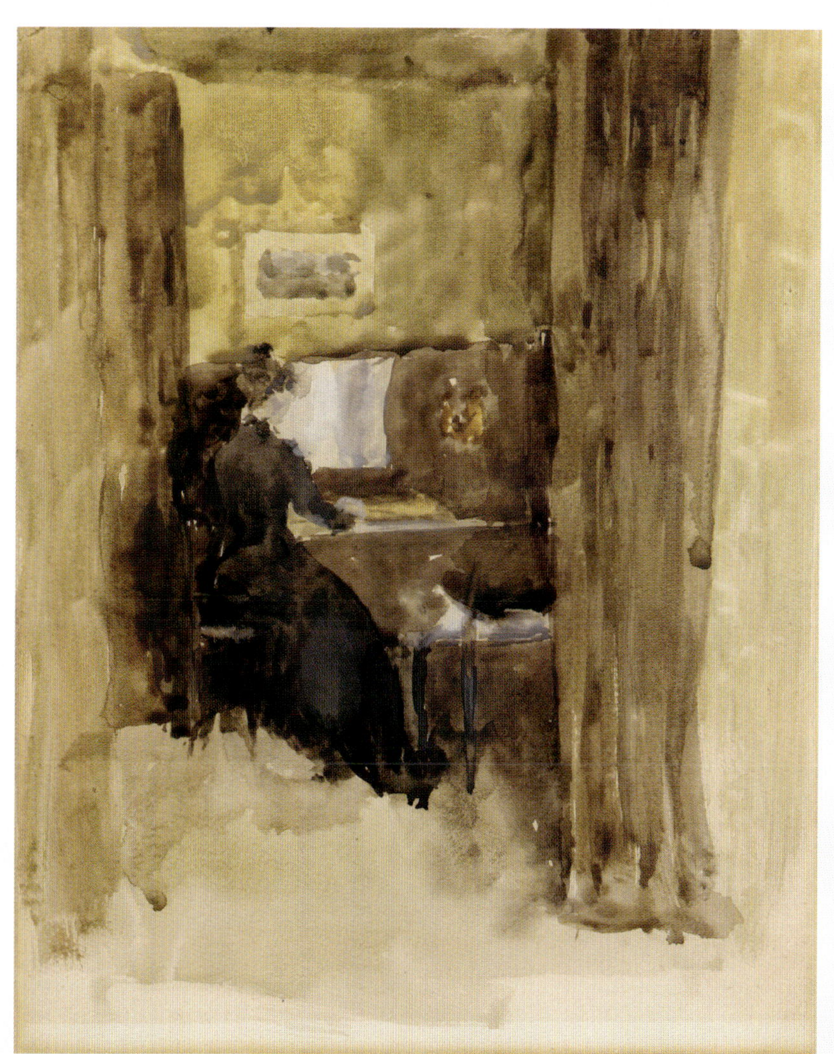

52 Bravura in brown

Moreby Hall

1883 or 1884
Pen, brown ink, and watercolor on cream paper,
$7^{11}/_{16} \times 11^{3}/_{16}$ in.
Freer Gallery of Art, Washington, D.C.
Gift of Charles Lang Freer
F1904.80
Dowdeswell 28

53 Moreby Hall

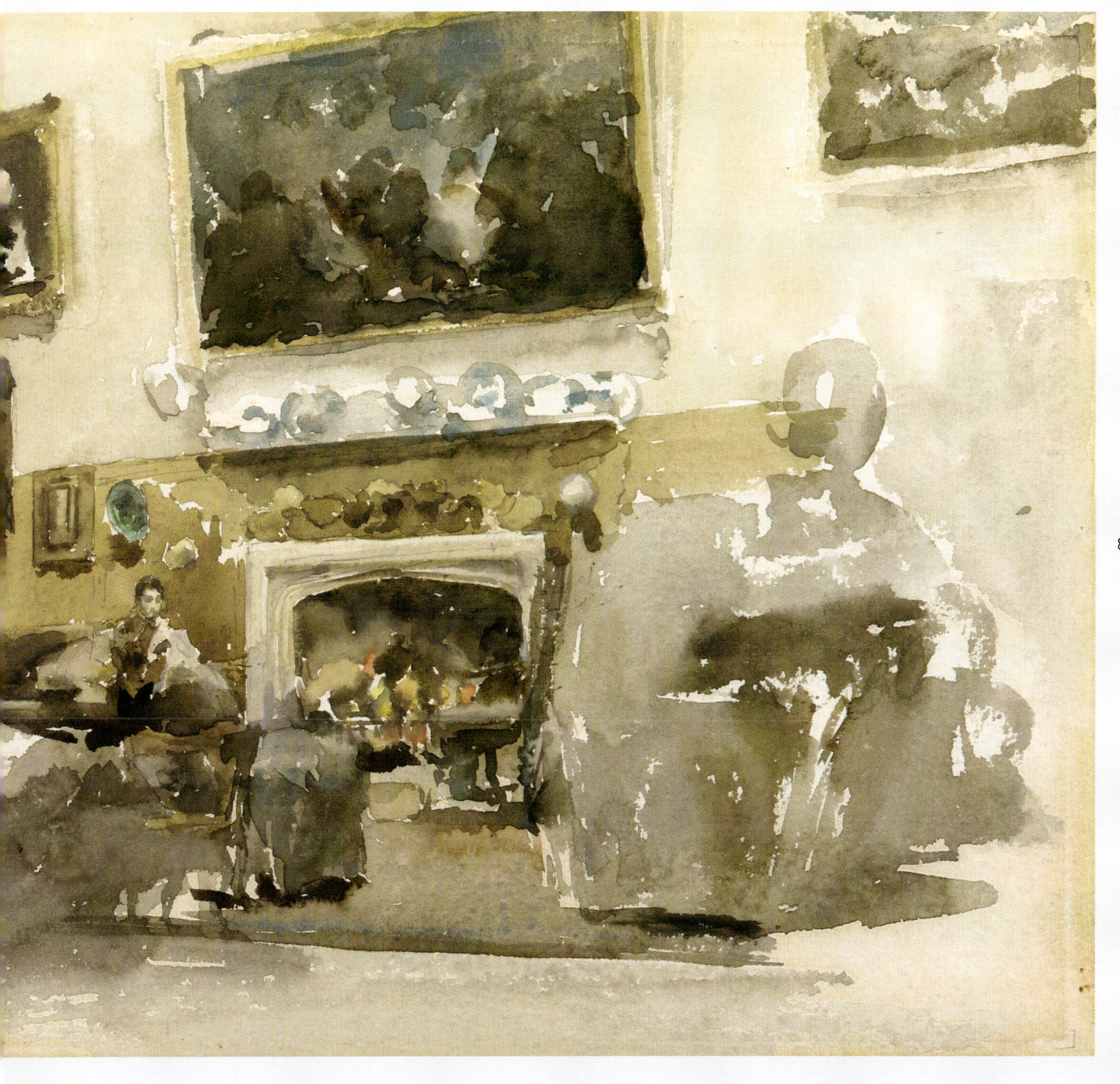

Identifying Paintings and Drawings Exhibited at the Dowdeswell and Dowdeswells Gallery in 1884

Paintings and drawings change over time. Oil paints flake and crackle. Varnishes darken. The pigments in watercolors fade from exposure to light. Watercolors and pastels are generally drawn on paper — and paper can fade, or darken, with exposure to light. But except in extreme instances, the basic appearance of an oil painting or drawing can remain recognizable for centuries.

The titles of works of art are much more evanescent. An artist completes a work, sends it to exhibition, and gives it a title. Some artists do not change the original titles. Many do. Whistler regularly changed his titles, and many of his major paintings have several different authoritative ones. Even artworks that are not renamed by their maker are often separated from their original titles. An artist finishes a work, titles it, and sells it. Maybe the original title is written on the back of the frame. This is especially common when a work is lent to an exhibition. Or maybe someone puts the original title on a tablet on the front of the frame. But artworks are often reframed, and when paintings and drawings are put into new frames, inscriptions on the backs of frames and tablets on their fronts are often lost. Inscriptions made directly onto the backs of paintings and drawings often survive longer, but even those get erased or obscured. Aging paintings and drawings are often attached to new canvas or board supports. This helps preserve the work of art, but conceals any information on the back of the original support. The first owners of artworks usually remember artist-given titles, but their descendents often forget them. And even the clearest of family memories are lost when artworks are sold. Paintings and drawings by well-known artists rarely get destroyed, but they are often separated from their original titles.

Sixty-four of the sixty-seven works that Whistler showed at the Dowdeswells' gallery in 1884 were small. Small works are even more vulnerable to title loss than big ones. Small paintings and drawings are generally completed more quickly than large ones, so artists rarely leave detailed descriptions of them in their journals or letters. Small works also tend to be less expensive, so galleries and collectors are less likely to pay for tablets when they are framed. Like nineteenth-century buyers of art, contemporary reviewers generally equated size with importance, so period reviews rarely offer detailed descriptions of small works. Whistler's aesthetic principles made his titles especially vulnerable. Whistler thought of his works as abstract studies in color and form, so he generally avoided descriptive titles, preferring to emphasize the formal, abstract qualities of his paintings and drawings. *Black and red* (no. 15), not 'Madge Seated'. But despite Whistler's preference and polemical purpose, collectors and dealers tend to describe representational works of art by their subject. Years pass, paintings change hands, and Whistler's *Harmony in violet and yellow* (no. 21) becomes *The Yellow Room*. *Sands; blue note* (no. 45) becomes *Low Tide*.

Collectors and art historians have been trying to identify the sixty-seven paintings shown at the Dowdeswells' gallery for more than one hundred years. The first person to play this game was the Detroit industrialist Charles Lang Freer (1854–1919), founder of the Freer Gallery of Art. Freer began collecting Whistler prints in 1887 and first met Whistler in 1890. Freer and Whistler became close friends in the late 1890s. By the time Freer retired in 1900, he had begun amassing what he hoped would become a comprehensive collection of Whistler's work. Freer devoted the rest of his life to collecting art, concentrating on work by Whistler and on works of Asian art that he thought were aesthetically sympathetic to Whistler's. Freer spent all of May and most of June 1902 in England and Scotland, purchasing a few Japanese paintings, but focusing his energies on the pursuit of work by Whistler. Freer bought from galleries, collectors, and the artist himself, acquiring major works from every period of Whistler's career including *The White Symphony: Three Girls* (ca. 1868), *Nocturne: Grey and Silver — Chelsea Embankment, Winter* (1879), and *Rose and Gold: The Little Lady Sophie of Soho* (1898–99), all three of which are now at the Freer. The most expensive purchase that Freer made during this buying spree was on June 3, 1902, when he bought thirty-one small Whistler oil paintings, watercolors, and pastels from the London barrister Sir Henry Studdy Theobald (1847–1934). Theobald had purchased most of these works from the Dowdeswells' gallery on July 1, 1885, and most — but not all — of them had been included in the 1884 exhibition.[1]

It seems unlikely that Freer had a chance to study the Theobald paintings and drawings while he was in London with Whistler, but after returning to Detroit he attempted to reconnect his purchases with their 1884 titles. Like subsequent art historians, Freer did this by trying to match the paintings and drawings with titles in the 1884 exhibition catalogue. Fortunately, the catalogue identified every work in the exhibition by title and medium: oil paintings were described by title alone, drawings were identified parenthetically by medium (as watercolors or pastels: see figure 2). In addition to the catalogue, Freer also used an 1887 manuscript that Theobald had sent him, in which Whistler provided titles for fifteen works that he hoped to borrow and exhibit at the *Exposition Internationale de Peinture et de Sculpture* at the Galerie Georges Petit in Paris. Unfortunately, Whistler's 1887 list has since disappeared.[2]

The results of Freer's research are clearly laid out in a typescript inventory titled "Oil Paintings, Water Colours and Pastels purchased from H. S. Theobald." Although undated, Freer probably created the inventory during the winter of 1906, when he was preparing lists of all objects he intended to donate to the Smithsonian Institution.[3] The inventory is organized by medium. Nothing on the sheet explains the parenthetical question marks that appear next to ten of the thirty-one titles — all located towards the bottom of one of the three categories — but a comparison of Freer's list with subsequent scholarly efforts to identify his purchases with titles in the 1884 catalogue makes clear that the question marks indicate works that he could not confidently connect to a specific work included in the 1884 exhibition. In making his identifications, Freer seems to have mainly relied on the 1884 catalogue and the now missing 1887 list, but he may have picked up additional information from his conversations with Theobald and Whistler. Even though Freer was working with the 1884 catalogue, his titles for works that he thought were in that show are not always an exact match for the published titles. In general, the titles he gives for the oils and pastels are much less exact than the titles he gives for the watercolors.

Given the limited information that was available, Freer did remarkably well. Of the ten titles he marked with a question mark, it now seems likely that none of the bottom three watercolors and none of the three pastels were in the 1884 exhibition. Three of the other titles with a question mark were probably in the show, but under different titles and — in one case — media. Thus, the painting Freer called *Low-Tide* was probably *Sands; blue note* (no. 45); *A Note in Red* was probably *Red and blue — Lindsey Houses* (no. 4); and the watercolor *A Note in Green* was probably *Yellow and grey* (no. 43), which was listed in the 1884 catalogue as an oil painting, but which period reviews suggest was actually a watercolor. Freer also seems to have mismatched two watercolors. The drawing he thought was *Petit Déjeuner: Note in opal* (no. 13), was probably in the 1884 exhibition as *Violet and amber — Tea* (no. 35). And the watercolor he thought was *The Studio — Note in pink and purple* (no. 27), seems to have been in the show as *Violet and red* (no. 6 or 10). Neither *Violet and amber — Tea* nor *Violet and red* seem to have been included in the 1887 Paris exhibition, so neither would have appeared on the missing 1887 list. The fact that Freer gave these two drawings titles taken directly from the 1884 catalogue suggests that while some of the identifications in the 1906 inventory may have derived from information that was supplied by Theobald or Whistler, others were based mainly or solely on Freer's efforts to match the Theobald paintings and drawings with titles he found in the 1884 catalogue.[4]

The one other title that Freer marked with a question mark, *The White House*, remains a puzzle. Freer's placement of this title well up from the bottom of his list of oils, and above three paintings that probably were in the 1884 exhibition, suggests that he thought *The White House* was probably in the Dowdeswell and Dowdeswells show but could not link it to any one title. The authors of the catalogue raisonné suggest that it was probably exhibited at Dowdeswell and Dowdeswells in either 1884 or 1886, but do not suggest any specific match. Style and provenance suggest that *The White House* might have been shown in the 1884 exhibition, but none of the period exhibition reviews contain a description that fits it. Moreover, *The White House* is not a good match for any of the unaccounted for oil paintings. Although far from conclusive, the existing evidence suggests that *The White House* was probably not included in the 1884 exhibition. Not counting *The White House*, twenty-four of the thirty-one paintings and drawings Freer purchased from Theobald were definitely or probably included in the 1884 exhibition. A strikingly high percentage of the small oils and watercolors Freer acquired between 1902 and his death in 1919 were also in the Dowdeswell and Dowdeswells exhibition, which suggests that after acquiring the Theobald collection he made some effort to reassemble as much of the 1884 show as possible.

Like Freer, modern scholars attempting to identify the paintings and drawings included in the 1884 exhibition rely on information in the exhibition catalogue and provenance. But contemporary art historians have access to an important source of information that Freer did not have. Like many successful artists today, Whistler hired clipping services to collect newspaper and magazine articles about him. Whistler had these cuttings pasted into scrapbooks, which were eventually given to the University of Glasgow. The Whistler press-cutting books contain hundreds of exhibition reviews, including almost forty of the 1884 Dowdeswell and Dowdeswells exhibition. Many of these reviews include descriptions of Whistler's work, enabling scholars to identify many of the paintings and drawings in the show. Art historians began mining the press-cutting books in the 1960s, and the fruits of their labors are summarized in two catalogues raisonné, which document almost all of Whistler's known oils, watercolors, pastels, and drawings. Many of my identifications derive from materials presented in these indispensable resources.[5]

Finally, frames too can be used to help identify paintings and drawings from the 1884 exhibition. As discussed in the main essay in this book, twenty-five of the paintings and watercolors at the Freer that can be traced back to the 1884 exhibition are housed in vintage frames, many of which still carry Dowdeswell and Dowdeswells labels on the reverse. The design and manufacture of all of these frames is consistent, suggesting that all were made at one time, although they exist in two sizes. Six of the twenty-five are 4⅜ inches wide. Four of the 4⅜ inch-wide frames hold tiny 3½ x 5¾ inch oil paintings, the smallest works in the Dowdeswell show. The nineteen other vintage frames have a molding width of 5 9⁄16 inches. Freer acquired three of the tiny paintings from Theobald who purchased most of the smallest paintings in the 1884 exhibition, so it seems likely that the vast majority of the works in the 1884 exhibition were housed in the 5 9⁄16 inch-wide frames — probably as many as fifty-five of the sixty-seven works in the show. A frame with a molding of 5 9⁄16 inches is unusually wide for a small oil painting, watercolor, or pastel , so it is not surprising that the reviewer for the *Globe* complained that the Dowdeswells' gallery frames were "massive."[6] By way of comparison, the similar frame Whistler designed for the 1881 exhibition of his Venice pastels at the Fine Art Society was only 4½ inches wide. The exaggerated width of the 1884 frames may explain why so many of them have been lost, but when they do survive they can be used to identify a work as having probably been in the exhibition. The fact that *Arrangement in Pink, Red and Purple* (Cincinnati Museum of Art) is in a vintage frame made from the same unusual 5 9⁄16 inch-wide molding found on many of the Freer paintings was a crucial clue contributing to my identification of it as probably being Dowdeswell numer 6 or number 10, both titled *Violet and red*.

Drawing on all these kinds of clues, I have identified fifty-seven of the sixty-seven works that were shown at the Dowdeswells' gallery in 1884. Some of my identifications seem certain. Others are more tentative. When I am unsure of an identification, I have qualified it as either "probable" or "possible." In order to let the reader join in the game of identification, reference catalogue entries include all relevant descriptions from contemporary reviews. Information about provenance, frames, inscriptions, and old exhibition labels is included only when it helps identify a painting or drawing as having been included in the 1884 Dowdeswell and Dowdewells exhibition.

Prices fixed May 1906

OIL PAINTINGS, WATER COLOURS and PASTELS purchased from

H. S. THEOBALD.

OIL PAINTINGS:

NOCTURNE. "OPAL AND SILVER."
"PETITE MEPHISTE."
"GREEN AND GOLD - THE GREAT SEA."
"CHELSEA SHOPS."
"BLUE AND GREY - UNLOADING."
"THE SEA AND SAND."
"HARMONY IN BROWN AND GOLD - OLD CHELSEA CHURCH."
"BLUE AND GREEN - THE COAL SHAFT."
"THE WHITE HOUSE." (?)
"WORTLEY - NOTE IN GREEN."
"LOW-TIDE." (?)
"A NOTE IN RED." (?)

WATER COLOUR:

"PINK NOTE - THE NOVELETTE."
NOCTURNE. "BLACK AND RED - BACK CANAL, HOLLAND."
NOCTURNE. "GREY AND GOLD - CANAL, HOLLAND."
NOCTURNE. "GRAND CANAL, AMSTERDAM."
"PETIT DEJEUNER - NOTE IN OPAL."
"THE STUDIO - NOTE IN PINK AND PURPLE."
"HARMONY IN VIOLET AND AMBER."
"A NOTE IN GREEN." (?)
"PINK NOTE - SHELLING PEAS."
"BRAVURA IN BROWN."
"FRITH - EVENING."
"GREY AND SILVER - PIER, SOUTHEND."
"OPAL BEACH."
"THE MOUTH OF THE RIVER." (?)
"THE BATHERS." (?)
"THE ANCHORAGE." (?)

PASTELS:

"VENETIAN COURTYARD." (?)
"DOORWAY." (?)
"RESTING." (?)

£ 3,000 $14,821.91

freight, duty, &c. 178.09 $15,000.00

Figure 1.
"Oil Paintings, Water Colours and Pastels purchased from H. S. Theobald", typescript, ca. 1906.
Charles Lang Freer Papers, Freer Gallery of Art Archives, Gift of the Estate of Charles Lang Freer.

Page 84
Figure 2.
"Notes" — "Harmonies" — "Nocturnes"
(London: Dowdeswell and Dowdeswells, 1884).
Freer Gallery of Art Library, Gift of Charles Lang Freer.
Marginal annotations are by Freer, and evidence his effort to match his purchases with their 1884 titles.

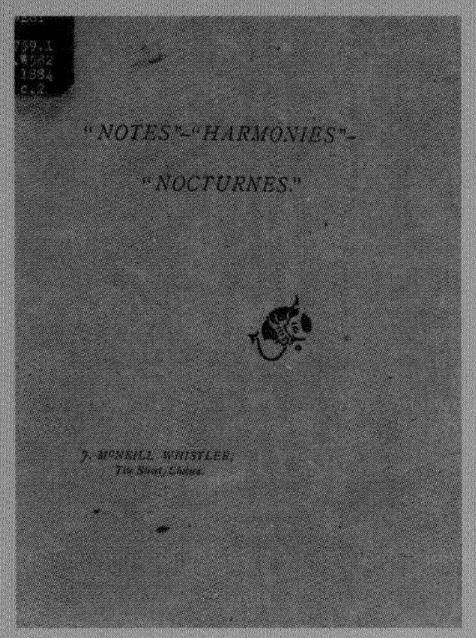

"NOTES"–"HARMONIES"–

"NOCTURNES."

J. McNEILL WHISTLER,
Tite Street, Chelsea.

"NOTES"—"HARMONIES"—

"NOCTURNES."

J. McNEILL WHISTLER,
Tite Street, Chelsea.

May, 1884.

L'ENVOIE.

A PICTURE is finished when all trace of the means used to bring about the end has disappeared.

To say of a picture, as is often said in its praise, that it shows great and earnest labour, is to say that it is incomplete and unfit for view.

Industry in Art is a necessity,—not a virtue,—and any evidence of the same, in the production, is a blemish, not a quality;—a proof, not of achievement, but of absolutely insufficient work, for work alone will efface the footsteps of work.

The work of the master reeks not of the sweat of the brow,—suggests no effort,—and is finished from its beginning.

The completed task of perseverance only has never been begun, and will remain unfinished to eternity,—a monument of goodwill and foolishness.

"There is one that laboureth, and taketh pains, and maketh haste, and is so much the more behind."

The masterpiece should appear as the flower to the painter,—perfect in its bud as in its bloom,—with no reason to explain its presence,—no mission to fulfil,—a joy to the artist,—a delusion to the philanthropist, a puzzle to the botanist, an accident of sentiment and alliteration to the literary man.

84

PAINTINGS—DRAWINGS—PASTELS.

1. The Pier; a grey note.
2. The Angry Sea.
3. Nocturne; grey and gold—Canal; Holland. (*Water-colour.*)
4. Red and blue—Lindsey Houses.
5. Grey and silver—Purfleet. (*Water-colour.*)
6. Violet and red.
7. Green and opal—The Village.
8. The Little Grocery, Chelsea; grey and red. (*Water-colour.*)
9. Nocturne in grey and gold—Piccadilly. (*Water-colour.*)
10. Violet and red.
11. Chelsea; yellow and grey.
12. Pink and opal—Harbour.
13. Petit Déjeuner; note in opal. (*Water-colour.*)
14. Erith—Evening. (*Water-colour.*)
15. Black and red. (*Water-colour.*)

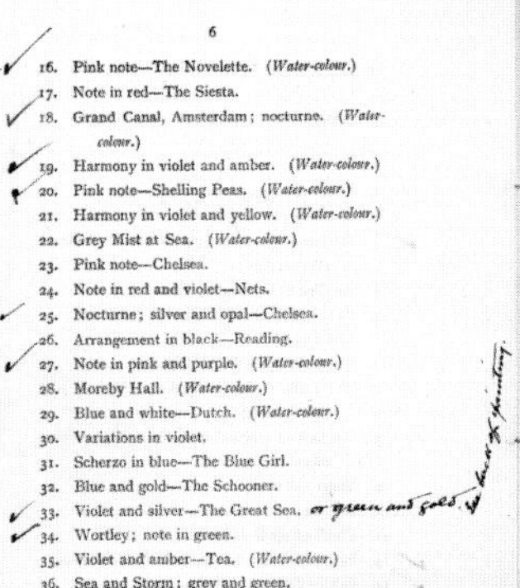

6

16. Pink note—The Novelette. (*Water-colour.*)
17. Note in red—The Siesta.
18. Grand Canal, Amsterdam; nocturne. (*Water-colour.*)
19. Harmony in violet and amber. (*Water-colour.*)
20. Pink note—Shelling Peas. (*Water-colour.*)
21. Harmony in violet and yellow. (*Water-colour.*)
22. Grey Mist at Sea. (*Water-colour.*)
23. Pink note—Chelsea.
24. Note in red and violet—Nets.
25. Nocturne; silver and opal—Chelsea.
26. Arrangement in black—Reading.
27. Note in pink and purple. (*Water-colour.*)
28. Moreby Hall. (*Water-colour.*)
29. Blue and white—Dutch. (*Water-colour.*)
30. Variations in violet.
31. Scherzo in blue—The Blue Girl.
32. Blue and gold—The Schooner.
33. Violet and silver—The Great Sea. or green and gold.
34. Wortley; note in green.
35. Violet and amber—Tea. (*Water-colour.*)
36. Sea and Storm; grey and green.
37. The Green Headland.

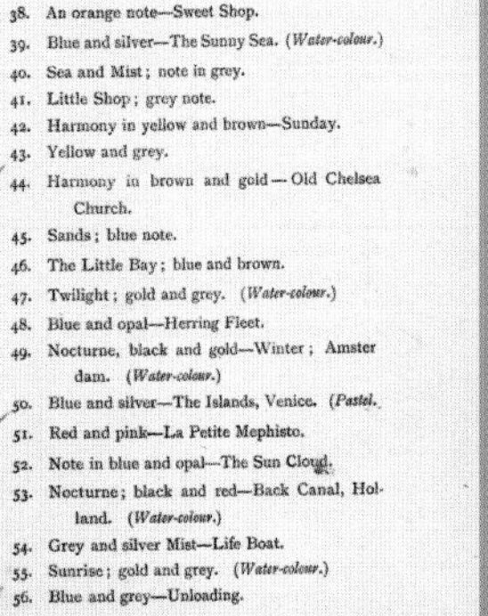

7

38. An orange note—Sweet Shop.
39. Blue and silver—The Sunny Sea. (*Water-colour.*)
40. Sea and Mist; note in grey.
41. Little Shop; grey note.
42. Harmony in yellow and brown—Sunday.
43. Yellow and grey.
44. Harmony in brown and gold—Old Chelsea Church.
45. Sands; blue note.
46. The Little Bay; blue and brown.
47. Twilight; gold and grey. (*Water-colour.*)
48. Blue and opal—Herring Fleet.
49. Nocturne, black and gold—Winter; Amsterdam. (*Water-colour.*)
50. Blue and silver—The Islands, Venice. (*Pastel.*)
51. Red and pink—La Petite Mephisto.
52. Note in blue and opal—The Sun Cloud.
53. Nocturne; black and red—Back Canal, Holland. (*Water-colour.*)
54. Grey and silver Mist—Life Boat.
55. Sunrise; gold and grey. (*Water-colour.*)
56. Blue and grey—Unloading.

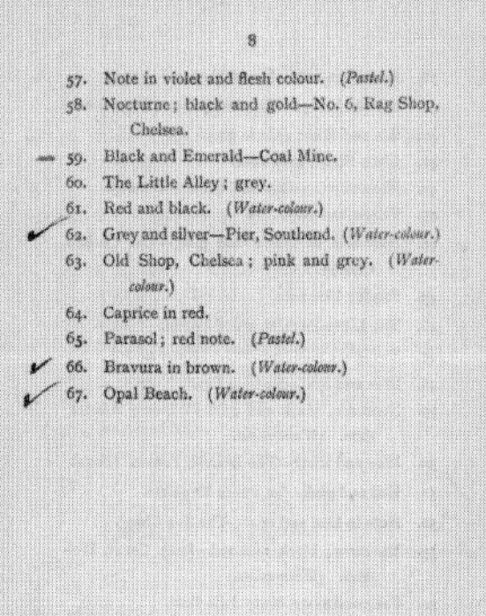

8

57. Note in violet and flesh colour. (*Pastel.*)
58. Nocturne; black and gold—No. 6, Rag Shop, Chelsea.
59. Black and Emerald—Coal Mine.
60. The Little Alley; grey.
61. Red and black. (*Water-colour.*)
62. Grey and silver—Pier, Southend. (*Water-colour.*)
63. Old Shop, Chelsea; pink and grey. (*Water-colour.*)
64. Caprice in red.
65. Parasol; red note. (*Pastel.*)
66. Bravura in brown. (*Water-colour.*)
67. Opal Beach. (*Water-colour.*)

The Pier; a grey note
December 1883 or January 1884
Oil on wood panel, $3\frac{7}{16} \times 5\frac{13}{16}$ in.
Fine Arts Museums of San Francisco
Plate 7 YMSM 286
Dowdeswell 1

"Some of the works he now exhibits have no more claim to be accounted pictures than an acorn to be described as an oak, or a heap of bricks as a house. From the contemplation of productions crude, immature, and like King Richard, 'but half made up,' such as 'The Pier,' 'The Angry Sea' [no. 2], 'Pink and Opal Harbour' [no. 12], 'Purfleet' [no. 5], and too many of the same class, we turn with pleasant sense of relief to performances which show their artist at his best, and prove of what fine work he is capable when he condescends to do himself justice." — "Messrs. Dowdeswell's Gallery," *Morning Post*, May 24, 1884

The Angry Sea
December 1883 or January 1884
Oil on wood panel, $4\frac{7}{8} \times 8\frac{1}{2}$ in.
Freer Gallery of Art, Washington, D.C.
Gift of Charles Lang Freer F1904.76
Plate 4 YMSM 282
Dowdeswell 2

HISTORY With Goupil Gallery (London) by 1901. Sold by Goupil Gallery to the art dealer John James Cowan (Edinburgh) as *Sky, steamer, sea & sandy shore*. Cowan sent Whistler a verbal description, a sketch and a photograph of the panel, and Whistler identified it as *The Angry Sea*, specifying that it was a view of St. Ives. (John James Cowan to Whistler, February 25, 1901 and November 19, 1902, GUL–WC). The painting is also discussed, as *The Angry Sea,* in Charles Lang Freer to John James Cowan, October 13, 1902 (FGAA–FP). Lent by Cowan to the annual exhibition of the Royal Scottish Academy of Painting, Sculpture and Architecture (Edinburgh 1904) as *The Angry Sea* (no. 314). Sold by Cowan (through William Marchant and Co., London dealers) to Charles Lang Freer (June 13, 1904). Bequeathed to Freer Gallery of Art in 1919.

"This wonderful artist uses frames of greenish gold wherever the picture requires such a setting, noticeably for his marine studies. A strip of angry grey-green sea, framed in green gold, against a dull pink background, is an exquisite arrangement of colour, worthy to be adopted by the costumiere [sic] of the period." — "Causerie," *Court Circular*, May 24, 1884

"What would Mr. Clark Russell say to the anger of 'The Angry Sea' (2)?" — Frederic Wedmore, "Mr Whistler's Arrangement in Flesh Colour and Gray," *Academy,* May 24, 1884

Nocturne; grey and gold — Canal; Holland
1883 or 1884
Watercolor on cream wove paper,
$11\frac{7}{16} \times 9\frac{1}{16}$ in.
Period Dowdeswell Gallery frame, $5\frac{9}{16}$ in. wide molding
Freer Gallery of Art, Washington, D.C.
Gift of Charles Lang Freer F1902.160
Plate 23 M945
Dowdeswell 3

HISTORY Exhibited at the Dublin Sketching Club (December 1884, as no. 235). Sold through Dowdeswell and Dowdeswells to Henry Studdy Theobald (July 1, 1885). Probably exhibited at the International Exposition of Painting and Sculpture (Paris: May 1887), as *Nocturne en gris et or* (no. 181). Sold by Theobald to Charles Lang Freer (June 3, 1902). Bequeathed to the Freer Gallery of Art in 1919.

Red and blue — Lindsey Houses
ca. 1882–84
Oil on wood panel, $5\frac{1}{4} \times 9\frac{1}{4}$ in.
Period Dowdeswell Gallery frame, $5\frac{9}{16}$ in. wide molding
Freer Gallery of Art, Washington, D.C.
Gift of Charles Lang Freer F1902.157
Plate 16 YMSM 306
Dowdeswell 4

HISTORY Probably sold by Dowdeswell and Dowdeswells to Henry Studdy Theobald (July 1, 1885). Sold by Theobald to Charles Lang Freer (June 3, 1902). Bequeathed to the Freer Gallery of Art in 1919.

Grey and silver — Purfleet
1883 or 1884
Watercolor on beige paper, laid down on card,
$6\frac{5}{16} \times 8\frac{3}{4}$ in.
Freer Gallery of Art, Washington, D.C.
Gift of Charles Lang Freer F1902.117
Plate 19 M883
Dowdeswell 5

HISTORY Exhibited at the Dublin Sketching Club (December 1884, as no. 256). Exhibited at the International Art Exhibition (Munich 1888). Exhibited in "Notes — Harmonies — Nocturnes" (New York: Wunderlich Gallery, 1889) as *Grey and Silver — Purlect* [sic] (no. 35). Sold by Whistler's Company of the Butterfly to Charles Lang Freer (1902). Bequeathed to the Freer in 1919.

"(5) Grey and Silver is a very beautiful little water-colour drawing ... representing chiefly pale broken clouds, in a wan and watery sky." — "Mr. Whistler's Gallery," *Standard*, May 20, 1884

"Some even of the slightest sketches have, in an eminent degree, the charm of colour and suggestiveness. The water-colour, 'Violet and Red,' for instance, in which the forms of two ladies seated at a table are vaguely indicated, and that called 'Grey and Silver,' Purfleet." — *Globe*, May 20, 1884

Grey and silver — Purfleet is "remarkably clever in indicating cloud effects." — *Home Journal*, March 15, 1889

Arrangement in Pink, Red and Purple
Probably 1884
Oil on wood, 12×9 in.
Period Dowdeswell Gallery frame, $5\frac{9}{16}$ in. molding
Cincinnati Art Museum
Plate 47 YMSM 324
Probably Dowdeswell 6 or 10, both titled "Violet and red"

HISTORY YMSM suggests that Whistler painted *Arrangement in Pink, Red and Purple* during a brief visit to Dieppe in the autumn of 1885, but this cannot be correct since the distinctive curved red couch appears in several paintings completed in Whistler's London studio. The couch appears in YMSM 254 and 255 (Dowdeswell 17 and 51) and M898 (Dowdeswell 10). The couch and the dress both appear in M907. All these works were probably completed between February and May 1884.

"When we come to study the paintings separately, of course there is much more room for difference of opinion. Some of them, though bearing such high-sounding and significant titles, are little better than daubs; others, which appear so at first view, and on close inspection, fall into their place wonderfully when viewed at what we take to be the distance the painter intended: numbers 6 and 9, for instance." — *The Builder,* May 24, 1884

Green and Silver: The Devonshire Cottages
1883 or 1884
Oil on canvas, $12\frac{5}{8} \times 24\frac{3}{4}$ in.
Freer Gallery of Art, Washington, D.C.
Gift of Charles Lang Freer F1906.227
Plate 9 YMSM 266
Possibly Dowdeswell 7, "Green and opal — the Village"

"How about the palette knife in 'Green and Opal — The Village' (7) — has it not played a heavy part?" — *Kensington News*, May 29, 1884

A Chelsea Street
Probably 1883 or 1884
Watercolor on white paper,
$4^{15}/_{16} \times 8^{9}/_{16}$ in.
Paul Mellon Collection, Yale Center For British Art, New Haven
Plate 29 M953
Probably Dowdeswell 8, "The Little Grocery, Chelsea; grey and red"

"'The Little Grocery' (8) appears to hint in the foreground at a small black figure without legs moving on an invisible bicycle; motiveless, missionless, a joy to the artist, and also a sweet boon to the literary man. With rare delicacy, Mr. Whistler commonly suppresses the legs of the figures in his designs, or merely generalises them into something vague, fleeting, attenuated, spiritual. He also avoids personal caricature by leaving the features of some of his models almost wholly to the fancy of the spectator. 'Leave it to you, sir,' as cabmen sometimes say, is on these occasions his motto." — "Mr. Whistler's Gallery," *Standard*, May 20, 1884

"We turn with [a] pleasant sense of relief to performances which show their artist at his best, and prove of what fine work he is capable when he condescends to do himself justice. In this honorable category may be mentioned,... 'The Little Grocery, Chelsea,' a small picture, lovely in tone and colour and full of quaint antique beauty." — "Messrs. Dowdeswell's Gallery," *Morning Post*, May 24, 1884

Nocturne in grey and gold — Piccadilly
1881–83
Watercolor on white wove paper,
$8^{3}/_{4} \times 11^{1}/_{2}$ in.
Period Dowdeswell Gallery frame, $5^{9}/_{16}$ in. wide molding
National Gallery of Ireland, Dublin
Plate 27 M862
Dowdeswell 9

HISTORY Exhibited at the Dublin Sketching Club (December 1884), as *Grey and Gold: Piccadilly* (no. 251). Acting as Whistler's agent, the organizer of the Dublin exhibition, William Booth Pearsall, sold *Nocturne in grey and gold — Piccadilly* and *Sunrise; gold and grey* (Dowdeswell 55) to Jonathan Hogg (Whistler to William Booth Pearsall, between December 19 and 26, 1884, LC-PC, box C, folder 8). After Whistler's death, Pearsall reported to Whistler's biographers, that during the Dublin exhibition he had induced Jonathan Hogg "to purchase *Piccadilly*, which had been No. 9, *Nocturne in Grey and Gold — Piccadilly* (watercolor) in his exhibition in Bond Street that May [Dowdeswell's]." Quoted in Elizabeth R. Pennell and Joseph Pennell, *The Life of James McNeill Whistler* (Philadelphia: Lippincott, 1911), pp. 239–40. Bequeathed by Jonathan Hogg to the National Gallery of Ireland (July 1930).

"(9) Piccadilly. Mr. Whistler calls this a 'Nocturne in grey and gold.' One faintly makes out the passengers on the top of an omnibus, and very yellow light streaming from windows. The horses are 'understood.'" — "Mr. Whistler's Gallery," *Standard*, May 20, 1884

"Mr. Whistler is ... the apostle of that artless art which portrays Piccadilly with a blur of grey and a dot of gold." — *Society*, May 22, 1884

"How tantalizing it is to pass on to the next work (9) 'Nocturne in grey and gold — Piccadilly,' and find one of the most enchanting little atmospheric gems one could well desire to possess." — *Kensington News*, May 29, 1884

"Whistler sent many of the paintings and drawings that did not sell at the spring 1884 exhibition at the Dowdeswells to a December, 1884 show at the Dublin Sketching Club: "*Silver and Gold, Chelsea* [no. 25]; *Grand Canal, Amsterdam* [no. 18]; *Grey and Gold, Piccadilly* — show a considerable range of effect, from the vaporous stillness (scene of twinkling lights) of quiet Dutch canals and the Thames at Chelsea to the gas illumined, smoky atmosphere of Piccadilly, bustling with laden omnibuses, Hansom cabs, and hurrying figures in the roar and activity of this great London thoroughfare." — *Daily Express*, January 12, 1885

Note in Pink and Purple: The Studio
1883 or 1884
Watercolor on cream wove paper,
$11^{15}/_{16} \times 8^{7}/_{8}$ in.
Period Dowdeswell Gallery frame,
$5^{9}/_{16}$ in. wide molding
Freer Gallery of Art, Washington, D.C.
Gift of Charles Lang Freer F1902.163
Plate 38 M898
Probably Dowdeswell 10 or 6, both titled "Violet and red"

HISTORY Probably sold by Dowdeswell and Dowdeswells to Henry Studdy Theobald (July 1, 1885). Sold by Theobald to Charles Lang Freer (June 3, 1902). Bequeathed to the Freer Gallery of Art in 1919.

"Some even of the slightest sketches have, in an eminent degree, the charm of colour and suggestiveness. The water-colour, 'Violet and Red,' for instance, in which the forms of two ladies seated at a table are vaguely indicated." — *Globe*, May 20, 1884

"Mr. Whistler['s] ... recent studies and sketches ... are varied in subject, and differ from each other very widely in merit. The majority are of the slightest kind, mere memoranda of effects of light and colour, such as other artists retain in their studios for reference. A few of these, vague as they are, and without any definition of form, are charming by reason of their subtle beauty of colour and suggestiveness. 'The Novelette' [no. 16], in which the figure of a lady reading in bed is faintly indicated, the figure of a girl seen through a doorway 'Shelling Peas' [no. 20], and the interior called 'Violet and Red' are among the best of these very slight watercolour sketches." — "Mr. Whistler's Exhibition," *Graphic*, May 24, 1884

Street in Old Chelsea
Early 1880s
Oil on wood panel, $5^{1}/_{4} \times 9^{1}/_{8}$ in.
Museum of Fine Arts, Boston
Plate 31 YMSM 249
Probably Dowdeswell 11, "Chelsea; yellow and grey"

"11. 'Chelsea, yellow and grey' is one of Mr. Whistler's rapid, suggestive studies of low-browed houses, shops, and the picturesque of drabs, yellows, dirty bricks, and dropping plaster." — "Mr. Whistler's Gallery," *Standard*, May 20, 1884

"I should think the marionettes are rather often in the streets of Chelsea from the figures that appear in (11) 'Chelsea: yellow and grey.'" [This joke apparently refers to the foreground figures who seem to lack legs and feet.] — *Kensington News*, May 29, 1884

Pink and opal — Harbour
Oil, support and size unknown
Whereabouts unknown
YMSM 272
Dowdeswell 12

"Some of the works he now exhibits have no more claim to be accounted pictures than an acorn to be described as an oak, or a heap of bricks as a house. From the contemplation of productions crude, immature, and, like King Richard, 'but half made up,' such as 'The Pier' [no. 1], 'The Angry Sea' [no. 2], 'Pink and Opal Harbour,' 'Purfleet' [no. 5], and too many of the same class, we turn with pleasant sense of relief to performances which show their artist at his best, and prove of what fine work he is capable when he condescends to do himself justice." — "Messrs. Dowdeswell's Gallery," *Morning Post*, May 24, 1884

Convalescent
1883 or 1884
Watercolor on off-white paper,
$9^{5}/_{8} \times 6^{3}/_{4}$ in.
Private Collection
Plate 41 M903
Probably Dowdeswell 13, "Petit Déjeuner; note in opal"

"Then there is the 'Petit Déjeuner' (No. 13), — otherwise 'note in opal' — in which the ghost of a warm-coloured blonde reads a pale blue book in bed, breakfast waiting on the table at her side." — "Mr. Whistler's Exhibition," *Standard*, May 19, 1884

"'Petit Déjeuner' indicates a lady who has breakfasted in bed, and is reading a novel. A fine frowsiness is delicately conveyed to the sense of the spectator." — "Mr. Whistler's Gallery," *Standard*, May 20, 1884

"'Petit Déjeuner,' a beautiful note in opal." — "Messrs. Dowdeswell's Gallery," *Morning Post*, May 24, 1884

"The 'Petit Déjeuner' (13) — a note in opal — is of a curious delicacy in slightness, such as hardly anybody but Mr. Whistler could command." — Frederic Wedmore, "Mr Whistler's Arrangement in Flesh Colour and Gray," *Academy*, May 24, 1884

"Let us turn from [*An orange note — Sweet Shop* (no. 38)] to 'Le Petit Déjeuner: note in opal.' Here we have a pale delicate water colour representing a young lady breakfasting in bed and reading a blue-covered book. This is one of the most graceful and refined drawings in the room. The face and hand are beautifully drawn, full of feeling, and are coloured with that fine sense the artist possesses in such a marked degree; and his nobility of 'style' and manner of work are shown in this drawing to great advantage. — [Walter Dowdeswell], "Mr. Whistler and His Art," *Artist and Journal of Home Culture*, June 1, 1884.

"In several [works], notably 'Le Petit Déjeuner' and a picture close by — a single girl figure — is found a curious effect (or defect). The face is skilfully [sic] and delicately drawn, and then washed over with a film of white, which seems to serve no purpose but that of obscuring the features." — "Philistine," "Mr. Whistler and His Artifices," *The Artist and Journal of Home Culture*, July 1, 1884.

Erith — Evening
1883 or 1884
Watercolor on beige paper, laid down on card, 5 11/16 × 9 7/16 in.
Period Dowdeswell Gallery frame, 5 9/16 in. wide molding
Freer Gallery of Art, Washington, D.C.
Gift of Charles Lang Freer F1902.168
Plate 20 M884
Dowdeswell 14

HISTORY Sold by Dowdeswell and Dowdeswells to Henry Studdy Theobald (July 1, 1885). Probably exhibited at the International Exposition of Painting and Sculpture (Paris: May 1887), as *Note en argent: Erith sur Tamise* (no. 182). Sold by Theobald to Charles Lang Freer (June 3, 1902). Bequeathed to the Freer Gallery of Art in 1919.

"... and the warm grey sunset of Erith (No. 14)." — "Mr. Whistler's Exhibition," *Standard*, May 19, 1884

"The colour in 'Erith — Evening' (14) is very good." — *Kensington News*, May 29, 1884

Black and red
1883 or 1884
Watercolor on white laid paper, 9 × 6 1/4 in.
National Gallery of Art, Washington, D.C.
Plate 42 M936
Dowdeswell 15

"How much dignity in the attitude, in the pose of the head, of the lady who sits up straight in her small straight chair and hangs one arm behind it!" — Frederic Wedmore, "Mr. Whistler's Arrangement in Flesh Colour and Gray," *Academy*, May 24, 1884

"We turn with [a] pleasant sense of relief to performances which show their artist at his best, and prove of what fine work he is capable when he condescends to do himself justice. In this honorable category may be mentioned, for example, ... 'Black and Red,' a charming study of a girl whose dress is arranged in those two hues." 'Messrs. Dowdeswells' Gallery,'" — "Messrs. Dowdeswell's Gallery," *Morning Post*, May 24, 1884

"Along side (no. 13, *Le Petit Déjeuner; note in opal*] hangs another water colour, striking as strong a note as 'Petit Déjeuner' strikes a sweet one. A girl, dressed in dull Indian violet, seated on a slim yellow chair, holds her black shawl and hat on her lap; the exquisitely modelled [*sic*] head and hair, simply but wonderfully delineated, set easily and happily on a graceful figure; a few bold, vigorous touches give us her black shawl and felt hat and feathers, and the folds of her dress. This drawing is one of the first that attracts the eye. It rings like a bell." — [Walter Dowdeswell], "Mr. Whistler and His Art," *Artist and Journal of Home Culture*, June 1, 1884.

Pink note — The Novelette
1883 or 1884
Watercolor on white wove paper, 9 15/16 × 6 1/16 in.
Period Dowdeswell Gallery frame, 5 9/16 in. wide molding.
Dowdeswell label on reverse
Freer Gallery of Art, Washington, D.C.
Gift of Charles Lang Freer F1902.158
Plate 44 M900
Dowdeswell 16

HISTORY Exhibited at the Dublin Sketching Club (December 1884, as no. 239). Sold by Dowdeswell and Dowdeswells to Henry Studdy Theobald (July 1, 1885). Exhibited at the International Exposition of Painting and Sculpture (Paris: May 1887), as *Rose et gris: Le Roman* (no. 166). Sold by Theobald to Charles Lang Freer (June 3, 1902). Bequeathed to the Freer Gallery of Art in 1919.

"Mr. Whistler's work this year is unusually varied in its apparent themes. All sorts of objects are pressed into the service of his brush — Southend pier [no. 62], the Cornish coast, a young woman dressed in a parasol and a red headgear [no. 65], a *grisette* reading a French novel, a fog in Piccadilly [no. 9], a shop in Chelsea [no. 38]." — "Mr. Whistler's Exhibition," *Standard*, May 19, 1884

"A good many contain figures of young girls reading, lounging, in various attitudes, their dresses and surroundings giving the colour combination which is denominated 'Pink Note' (N.B. Not a billet-doux, but a 'note' in the scale of colour), or 'Harmony in Violet and Amber' [no. 19]. These figures are very slightly sketched, and their faces will certainly not bear looking close at; but they nearly all have character in pose, and show that there is good drawing underlying their shadowy similitude; one in particular, 'Yellow and Grey' (43), a girl standing before a background of yellow, is charming in attitude and in the masterly indication of the figure." — *The Builder*, May 24, 1884

"Mr. Whistler['s] ... recent studies and sketches ... are varied in subject, and differ from each other very widely in merit. The majority are of the slightest kind, mere memoranda of effects of light and colour, such as other artists retain in their studios for reference. A few of these, vague as they are, and without any definition of form, are charming by reason of their subtle beauty of colour and suggestiveness. 'The Novelette,' in which the figure of a lady reading in bed is faintly indicated, the figure of a girl seen through a doorway 'Shelling Peas' [no. 20], and the interior called 'Violet and Red' [no. 6 or no. 10], are among the best of these very slight watercolour sketches." — "Mr. Whistler's Exhibition," *Graphic*, May 24, 1884

"The color in 'Erith — Evening' (14) is very good. So is it in (16), 'Pink note — The Novelette' in which, however, a delighted devourer of penny sentimentalities is seen reading upon a bed. Of course a girl with legs about six feet long might be expected to develop strange *penchants*." — *Kensington News*, May 29, 1884

Note in red — The Siesta
Probably 1883 or 1884
Oil on wood panel, 8 1/2 × 12 in.
Terra Museum of American Art, Chicago
Plate 46 YMSM 254
Dowdeswell 17

HISTORY Exhibited at the Dublin Sketching Club (December 1884, as no. 236) . Exhibited at the International Art Exhibition (Munich 1888), as *Eine rote Stimmung* (no. 58). Exhibited in "Notes — Harmonies — Nocturnes" (New York: Wunderlich Gallery, 1889), as *A Red Note — The Sofa* (no. 26). Sold by Goupil Gallery, London to Sir George Drummond (December 21, 1891). Through several private owners, detailed in catalogue raisonnée, to Daniel Terra (1982). Bequeathed to the Terra Foundation for the Arts (1996).

"Stronger still [than no. 15] is a 'Note in Red—The Siesta,' in oil; a girl in red and white drapery lies huddled up on a red and grey covered sofa, painted in a most masterful manner."—[Walter Dowdeswell], "Mr. Whistler and His Art," *Artist and Journal of Home Culture*, June 1, 1884

"'A Red Note—The Sofa,' an oil sketch of a young woman asleep on cushions."—"Etchings, Drawings, Pastels," *New York Times*, March 3, 1889

Grand Canal, Amsterdam; nocturne
1883 or 1884
Watercolor on cream wove paper,
$8^{7}/_{8} \times 11^{3}/_{16}$ in.
Period Dowdeswell Gallery frame, $5^{9}/_{16}$ in. wide molding
Freer Gallery of Art, Washington, D.C.
Gift of Charles Lang Freer F1902.161
Plate 24 M944
Dowdeswell 18

HISTORY Exhibited at the Dublin Sketching Club (December 1884, as no. 232). Probably sold by Dowdeswell and Dowdeswells to Henry Studdy Theobald (July 1, 1885). Sold by Theobald to Charles Lang Freer (June 3, 1902). Bequeathed to the Freer Gallery of Art in 1919.

"'The Grand Canal, Amsterdam,' is a 'nocturne' not without picturesque effect, but in the absence of those schuyts, tjalks, &c., which give such bustle and animation to the actual scene, the picture can hardly be said to present a characteristic view. As well might Cheapside be painted, without cabs and omnibuses."—"Messrs. Dowdeswell's Gallery," *Morning Post*, May 24, 1884

"18, 'The Grand Canal at Amsterdam,' with luminous yellow lights and reflections."—"Whistles," *Topical Times*, May 24, 1884

"Whistler sent many of the paintings and drawings that did not sell at the spring 1884 exhibition at the Dowdeswells to a December, 1884 show at the Dublin Sketching Club: *Silver and Gold, Chelsea* [no. 25]; *Grand Canal, Amsterdam*; *Grey and Gold, Piccadilly* [no. 9]—show a considerable range of effect, from the vaporous stillness (scene of twinkling lights) of quiet Dutch canals and the Thames at Chelsea to the gas illumined, smoky atmosphere of Piccadilly...."—*Daily Express*, January 12, 1885

Harmony in violet and amber
1883 or 1884
Watercolor on cream paper, laid down on card,
$9^{13}/_{16} \times 6^{7}/_{16}$ in.
Period Dowdeswell Gallery frame, $5^{9}/_{16}$ in. wide molding
Dowdeswell label on reverse
Freer Gallery of Art, Washington, D.C.
Gift of Charles Lang Freer F1902.164
Plate 43 M906
Dowdeswell 19

HISTORY Possibly sold by Dowdeswell and Dowdeswells to E.J. Poole (ca. 1885). Sold by Poole or Dowdeswell and Dowdeswells to Henry Studdy Theobald (by 1888). Probably exhibited at the International Art Exhibition (Munich 1888) as *Variation in Violet und Gold*. Sold by Theobald to Charles Lang Freer (June 3, 1902). Bequeathed to the Freer Gallery of Art in 1919.

"A good many contain figures of young girls reading, lounging, in various attitudes, their dresses and surroundings giving the colour combination which is denominated 'Pink Note' [no. 16] (N.B. Not a billet-doux, but a 'note' in the scale of colour), or 'Harmony in Violet and Amber.' These figures are very slightly sketched, and their faces will certainly not bear looking close at; but they nearly all have character in pose, and show that there is good drawing underlying their shadowy similitude; one in particular, 'Yellow and Grey' (43), a girl standing before a background of yellow, is charming in attitude and in the masterly indication of the figure."—*The Builder*, May 24, 1884

Pink note—Shelling Peas
1883 or 1884
Watercolor on cream wove paper, $9^{1}/_{2} \times 5^{5}/_{8}$ in.
Period Dowdeswell Gallery frame, $5^{9}/_{16}$ in. wide molding
Dowdeswell label on reverse
Freer Gallery of Art, Washington, D.C.
Gift of Charles Lang Freer F1902.166
Plate 45 M925
Dowdeswell 20

HISTORY Probably sold by Dowdeswell and Dowdeswells to Henry Studdy Theobald (July 1, 1885). Sold by Theobald to Charles Lang Freer (June 3, 1902). Bequeathed to the Freer Gallery of Art in 1919.

"Then there is the charming little water colour, No. 20, which Mr. Whistler, addressing the initiated, calls 'Pink note,' but which, remembering the outsider with a measure of tenderness, he styles also 'Shelling Peas'—what a pretty little vision of the coolest of sunny light."—"Mr. Whistler's Exhibition," *Standard,* May 19, 1884

"Mr. Whistler['s] ... recent studies and sketches ... are varied in subject and differ from each other very widely in merit. The majority are of the slightest kind, mere memoranda of effects of light and colour, such as other artists retain in their studios for reference. A few of these, vague as they are, and without any definition of form, are charming by reason of their subtle beauty of colour and suggestiveness. 'The Novelette' [no. 16], in which the figure of a lady reading in bed is faintly indicated, the figure of a girl seen through a doorway 'Shelling Peas,' and the interior called 'Violet and Red' [no. 6 or no. 10], are among the best of these very slight watercolour sketches."—"Mr. Whistler's Exhibition," *Graphic*, May 24, 1884

"We turn with [a] pleasant sense of relief to performances which show their artist at his best, and prove of what fine work he is capable when he condescends to do himself justice. In this honorable category may be mentioned, for example,... 'Shelling Peas,' a pretty drawing, especially to be commended for the daylight outlook and the tenderly painted figure of the girl who is shelling."—"Messrs. Dowdeswell's Gallery," *Morning Post*, May 24, 1884

"Perhaps (20) 'Pink Note—Shelling Peas' is the best work of all, the effect of sunlight is so good."—*Kensington News*, May 29, 1884

The Yellow Room
1883 or 1884
Watercolor on off-white paper, $9^{13}/_{16} \times 7$ in.
Museum of Fine Arts, St. Petersburg, Florida.
Anonymous Loan
Plate 40 M881
Possibly Dowdeswell 21, "Harmony in violet and yellow"

"The 'Petit Dejeuner' (13)—a note in opal—is of a curious delicacy in slightness, such as hardly anybody but Mr. Whistler could command. No. 21 is, in its own way, as successful and as exquisite."—Frederic Wedmore, "Mr. Whistler's Arrangement in Flesh Colour and Gray," *Academy,* May 24, 1884

Grey Mist at Sea
1883 or 1884
Watercolor on white wove paper, $5^{9}/_{16} \times 9^{7}/_{16}$ in.
Birmingham Museums and Art Gallery
Plate 17 M938
Dowdeswell 22

HISTORY Sold by Dowdeswell and Dowdeswells to Wilson King, American consul in Birmingham, England, July 1884 (Dowdeswell and Dowdeswells to Whistler, between July 1885 and late 1886, GUL-WC). Given by King's daughter, Mrs. Giles, to the Birmingham City Art Gallery in 1930.

"ship sailing on some flat very sandy [dunes]."—Charles Lang Freer, manuscript annotation in Dowdeswell and Dowdeswells, "Notes"—"Harmonies"—"Nocturnes" (1884), Freer Gallery of Art Library [Rare: 759.1 W582 1884 c.1]

Chelsea Shops
Early 1880s
Oil on wood panel, $5^{1}/_{4} \times 9^{1}/_{4}$ in.
Period Dowdeswell Gallery frame, $5^{9}/_{16}$ in. wide molding
Freer Gallery of Art, Washington, D.C.
Gift of Charles Lang Freer F1902.149
Plate 32 YMSM 246
Probably Dowdeswell 23, "Pink note—Chelsea;" or, possibly, Dowdeswell 42, "Harmony in yellow and brown—Sunday"

HISTORY Probably sold by Dowdeswell and Dowdeswells to Henry Studdy Theobald (July 1, 1885). Probably exhibited at the International Exposition of Painting and Sculpture (Paris: May 1887), as *Rose et brun: Les Boutiques de Chelsea* (no. 208). Sold by Theobald to Charles Lang Freer (June 3, 1902). Bequeathed to the Freer Gallery of Art in 1919.

"A clever study of a sweetshop is called an orange note [no. 38]. A study of Old Chelsea Church is called a harmony in brown and gold [no. 44]. Another view of Chelsea, described as a pink note, is more elaborate than the others ..." — "Art Notes," *Liverpool Mercury*, July 3, 1884

Note in red and violet — Nets
1884
Oil on wood panel, 4¾ × 8½ in.
Whereabouts unknown
YMSM 269
Dowdeswell 24

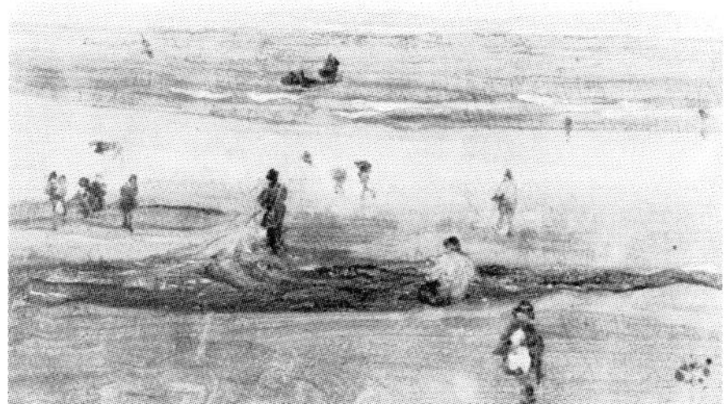

Reproduced from a photograph in the J. & E. R. Pennell Collection, Library of Congress, Washington, D.C.

Nocturne; silver and opal — Chelsea
ca. 1880–84
Oil on wood panel, 8 × 10⅛ in.
Period Dowdeswell Gallery frame, 5⁹⁄₁₆ in. wide molding
Freer Gallery of Art, Washington, D.C.
Gift of Charles Lang Freer F1902.146
Plate 28 YMSM 309
Dowdeswell 25

HISTORY Sold by Dowdeswell and Dowdeswells to Henry Studdy Theobald (July 1, 1885). Exhibited at the International Exposition of Painting and Sculpture (Paris: May 1887), as *Nocturne en opale: Chelsea* (no. 165). Exhibited at the Goupil Gallery (London 1891) as *Nocturne: Opal and Silver* (no. 11). Sold by Theobald to Charles Lang Freer (June 3, 1902). Bequeathed to the Freer Gallery of Art in 1919.

"Than the 'Nocturne, Silver and Opal,' Mr. Whistler has never painted a finer work. It is preferable to his 'Valparaiso.' There is not an artist with as true or fine a sense of the mystery and infinity of night as Mr. Whistler, and this little picture, full of space and atmosphere, is impressive in its solemnity." — [Walter Dowdeswell], "Mr. Whistler and His Art," *Artistist and Journal of Home Culture*, June 1, 1884

"On the left hand [as you enter the gallery] is a 'Nocturne, Silver and Opal'; ('Mr. Whistler never painted a finer work!' Enthus.: loq.:) The moment I saw this, there came into my mind an old joke from 'Punch' — 'Policeman to cabby with half-starved bony horse, "Going to have a new horse, Cabby?" The son of Nimshi, "What d'yer mean?" Apollo Agyieus, "Well, I see you've got the frame work together."' Here is a prepared ground of a strange, hazy, smoky, colour, but where is the picture? has Chelsea melted not into thin, but thick air? is this the blank in nature which Chelsea used to fill? Careful, close study shews a blackish line, which may be meant for Chelsea-bridge, or is this a kind of 'Pons Asinorum' over which we must pass before becoming admirers? The plain truth is, that if, knowing Chelsea well, you stand about five yards from the wall, with the aid of Mr. Whistler's work, you can conjure up a picture, of which three-quarters will be of your own mind's painting." "Philistine," "Mr. Whistler and His Artifices," — *The Artist and Journal of Home Culture*, July 1, 1884

"A study of Old Chelsea Church is called a harmony in brown and gold [no. 44]. Another view of Chelsea, described as a pink note [no. 23], is more elaborate than the others; but there is an evening effect of Chelsea, called 'Nocturne in Silver and Opal,' which shows the painter's penchant for vague indistinctness. The study represents mist or smoke, with a dark line which may be meant for Chelsea or any other bridge." — "Art Notes," *Liverpool Mercury*, July 3, 1884

Whistler sent many of the paintings and drawings that did not sell at the spring 1884 exhibition at the Dowdeswells to a December, 1884 show at the Dublin Sketching Club: "Silver and Gold, Chelsea; Grand Canal, Amsterdam [no. 18]; Grey and Gold, Piccadilly [no. 9] — show a considerable range of effect, from the vaporous stillness (scene of twinkling lights) of quiet Dutch canals and the Thames at Chelsea to the gas illumined, smoky atmosphere of Piccadilly ..." — *Daily Express*, January 12, 1885

Arrangement in black — Reading
Early 1880s
Oil on wood panel, 9¾ × 7½ in.
Jim and Gina Liautaud
Plate 51 YMSM 224
Dowdeswell 26

HISTORY Exhibited at the Dublin Sketching Club (December 1884, as no. 254). Exhibited at the International Art Exhibition (Munich 1888), as *Eine schwarze Stimmung* (no. 59). Exhibited in "Notes — Harmonies — Nocturnes" (New York: Wunderlich Gallery, 1889), as no. 25. Acquired by Alexander Henderson by 1905. Through several private owners, detailed in catalogue raisonnée, to Christie's, New York, May 22, 1991 (lot 245). To current owner.

In a review of "Notes — Harmonies — Nocturnes" (New York: Wunderlich Gallery, 1889), Whistler's first one-man show of paintings and drawings in the United States, this painting was described as "'An Arrangement in Blacks,' a woman reading, dimly perceived against the black ground, but yet revealing all the modelling [*sic*] of her face, which is so ugly as to be interesting." — *Evening Sun*, March 16, 1889

Note in pink and purple
1883 or 1884
Watercolor on white laid paper,
9¾ × 6¼ in.
Cincinnati Art Museum
Plate 48 M935
Probably Dowdeswell 27, "Note in pink and purple"

HISTORY Exhibited in "Notes — Harmonies — Nocturnes" (New York: Wunderlich Gallery, 1889), as *Pink and Violet* (no. 15). Acquired by Otto Goldschmidt, possible from Whistler, in the 1890s. Sold by Mme. B. Max Goldschmidt to Colnaghi, London art dealers (December 1, 1912). Through several owners, detailed in catalogue raisonnée, to Miss M. Hanna, Cincinnati (1928). Bequeathed to Cincinnati Art Museum in 1956.

"[no. 27, a watercolor], called 'A note in Pink and Purple' is really Lady Archie Campbell, or, at all events a portion of that lady." — "Whistles," *Topical Times*, May 24, 1884

"In [other works], the artist's love of the *bizarre* and his perversity are evident; in the amazingly ill-drawn nude figure, 'The Parasol' [no. 65], for instance, and in the inchoate adumbration of a group called 'Note in Pink and Purple.'" — "Mr. Whistler's Exhibition," *Graphic*, May 24, 1884

Moreby Hall
1883 or 1884
Pen, brown ink, and watercolor on cream paper,
7¹¹⁄₁₆ × 11³⁄₁₆ in.
Period Dowdeswell Gallery frame, 5⁹⁄₁₆ in. wide molding
Freer Gallery of Art, Washington, D.C.
Gift of Charles Lang Freer F1904.80
Plate 53 M908
Dowdeswell 28

HISTORY Possibly sold by Dowdeswell and Dowdeswells to E.J. Poole, ca. 1885. (Dowdeswell and Dowdeswells to Whistler, between July 1885 and early 1886, GUL–WC). Possibly reacquired by Whistler. With E. J. van Wissenlingh (London art dealer), probably by the 1890s. Sold by van Wissenlingh to Edinburgh art dealer John

James Cowan as *Morby Hall* [*sic*], by 1902. (Cowan to Charles Lang Freer, November 7, 1902, FGAA–FP; and Cowan to J. M. Whistler, November 19, 1902, GUL–WC) Sold by Cowan (through William Marchant and Co., London dealers) to Charles Lang Freer (June 13, 1904). Bequeathed to the Freer Gallery of Art in 1919.

Zuyder Zee
ca. 1883–85
Watercolor on white wove paper,
$5^3/_8$ x 11 in.
Period Dowdeswell Gallery style frame,
$5^9/_{16}$ in. molding
Dr. and Mrs. John E. Larkin, Jr.
M962
Possibly Dowdeswell 29, "Blue and white—Dutch" (M941)

HISTORY Possibly exhibited at the Dublin Sketching Club (December 1884) as *Blue and white—Dutch* (no. 254). Sold by Whistler to Frank J. Hecker, 13 July 1891, as *Zuyder Zee*. Lent by Hecker to Whistler Memorial Exhibition (Boston 1904) as *Zuyder Zee* (no. 97). Sold at auction, Parke Bernet, 27–8 October 1971 (no. 81). Through several galleries, detailed in catalogue raisonnée, to current owner.

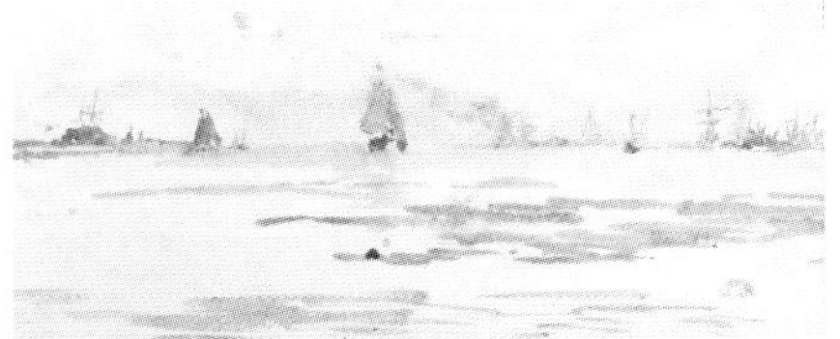

Photograph courtesy of Berry-Hill Galleries, Inc.

Variations in violet
Oil, support and size unknown
Whereabouts unknown
YMSM 301
Dowdeswell 30

"After the 'Scherzo in Blue' [no. 31], it seems natural to come across 'Variations in Violet' in the form of a clever flower study."—"Art Notes," *Liverpool Mercury*, July 3, 1884

Scherzo in blue—The Blue Girl
1882
Oil on canvas, "life-size"
Presumed destroyed
For illustration, see figure 11 YMSM 226
Dowdeswell 31

"The large portrait called, with unnecessary tautology, 'Scherzo in Blue—The Blue Girl,' would be more satisfactory if the girl's right eye were more nearly on a level with her left, and if her feet appeared to touch the ground on which she is supposed to stand; but the modulations of colour in the dress are managed with subtle skill, and the general tone of the picture is agreeable."—*Globe*, May 20, 1884

"I soon got tired of guessing Whistler's puzzles, for I am an ordinary Philistine, and cannot see why a grass field should be dignified with the name of a 'note in green' [no. 34], or a splashy mess of black with a light here and there a nocturne, much less a blue girl a 'scherzo'. ... No, I shall not choose Mr. Whistler's gallery to spend a happy day in. 'Scherzo, he calls it,' remarked a wondering onlooker, 'it looks a darned sight more like a chemise!'" —*Life* (?), May 22, 1884

"A life-size oil painting of a child called 'The Blue Girl' is admirable in its way, both in colour and drawing, except (in regard to colour) the shaded side of the face, which looks as if not clean."—*The Builder* May 24, 1884

"The one big picture, 'The Blue Girl,' is to me impossible. 'Scherzo indeed!' said one Philistine critic, glancing at the catalogue, 'she never wore *anything of the sort*!' and other people, associating her with a 'girl' of another color that hung in the Grosvenor some years ago, made even still ruder remarks."—"Whistles," *Topical Times*, May 24, 1884

"The only large work in the collection, 'The Blue Girl,' is not a favourable example of Mr. Whistler's skill in portraiture. His fine sense of colour is shown in the treatment of delicately modulated local tints, but the girl's head is ill-drawn, one eye being considerably higher than the other." —"Mr. Whistler's Exhibition," *Graphic*, May 24, 1884

"A scherzo (why not a perielesis or a canon ad hypodiapente) in blue is the first thing you see. A full length picture of a girl, dressed in blue: when you are at the right distance (about three yards out of the gallery) the picture looks well, for the pose is masterly, the drawing fine, and the colour very pleasant; but when you come closer, in order to see the face, you are shocked to find that the young lady is suffering from eczema, or some other skin disease on the left cheek, and has a cataract in the left eye. This discovery, doubtless due to the fact that Mr. Whistler did not think it worth while to finish the picture, robs you of nearly all pleasure in it."—"Philistine," "Mr. Whistler and His Artifices," *The Artist and Journal of Home Culture*, July 1, 1884.

"The pièce de résistance of the Whistler exhibition is a full-length portrait of a young girl dressed in blue, and is called a scherzo in that colour. This is a dignified canvas, fine in execution and marked by a more thoughtful insight into the problem of portraiture than has characterised some of his pictures of this class. It might make a pendant for Gainsborough's 'Blue Boy.'"—"Art Notes," *Liverpool Mercury*, July 3, 1884

Blue and gold—The Schooner
December 1883 or January 1884
Oil on wood panel, $3^3/_8 \times 5^7/_8$ in.
Private collection
Plate 8 YMSM 276 and 368
Dowdeswell 32

HISTORY Exhibited at the Dublin Sketching Club (December 1884), as *Blue and gold—The Schooner* (no. 252). Exhibited at the International Exposition of Painting and Sculpture (Paris: May 1887), as *Bleu et argent: La Chaloupe aux docks* (no. 195). Exhibited at the Exposition General des Beaux Arts (Brussels 1890) as *La Chaloupe* (no. 844a). With Siegfried Bing, Paris art dealer, in 1897, as *Green and Gold: The Sloop* (Whistler to Bing, May 20 [1890], private collection; and ca. May 29, 1897, GUL–WC). Sold by Bing, probably about 1897, probably to Miss A. B. Jennings, New York. Lent by Miss A. B. Jennings to Whistler Memorial Exhibition (Boston 1904), as *The Schooner* (no. 77). Through at least one more private owner, listed in Christie's sale catalogue, to Christie's, New York, May 23, 1990 (lot 43). To current owner.

"Beauty of handling and high finish will be specially noticed in the landscapes, principally Cornish, particularly 'Blue and gold—the Schooner;' 'Harmony in brown and gold—Old Chelsea Church' [no. 44]; 'Grey and silver mist' [no. 54]; and 'Blue and grey—Unloading' [no. 56]; the most brilliant in colour being a 'Note in blue and opal—the Sun Cloud' [no. 52]"—[Walter Dowdeswell], "Mr. Whistler and His Art," *The Artist and Journal of Home Culture*, June 1, 1884

Violet and silver—The Great Sea
ca. 1884
Oil on wood panel, $5^3/_8 \times 9^1/_4$ in.
Period Dowdeswell Gallery frame, $5^9/_{16}$ in. wide molding
Freer Gallery of Art, Washington, D.C.
Gift of Charles Lang Freer F1902.148
Plate 12 YMSM 298
Dowdeswell 33

HISTORY Sold by Dowdeswell and Dowdeswells to Henry Studdy Theobald (July 1, 1885). Exhibited at the International Exposition of Painting and Sculpture (Paris: May 1887), as *Bleu et argent: La grande Mer* (no. 168). Sold by Theobald to Charles Lang Freer (June 3, 1902). Bequeathed to the Freer Gallery of Art in 1919.

"'The Great Sea,' a rough, vigorous study of the seashore."—"Messrs. Dowdeswell's Gallery," *Morning Post*, May 24, 1884

Wortley; note in green
ca. 1883
Oil on wood panel, $5^1/_4 \times 9^1/_4$ in.
Period Dowdeswell Gallery frame, $4^3/_8$ in. molding
Freer Gallery of Art, Washington, D.C.

Gift of Charles Lang Freer F1902.155
Plate 3 YMSM 303
Dowdeswell 34

HISTORY For dating, see Whistler to Waldo Story, nd [1883–84?], LC–PC. Sold by Dowdeswell and Dowdeswells to Henry Studdy Theobald (July 1, 1885). Exhibited at the International Exposition of Painting and Sculpture (Paris: May 1887), as *Note en vert: Le Village de Wortley* (no. 163). Sold by Theobald to Charles Lang Freer (June 3, 1902). Bequeathed to the Freer Gallery of Art in 1919.

"I soon got tired of guessing Whistler's puzzles, for I am an ordinary Philistine, and cannot see why a grass field should be dignified with the name of a 'note in green,' or a splashy mess of black with a light here and there a nocturne, much less a blue girl a 'scherzo' [no. 31]. —*Life* (?), May 22, 1884

Note in Opal: Breakfast
1883 or 1884
Watercolor on cream paper,
laid down on card, 9⅞ × 6⅞ in.
Period Dowdeswell Gallery frame, 5 9/16 in. wide molding.
Original Dowdeswell label on reverse
Freer Gallery of Art, Washington, D.C.
Gift of Charles Lang Freer F1902.162
Plate 39 M897
Probably Dowdeswell 35, "Violet and Amber—Tea"

HISTORY Possibly sold by Dowdeswell and Dowdeswells to E.J. Poole (ca. 1885). Sold by Poole or Dowdeswell and Dowdeswells to Henry Studdy Theobald (probably by 1888). Sold by Theobald to Charles Lang Freer (June 3, 1902). Bequeathed to the Freer Gallery of Art in 1919.

"'Violet and Amber—Tea' (35), might also be styled 'an essay in smudge.'"—"Mr. Whistler's Gallery," *Standard*, May 20, 1884

The Sea and Sand
Probably December 1883 or January 1884
Oil on wood panel, 5¼ × 9¼ in.
Period Dowdeswell Gallery frame, 3⅜ in. molding
Freer Gallery of Art, Washington, D.C.
Gift of Charles Lang Freer F1902.151
Plate 5 YMSM288
Probably Dowdeswell 36,
"Sea and Storm; grey and green"

HISTORY Sold by Dowdeswell and Dowdeswells to Henry Studdy Theobald (July 1, 1885). Sold by Theobald to Charles Lang Freer (June 3, 1902). Bequeathed to the Freer Gallery of Art in 1919.

Cliffs and Breakers
Probably December 1883 or January 1884
Oil on wood panel, 4⅞ × 8½ in.
Hunterian Art Gallery, University of Glasgow
Plate 2 YMSM 278
Possibly Dowdeswell 37, "The Green Headland"

HISTORY In Whistler's studio at his death (1903). Bequeathed to Miss R. Birnie Philip. Bequeathed by Miss Birnie Philip to the University of Glasgow (1958).

An orange note—Sweet Shop
December 1883 or January 1884
Oil on wood panel, 4¾ × 8½ in.
Freer Gallery of Art, Washington, D.C.
Gift of Charles Lang Freer F1904.315
Plate 33 YMSM 264
Dowdeswell 38
Inscribed on the reverse of the panel (covered by wooden backing that was added in 1938), in Whistler's writing, "An Orange Note—Sweet Shop. No. 38 Catalogue, 'Notes, Harmonies, Nocturnes' 1884 [signed] Whistler butterfly monogram;" inscribed in another hand is "W. Flower. Old Swan House. Chelsea." (Description of covered reverse of panel from notes in the Registrar's Object File, Freer Gallery of Art)

HISTORY Sold by Dowdeswell and Dowdeswells to Wickham Flower, in 1884. (Flower to Whistler, August 15 [1884]; Whistler to Flower, ca. August 1884; and Dowdeswell and Dowdeswells to Whistler between July 1885 and early 1886; all in GUL–WC. Reproduced as "An Orange Note—Sweet Shop," in Walter Dowdeswell, "Whistler," *Art Journal* 13 (April 1887), 97. Exhibited at the International Exposition of Painting and Sculpture (Paris: May 1887) as *Note en orange: Boutique de bonbons* (no. 206). Cited as "*The Little Sweetstuff Shop*, in the possession of Mr. Wickham Flower," in Walter Sickert, "Whistler To-day," *The Fortnightly Review* (April 1892). Purchased at the Wickam Flower estate auction (London, Christie's, December 17, 1904), by Colnaghi (London art gallery). Sold by Colnaghi to Charles Lang Freer (January 4, 1905). Bequeathed to the Freer Gallery of Art in 1919.

"Mr. Whistler's work this year is unusually varied in its apparent themes. All sorts of objects are pressed into the service of his brush—Southend pier [no. 62], the Cornish coast, a young woman dressed in a parasol and a red headgear [no. 65], a *grisette* reading a French novel [no. 16], a fog in Piccadilly [no. 9], a shop in Chelsea. The shop is probably the most perfect little thing of its kind that was ever wrought by an artist who has learnt how to see. It is numbered 38 in the present Exhibition. It is without detail, without apparent labour, without dramatic interest; but it is exquisite in colour, faultless in tone, and its well-considered mystery has, at least, the interest of suggestiveness."—"Mr. Whistler's Exhibition," *Standard*, May 19, 1884

"Mr. Whistler's fine sense of colour and his power of rapidly recording his impression of a scene, are, however, best shown in the studies made in the streets about Chelsea. The rows of old houses, 'Sunday' [no. 42], 'Old Chelsea Church' [no. 44], and the little 'Sweet Shop,' with a pile of oranges in the window, are admirable studies, most harmonious in tone, produced with little apparent labour, but conveying an impressions of completeness.—*Globe*, May 20, 1884

"...of the oils my fancy was struck with 38, 'An Orange Note.' It is only a 'sweet shop,' but there is both harmony and humor of a subtle sort in it."—"Whistles," *Topical Times*, May 24, 1884

"'A Sweet Shop,' excellent in tone and wonderfully clever in the suggestion of minute detail without extravagant elaboration."—"Messrs. Dowdeswell's Gallery," *Morning Post*, May 24, 1884

"Very much better than any of ... [the other] works are three or four studies in oil made in the streets of Chelsea. The 'Sweet Shop,' with a pile of oranges forming the keynote of colour, is an exquisite work of its kind; and the views of 'Old Chelsea Church' [no. 44], and of a row of houses, 'Sunday' [no. 42], are scarcely inferior to it. Painted with obvious ease and with little labour, they leave no sense of incompleteness, and they are remarkable besides for their perfect harmony of low-toned colour."—"Mr. Whistler's Exhibition," *Graphic*, May 24, 1884

"Perhaps the most remarkable [work] is 'The Sweet-Shops: Orange Note,' a simple subject—a doorway, a tiny shop window piled with oranges and cakes, a shelf full of bottles containing lollipops, and three little figures; but for tone and wonderful breadth of detail, which gives us the contents even of the bottles, this little gem can hold its own with canvases a hundred times its size, and will doubtless become historical, as one of the most beautiful, refined, and powerful creations by the author of the Peacock Room."—[Walter Dowdeswell], "Mr. Whistler and His Art," *Artist and Journal of Home Culture*, June 1, 1884

"The 'Sweet Shop—orange note,' as a piece of clever painting cannot be too highly praised: but to talk of it as a powerful creation is to ludicrously ignore the fact that it is a picture about eight inches by four of some oranges, goodies, and bottles."—"Philistine," "Mr. Whistler and His Artifices," *The Artist and Journal of Home Culture*, July 1, 1884

Blue and silver—The Sunny Sea
Watercolor on paper, size unknown
Whereabouts unknown
M942
Dowdeswell 39

Sea and Mist; note in grey
Oil, support and size unknown
Whereabouts unknown
YMSM 284
Dowdeswell 40

A Grey Note: Village Street
Probably December 1883 or January 1884
Oil on wood panel, 4⅞ × 8½ in.
Hunterian Art Gallery, University of Glasgow
Plate 34 YMSM 265
Possibly Dowdeswell 41, "Little Shop; grey note"

HISTORY Possibly exhibited at the International Exposition of Painting and Sculpture (Paris: May 1887), as *Note grise: La petite Boutique* (no. 167). Possibly exhibited at the International Art Exhibition (Munich 1888), as *Eine graue Stimmung: Strassen-Ecke* (no. 64). In Whistler's studio at the time of his death (1903). Bequeathed to Miss R. Birnie Philip. Given by Miss R. Birnie Philip to the University of Glasgow (1935)

"'Little Shop—grey note' offers a puzzle in the foreground. Is the white object a cat, a hen in the first pride of maternity, or a newspaper blown by the winds?"—"Mr. Whistler's Gallery," *Standard*, May 20, 1884

"Some of [Whistler's] arrangements in colour, such as the 'Little Grey Note,' or the 'Note in Blue and Opal,' [no. 52] have all the delicate loveliness of lyrics."—[Oscar Wilde], "The Butterfly's Boswell," *Court and Society Review*, April 20, 1887

Harmony in yellow and brown—Sunday
Early 1880s
Oil, support and size unknown
Whereabouts unknown
YMSM 248
Dowdeswell 42

"Mr. Whistler's fine sense of colour and his power of rapidly recording his impression of a scene, are, however, best shown in the studies made in the streets about Chelsea. The rows of old houses, 'Sunday,' 'Old Chelsea Church' [no. 44], and the little 'Sweet Shop' [no. 38], with a pile of oranges in the window, are admirable studies, most harmonious in tone, produced with little apparent labour, but conveying an impression of completeness."—*Globe*, May 20, 1884

"Very much better than any of ... [the other] works are three or four studies in oil made in the streets of Chelsea. The 'Sweet Shop' [no. 38], with a pile of oranges forming the key note of colour, is an exquisite work of its kind; and the views of 'Old Chelsea Church' [no. 44], and of a row of houses, 'Sunday,' are scarcely inferior to it. Painted with obvious ease and with little labour, they leave no sense of incompleteness, and they are remarkable besides for their perfect harmony of low-toned colour."—"Mr. Whistler's Exhibition," *Graphic*, May 24, 1884

Yellow and grey (A Note in Green)
1883 or 1884
Watercolor on cream wove paper, $9^{13}/_{16}$ × 6⅞ in.
Period Dowdeswell Gallery frame, $5^{9}/_{16}$ in. wide molding.
Original Dowdeswell label on reverse
Freer Gallery of Art, Washington, D.C.
Gift of Charles Lang Freer F1902.165
Plate 50 M905
Dowdeswell 43

HISTORY Probably sold by Dowdeswell and Dowdeswells to Henry Studdy Theobald (July 1, 1885). Sold by Theobald to Charles Lang Freer (June 3, 1902). Bequeathed to the Freer Gallery of Art in 1919.

"Then there is 'yellow and grey' (No. 43), a girl in yellowish grey raiment, just touched with vivid green—she stands in front of a blazing greenish-yellow background."—"Mr. Whistler's Exhibition," *Standard*, May 19, 1884

"A good many contain figures of young girls reading, lounging, in various attitudes, their dresses and surroundings giving the colour combination which is denominated 'Pink Note' [no. 16] (N.B. Not a billet-doux, but a 'note' in the scale of colour), or 'Harmony in Violet and Amber' [no. 19]. These figures are very slightly sketched, and their faces will certainly not bear looking close at; but they nearly all have character in pose, and show that there is good drawing underlying their shadowy similitude; one in particular, 'Yellow and Grey,' (43) a girl standing before a background of yellow, is charming in attitude and in the masterly indication of the figure.—*The Builder*, May 24, 1884

Harmony in brown and gold—Old Chelsea Church
Probably 1884
Oil on wood panel, 3½ × $5^{13}/_{16}$ in.
Period Dowdeswell Gallery frame, 4⅜ in. wide molding
Freer Gallery of Art, Washington, D.C.
Gift of Charles Lang Freer F1902.152
Plate 15 YMSM 305
Dowdeswell 44

HISTORY Exhibited at the Dublin Sketching Club (December 1884, as no. 247). Sold by Dowdeswell and Dowdeswells to Henry Studdy Theobald (July 1, 1885). Sold by Theobald to Charles Lang Freer (June 3, 1902). Bequeathed to the Freer Gallery of Art in 1919.

"Mr. Whistler's fine sense of colour and his power of rapidly recording his impression of a scene, are, however, best shown in the studies made in the streets about Chelsea. The rows of old houses, 'Sunday' [no. 42], 'Old Chelsea Church,' and the little 'Sweet Shop' [no. 38], with a pile of oranges in the window, are admirable studies, most harmonious in tone, produced with little apparent labour, but conveying an impression of completeness."—*Globe*, May 20, 1884

"Very much better than any of ... [the other] works are three or four studies in oil made in the streets of Chelsea. The 'Sweet Shop' [no. 38], with a pile of oranges forming the key-note of colour, is an exquisite work of its kind; and the views of 'Old Chelsea Church,' and of a row of houses, 'Sunday' [no. 42], are scarcely inferior to it. Painted with obvious ease and with little labour, they leave no sense of incompleteness, and they are remarkable besides for their perfect harmony of low-toned colour."—"Mr. Whistler's Exhibition," *Graphic*, May 24, 1884

"Beauty of handling and high finish will be specially noticed in the landscapes, principally Cornish, particularly 'Blue and gold—The Schooner' [no. 32]; 'Harmony in brown and gold—Old Chelsea Church'; 'Grey and silver mist' [no. 54]; and 'Blue and grey—Unloading' [no. 56]; the most brilliant in colour being a 'Note in blue and opal—the Sun Cloud' [no. 52]."—[Walter Dowdeswell], "Mr. Whistler and His Art," *Artist and Journal of Home Culture*, June 1, 1884

Low Tide
Probably December 1883 or January 1884
Oil on wood panel, 5⅜ × 9¼ in.
Period Dowdeswell Gallery frame, $5^{9}/_{16}$ in. wide molding
Freer Gallery of Art, Washington, D.C.
Gift of Charles Lang Freer F1902.156
Plate 10 YMSM 280
Probably Dowdeswell 45, "Sands; blue note"

HISTORY Probably sold by Dowdeswell and Dowdeswells to Henry Studdy Theobald (July 1, 1885). Sold by Theobald to Charles Lang Freer (June 3, 1902). Bequeathed to the Freer Gallery of Art in 1919.

The Little Bay; blue and brown
Probably 1881
Oil, support and size unknown
Whereabouts unknown
YMSM 232
Dowdeswell 46

Twilight; gold and grey
Watercolor
Whereabouts unknown
M917
Dowdeswell 47 (see Dowdeswell 55)

Blue and opal—Herring Fleet
Probably 1883 or 1884
Oil on wood, 4⅞ × 8¾ in
Whereabouts unknown

YMSM 273
Dowdeswell 48

"What a placid charm in that delicate, ghostly vision of the 'Herring Fleet' (48). Poetical, we should desire to call it, only that to be poetical is to be literary." — Frederic Wedmore, "Mr. Whistler's Arrangement in Flesh Colour and Gray," *Academy*, May 24, 1884

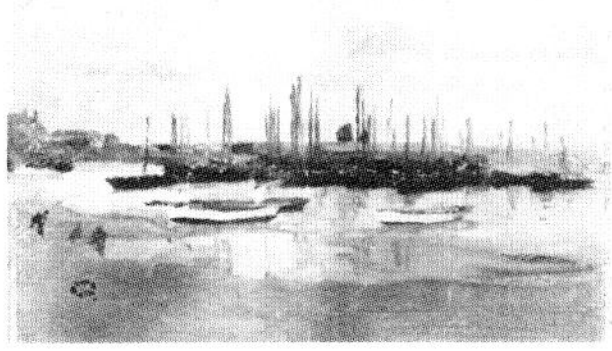

Reproduced from a photograph in Young, Paintings of James McNeill Whistler, *plate 185*

Amsterdam in Winter
December 1882
Watercolor on cream paper,
laid down on card, 8 × 10 7/8 in.
Period Dowdeswell Gallery frame, 5 9/16 in. wide molding
Freer Gallery of Art, Washington, D.C.
Gift of Charles Lang Freer F1904.81
Plate 22 M877
Probably Dowdeswell 49,
"Nocturne, black and gold — Winter; Amsterdam"

HISTORY Possibly sold by Dowdeswell and Dowdeswells to E. J. Poole, in 1884 (Dowdeswell and Dowdeswells to Whistler, between July 1885 and early 1886, GUL-WC). Through several owners, detailed in catalogue raisonnée, to John James Cowan, Edinburgh art dealer (January 26, 1903). Lent by Cowan to the annual exhibition of the Royal Scottish Academy of Painting, Sculpture and Architecture (Edinburgh 1904) as *Amsterdam in Winter* (no. 75).Sold by Cowan (through William Marchant and Co., London dealers) to Charles Lang Freer (June 13, 1904). Bequeathed to the Freer Gallery of Art in 1919.

"There was one picture which really frightened me. It is called a 'nocturne in black and gold — Winter: Amsterdam.' An awful thing is rising out of space on the left, the sort of genius which came out of the stone bottle in the Arabian Nights, and the inhabitants are flying terror-stricken in all directions." — *Life* (?), May 22, 1884

Blue and silver — The Islands, Venice
1880
Chalk and pastel on brown paper,
3 9/16 × 11 3/16 in.
Freer Gallery of Art, Washington, D.C.
Gift of Charles Lang Freer F1905.215
Plate 1 M822
Dowdeswell 50

HISTORY Sold by Dowdeswell and Dowdeswells to W. Baptiste Scoones in 1884 (Dowdeswell and Dowdeswells to Whistler, between July 1885 and early 1886, GUL-WC). Lent by Scoones to Whistler Memorial Exhibition (London 1905) as "The Isles of Venice" (no. 92). Sold by Scoones (through William Marchant and Co., London dealers), to Charles Lang Freer (July 28, 1905). Bequeathed to the Freer Gallery of Art in 1919.

"A delightful Venetian pastel, as charming as any that Mr. Whistler exhibited some years ago is (50) 'Blue and Silver, the Isles, Venice.'" — "Mr. Whistler's Gallery," *Standard*, May 20, 1884

"A pastel sketch 'Blue and Silver — The Islands, Venice' (50) is another fine piece of luscious colour." — *Kensington News*, May 29, 1884

Red and pink — La Petite Mephisto
Probably 1884
Oil on wood panel, 10 × 8 in.
Period Dowdeswell Gallery frame, 5 9/16 in. wide molding
Freer Gallery of Art, Washington, D.C.
Gift of Charles Lang Freer F1902.147
Plate 36 YMSM 255
Dowdeswell 51

HISTORY Exhibited at the Dublin Sketching Club (December 1884, as no. 238). Sold by Dowdeswell and Dowdeswells to Henry Studdy Theobald (July 1, 1885). Exhibited at the International Exposition of Painting and Sculpture (Paris: May 1887), as *Note en rouge: La petite Méphisto* (no. 164). Sold by Theobald to Charles Lang Freer (June 3, 1902). Bequeathed to the Freer Gallery of Art in 1919.

"Then there was a Lifeboat (54), and a Sea and Mist (40), and a queer thing in red and pink, 'La Petite Mephisto' (51) a sulky diavoletta of a girl [boudling] in a boudoir — I often wondered what a boudoir was for; its definition is now obvious." — "Whistles," *Topical Times*, May 24, 1884

"With 'La Petite Mephisto' (51) we are back again among triumphant boldness and dash." — Frederic Wedmore, "Mr Whistler's Arrangement in Flesh Colour and Gray," *Academy* May 24, 1884

Note in blue and opal — The Sun Cloud
Probably December 1883 or January 1884
Oil on wood panel, 4 7/8 × 8 1/2 in.
Freer Gallery of Art, Washington, D.C.
Gift of Charles Lang Freer F1904.314
Plate 13 YMSM 271
Dowdeswell 52
Inscribed on reverse of panel (covered by wooden backing added in 1938), in Whistler's writing, "No. 52 Catalogue 'Notes, Harmonies, Nocturnes' 1884. The Sun Cloud, Note in blue and opal. J. McN. Whistler."; inscribed in another hand, "W. Flower. Old Swan House. Chelsea." (Description of covered reverse of panel from notes in the Registrar's Object File, Freer Gallery of Art).

HISTORY Sold by Dowdeswell and Dowdeswells to Wickham Flower (August 1884). (Flower to Whistler, August 15, [1884]; Whistler to Flower, ca. August 1884; and Dowdeswell and Dowdeswells to Whistler, between July 1885 and early 1886; all in GUL-WC). Purchased at the Wickam Flower estate auction (London, Christie's, December 17, 1904) by Colnaghi (London art gallery). Sold by Colnaghi to Charles Lang Freer (January 4, 1905). Bequeathed to the Freer Gallery of Art in 1919.

"Excellent also in colour and keeping is the low-toned study of a green meadow with a row of cottages behind; but why does Mr. Whistler call it 'The Sun Cloud'? There is no suggestion of sunshine on the cloud or any part of the work." — *Globe*, May 20, 1884

"Beauty of handling and high finish will be specially noticed in the landscapes, principally Cornish, particularly 'Blue and gold — The Schooner' [no. 32]; 'Harmony in brown and gold — Old Chelsea Church' [no. 44]; 'Grey and silver mist' [no. 54]; and 'Blue and grey — Unloading' [no. 56]; the most brilliant in colour being a 'Note in blue and opal — the Sun Cloud.'" — [Walter Dowdeswell], "Mr. Whistler and His Art," *Artist and Journal of Home Culture*, June 1, 1884

"Some of [Whistler's] arrangements in colour, such as the 'Little Grey Note' [no. 41], or the 'Note in Blue and Opal,' have all the delicate loveliness of lyrics." — [Oscar Wilde], "The Butterfly's Boswell," *Court and Society Review,* April 20, 1887

Nocturne; black and red — Back Canal, Holland
1883 or 1884
Watercolor on cream wove paper,
8 5/8 × 11 1/8 in.
Period Dowdeswell Gallery frame, 5 9/16 in. wide molding
Freer Gallery of Art, Washington, D.C.
Gift of Charles Lang Freer F1902.159
Plate 21 M946
Dowdeswell 53

HISTORY Exhibited at the Dublin Sketching Club (December 1884), as *Nocturne, black and red — Grand Canal, Holland* (no. 237). Probably sold by Dowdeswell and Dowdeswells to Henry Studdy Theobald (July 1, 1885). Sold by Theobald to Charles Lang Freer (June 3, 1902). Bequeathed to the Freer Gallery of Art in 1919.

Grey and silver Mist — Life Boat
Probably December 1883 or January 1884
Oil on wood panel, 4 7/8 × 8 1/2 in.
Freer Gallery of Art, Washington, D.C.

Gift of Charles Lang Freer F1914.1
Plate 11 YMSM 287
Dowdeswell 54
Inscribed on the exhibition label on the back of the frame (removed ca. 1923), in Whistler's handwriting, "Gris et Argent — Le Bateau de Sauvetage. (signed) J. McNeill Whistler, 21 Cheyne Walk, Chelsea, London." (Registrar's Object File, Freer Gallery of Art).

HISTORY Exhibited at the Dublin Sketching Club (December 1884) as *Grey and silver Mist — Life Boat* (no. 246). Exhibited at the International Exposition of Painting and Sculpture (Paris: May 1887), as *Gris et argent: Mer et Pluie. Batteau de sauvetage* (no. 199). Exhibited at the International Art Exhibition (Munich 1888), as *Grau und silber* (no. 60). Exhibited in "Notes — Harmonies — Nocturnes" (New York: Wunderlich Gallery, 1889) as *A Grey Note: the Life Boat* (no. 29). Exhibited at Exposition General des Beaux Arts (Brussels 1890) as *Le Bateau de sauvetage* (no. 843). Sold, probably by Whistler, to Otto Goldschmidt (by November 1892). After Goldschmidt's death, sold to New York art gallery Knoedler (November 1913). Sold by Knoedler to Charles Lang Freer (January 1914). Bequeathed to the Freer Gallery of Art in 1919.

"Beauty of handling and high finish will be specially noticed in the landscapes, principally Cornish, particularly 'Blue and gold — The Schooner' [no. 32]; 'Harmony in brown and gold — Old Chelsea Church' [no. 44]; 'Grey and silver mist'; and 'Blue and grey — Unloading' [no. 56]; the most brilliant in colour being a 'Note in blue and opal — the Sun Cloud' [no. 52]." — [Walter Dowdeswell], "Mr. Whistler and His Art," *Artist and Journal of Home Culture*, June 1, 1884

Sunrise; gold and grey
Probably December 1883 or January 1884
Watercolor on white wove paper, $6^7/_8 \times 4^{15}/_{16}$ in.
Period Dowdeswell Gallery frame, $5^9/_{16}$ in. molding
National Gallery of Ireland
Plate 18 M917
Probably Dowdeswell 55, "Sunrise; gold and grey;" or, possibly, Dowdeswell 47, "Twilight; gold and grey"

HISTORY Exhibited at the Dublin Sketching Club (December 1884), as *Sunrise — gold and grey* (no. 231); or, less probably, as *Twilight; gold and grey* (no. 55). Acting as Whistler's agent, the organizer of the Dublin exhibition, William Booth Pearsall, sold this painting and *Nocturne in grey and gold — Piccadilly* (Dowdeswell no. 9) to Jonathan Hogg. (Whistler to William Booth Pearsall, between December 19 and 26, 1884, LC-PC, box C, folder 8). Bequeathed by Jonathan Hogg to the National Gallery of Ireland in July 1930.

Blue and grey — Unloading
Probably December 1883 or January 1884
Oil on wood panel, $3^1/_2 \times 5^7/_8$ in.
Period Dowdeswell Gallery frame, $4^3/_8$ in. wide molding
Freer Gallery of Art, Washington, D.C.
Gift of Charles Lang Freer F1902.150
Plate 14 YMSM 296
Dowdeswell 56

HISTORY Sold by Dowdeswell and Dowdeswells to Henry Studdy Theobald (July 1, 1885). Exhibited at the International Exposition of Painting and Sculpture (Paris: May 1887), as *Bleu et argent: Le Débarquement* (no. 171). Sold by Theobald to Charles Lang Freer (June 3, 1902). Bequeathed to the Freer Gallery of Art in 1919.

"Beauty of handling and high finish will be specially noticed in the landscapes, principally Cornish, particularly 'Blue and gold — The Schooner' [no. 32]; 'Harmony in brown and gold — Old Chelsea Church' [no. 44]; 'Grey and silver mist' [no. 54]; and 'Blue and grey — Unloading'; the most brilliant in colour being a 'Note in blue and opal — the Sun Cloud' [no. 52]." — [Walter Dowdeswell], "Mr. Whistler and His Art," *Artist and Journal of Home Culture*, June 1, 1884

Note in violet and flesh colour
Pastel
Whereabouts unknown
M956
Dowdeswell 57

Nocturne; black and gold — No. 6, Rag Shop, Chelsea
ca. 1878
Oil on canvas, $14^1/_2 \times 20$ in.
Fogg Art Museum, Harvard University
Plate 35 YMSM 204
Dowdeswell 58

HISTORY Sold by Whistler to Edinburgh art dealer John James Cowan in January 1899. Exhibited by Cowan at International Society of Sculptors, Painters, and Gravers Exhibition (London 1899) as *Nocturne in Brown and Gold — Chelsea Rags* (no. 134). Exhibited by Cowan at the Whistler Memorial Exhibition (London 1905) as *Nocturne — Chelsea Rags* (no. 90). Sold at Cowan estate sale, (London, Christie's, July 2, 1926). By descent through several art dealers, described in catalogue raisonnée, to Grenville L. Winthrop (1930). Bequeathed by Winthrop to Fogg Art Museum in 1943.

"Mr. Whistler does but little justice to his sitters, or he must be singularly unfortunate in his models. Surely such long-legged children, such elephantine-footed females were never seen before. Their costumes seem to have been purchased, too, at that Rag shop in Chelsea, a picture of which, taken seemingly in the middle of the night, Mr. Whistler obligingly christens a Nocturne in black and gold." — "Notes — Harmonies — Nocturnes," *Sunday Times*, May 18, 1884

Black and Emerald — Coal Mine
Probably December 1883 or January 1884
Oil on wood panel, $3^7/_{16} \times 5^7/_8$ in.
Period Dowdeswell Gallery frame, $4^3/_8$ in. wide molding
Freer Gallery of Art, Washington, D.C.
Gift of Charles Lang Freer F1902.153
Plate 6 YMSM 302
Dowdeswell 59

HISTORY Exhibited at the Dublin Sketching Club (December 1884), as *Black and Emerald — Coal Mine* (no. 248). Sold by Dowdeswell and Dowdeswells to Henry Studdy Theobald (July 1, 1885). Exhibited at the International Exposition of Painting and Sculpture (Paris: May 1887), as *Vert et noir: La Mine abandonnée* (no. 174). Sold by Theobald to Charles Lang Freer (June 3, 1902). Bequeathed to the Freer Gallery of Art in 1919.

The Little Alley; grey
Oil, support and size unknown
Whereabouts unknown
YMSM 291
Dowdeswell 60

Red and black
1883 or 1884
Watercolor on brown paper, $9^3/_{16} \times 5^1/_8$ in.
Fogg Art Museum, Harvard University
Plate 49 M934
Dowdeswell 61

"In looking at the figure subjects one gets caught in a dilemma; the faces are often very expressive, but being small must be examined at a distance of a very few feet. At this range, the rest of the picture, painted in a slashing, dashing style, is an unintelligible, amorphous mass. When you retire some yards the picture shapes itself: it may be compared to one of those pictures drawn for children to use with a distorting mirror, which, to the naked eye, seems shapeless, but when seen in the mirror look all right: distance in our case acting as the mirror. At the distance required for general effect you cannot see what the face is like: so you must sacrifice face for general effect, or vice versa. 'Bravura in Brown' [no. 66] and 'Red and Black' shew this strongly." — "Philistine," "Mr. Whistler and His Artifices," *The Artist and Journal of Home Culture*, July 1, 1884

Grey and silver — Pier, Southend
1883 or 1884
Watercolor on cream paper, laid down on card, $6^1/_4 \times 9^{11}/_{16}$ in.
Period Dowdeswell Gallery frame, $5^9/_{16}$ in. wide molding.
Original Dowdeswell label on reverse
Freer Gallery of Art, Washington, D.C.

Gift of Charles Lang Freer F1902.169
Plate 26 M890
Dowdeswell 62

HISTORY Probably sold by Dowdeswell and Dowdeswells to Henry Studdy Theobald (July 1, 1885). Sold by Theobald to Charles Lang Freer (June 3, 1902). Bequeathed to the Freer Gallery of Art in 1919.

"Mr. Whistler's work this year is unusually varied in its apparent themes. All sorts of objects are pressed into the service of his brush—Southend pier [no. 62], the Cornish coast, a young woman dressed in a parasol and a red headgear [no. 65], a *grisette* reading a French novel [no. 16], a fog in Piccadilly [no. 9], a shop in Chelsea [no. 38]."—"Mr. Whistler's Exhibition," *Standard,* May 19, 1884

Village Shops, Chelsea
1883 or 1884
Watercolor on off-white paper,
laid down on card, 5 × 8½ in.
National Gallery of Art, Washington, D.C.
Plate 30 M950
Possibly Dowdeswell 63,
"Old Shop, Chelsea; pink and grey" (M951)

"A particularly pleasing effect is produced by a delicate little sketch of an old shop in Chelsea, in which there is a good deal of pink, with the paper left white in the background and foreground, and a broad, flat frame of buff silver."—*The Nation*, June 26, 1884

Note en rouge: L'Éventail
Probably 1884
Oil on wood, 3 7/16 × 5 13/16 in.
Period Dowdeswell Gallery frame, 4⅛ in. wide molding
Freer Gallery of Art, Washington, D.C.
Gift of Charles Lang Freer F1913.91
Plate 37 YMSM 256
Possibly Dowdeswell 64, "Caprice in red" (YMSM 257)

HISTORY Possibly exhibited at the Dublin Sketching Club (December 1884), as *Caprice in red* (no. 249). Exhibited at the International Exposition of Painting and Sculpture (Paris: May 1887), as *Note en rouge: L'Éventail* (no. 170). Lent by H. Cust to the Whistler Memorial Exhibition (Paris, 1905) as *The Little Red Note* (no. 54). Sold by H. Cust to Dr. Hogarth, Oxford (probably in 1913). Sold by Dr. Hogarth to Charles Lang Freer (December 1913). Bequeathed to the Freer Gallery of Art in 1919.

Parasol; red note
Pastel on brown paper, 11 7/16 × 4¼ in.
Whereabouts unknown
M957
Dowdeswell 65

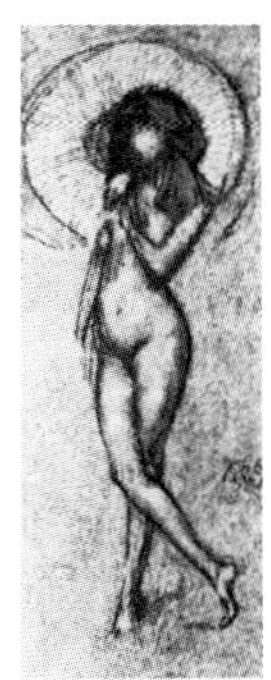

Reproduced from La Revue Indépendent de Littérature et d'Art, *nouvelle série, tome 1 (1886). L'édition de luxe contient, en double triage, sur japon et chine, quatre études de James M. R. Whistler [sic]*

"Mr. Whistler's work this year is unusually varied in its apparent themes. All sorts of objects are pressed into the service of his brush—Southend pier [no. 62], the Cornish coast, a young woman dressed in a parasol and a red headgear, a *grisette* reading a French novel [no. 16], a fog in Piccadilly [no. 9], a shop in Chelsea [no. 38]."—"Mr. Whistler's Exhibition," *Standard*, May 19, 1884

"In [other works], the artist's love of the *bizarre* and his perversity are evident; in the amazingly ill-drawn nude figure, 'The Parasol,' for instance, and in the inchoate adumbration of a group called 'Note in Pink and Purple' [no. 27]."—"Mr. Whistler's Exhibition," *Graphic*, May 24, 1884

"Is there much suggestion of the real figure in the young woman dressed in a parasol and a red head-gear (65)? It appears not a fortunate transcript, but an imperfect and graceless recollection."—Frederic Wedmore, "Mr Whistler's Arrangement in Flesh Colour and Gray," *Academy,* May 24, 1884

"I don't admire the young lady who considers a parasol full dress costume (65), she is hardly classical."—*Kensington News*, May 29, 1884

"I have not space to speak in detail of any more of the works. In most cases the colouring is beautiful, though sometimes the relation between the colours is so subtle as to produce a monotonous effect; the drawing is execrable; see, for instance, a "Parasol—red note," in which the right leg is much longer than the left; the posing is clever, and the painting slipshod but effective."—"Philistine," "Mr. Whistler and His Artifices," *The Artist and Journal of Home Culture*, July 1, 1884

Bravura in brown
1883 or 1884
Watercolor on cream wove paper,
8 9/16 × 6 15/16 in.
Freer Gallery of Art, Washington, D.C.
Gift of Charles Lang Freer F1902.167
Plate 52 M928
Possibly Dowdeswell 66, "Bravura in brown"

HISTORY Probably sold by Dowdeswell and Dowdeswells to Henry Studdy Theobald (July 1, 1885). Sold by Theobald to Charles Lang Freer (June 3, 1902). Bequeathed to the Freer Gallery of Art in 1919.

"'A Bravura,' a subtle arrangement of colours in warm brown and grey.—"Messrs. Dowdeswell's Gallery," *Morning Post*, May 24, 1884

"The spirit and fire of the 'Bravura in Brown'—an 'accident of alliteration,' Mr. Whistler, but how serviceable, is it not?—are not for a moment to be gainsaid."—Frederic Wedmore, "Mr. Whistler's Arrangement in Flesh Colour and Gray," *Academy*, May 24, 1884

"In looking at the figure subjects one gets caught in a dilemma; the faces are often very expressive, but being small must be examined at a distance of a very few feet. At this range, the rest of the picture, painted in a slashing, dashing style, is an unintelligible, amorphous mass. When you retire some yards the picture shapes itself: it may be compared to one of those pictures drawn for children to use with a distorting mirror, which, to the naked eye, seems shapeless, but when seen in the mirror look all right: distance in our case acting as the mirror. At the distance required for general effect you cannot see what the face is like: so you must sacrifice face for general effect, or vice versa. 'Bravura in Brown' and 'Red and Black' [no. 61] shew this strongly."—"Philistine," "Mr. Whistler and His Artifices," *The Artist and Journal of Home Culture*, July 1, 1884

"After the 'Scherzo in Blue' [no. 31], it seems natural to come across 'Variations in Violet' [no. 30] in the form of a clever flower study and a 'Bravura in Brown' in water colour."—"Art Notes," *Liverpool Mercury*, July 3, 1884

Opal Beach
1883 or 1884
Watercolor on cream paper,
laid down on card, 6 15/16 × 9 15/16 in.
Freer Gallery of Art, Washington, D.C.
Gift of Charles Lang Freer F902.170
Plate 25 M886
Dowdeswell 67

HISTORY Probably sold by Dowdeswell and Dowdeswells to Henry Studdy Theobald (July 1, 1885). Sold by Theobald to Charles Lang Freer (June 3, 1902). Bequeathed to the Freer Gallery of Art in 1919.

Abbreviations

AAA
Archives of American Art, Smithsonian Institution
FAS
Fine Art Society, London
FGAA-FP
Freer Gallery of Art Archives, Charles Lang Freer Papers
GUL-WC
Glasgow University Library, Whistler Collection
LC-PC
Library of Congress, Washington, D.C., J. & E. R. Pennell Collection
LC-RC
Library of Congress, Washington, D.C., Rosenwald Collection
M
MacDonald, Margaret F. *James McNeill Whistler, Drawings, Pastels, and Watercolours, a Catalogue Raisonné*, New Haven, CT and London, Yale University Press, 1995
PCB
Press-Cutting Books, Whistler Collection, Glasgow University Library
YMSM
Young, Andrew McLaren, Margaret F. MacDonald, Robin Spencer, and Hamish Miles. *The Paintings of James McNeill Whistler*, 2 vols., New Haven, CT and London, Yale University Press, 1980

Notes

Mr. Whistler's Gallery

1. On the history of art exhibition design, see Carol Duncan and Allan Wallach, "The Universal Survey Museum", *Art History* 3 (1980), 447–69; and Carol Duncan, *Civilizing Rituals: Inside Public Art Museums* (London and New York: Routledge, 1995), 7–20. For the development of twentieth-century modernist exhibition design, see Brian O'Doherty, *Inside the White Cube: The Ideology of the Gallery Space* (Berkeley: University of California Press, 1986); and Mary Anne Staniszewski, *The Power of Display: A History of Exhibition Installations at the Museum of Modern Art* (Cambridge, Mass.: MIT Press, 1998). On changes in exhibition lighting in the nineteenth and twentieth centuries, see Andreas Blühm and Louise Lippincott, *Light!: The Industrial Age 1750–1900, Art and Science, Technology and Science* (New York: Thames and Hudson, 2001).

2. Wildenstein and Company, *One Hundred Years of Impressionism: A Tribute to Durand-Ruel* (New York: Wildenstein and Company, 1970); Jeremy Maas, *Gambart: Prince of the Victorian Art World* (London: Barrie & Jenkins, 1975), 15–21; and Colleen Denney, "The Grosvenor Gallery as Palace of Art: An Exhibition Model," in Susan P. Casteras and Colleen Denney, eds., *The Grosvenor Gallery, A Palace of Art in Victorian England* (New Haven and London: Yale University Press, 1996), 11–15.

3. For exhibition practices at the Académie des Beaux-Arts, see Elizabeth Gilmore Holt, ed., *The Art of All Nations: 1850–73: The Emerging Role of Exhibitions and Critics* (Princeton: Princeton University Press, 1982) and Albert Boime, *The Academy and French Painting in the Nineteenth Century* (London: Phaidon, 1971). For exhibition practices at the Royal Academy, see David H. Solkin, ed. *Art on the Line: The Royal Academy Exhibitions at Somerset House, 1780–1836* (New Haven and London: Yale University Press, 2001).

4. James Jackson Jarves, "Art of the Whistler Sort," *New York Times*, January 12, 1879, 10. In his review, Jarves complained about the installation of a Whistler nocturne that he apparently saw at the Grosvenor Gallery in either 1877 or 1878.

5. For Whistler's development of the nocturne motif, see especially John Siewert, "Whistler's Nocturnes and the Aesthetic Subject," (Ph.D. diss., University of Michigan, 1994), 57–60; and Robin Spencer, "Whistler, Swinburne, and art for art's Sake," in *After the Pre-Raphaelites: Art and Aestheticism in Victorian England*, ed. Elizabeth Prettejohn (New Brunswick, N.J.: Rutgers University Press, 1999), 72–75. The Dudley Gallery was a non-profit artists' cooperative.

6. Although Whistler did not begin to rely on private galleries as the main mechanism for promoting his work until the 1870s, he had used them from the beginning of his career. He sent etchings to a print gallery that was operated by the etcher Achille-Louis Martinet in Paris (1861, 1862, and 1863), showed *The White Girl* at Morgan's Berners Street Gallery in London in July 1862 (after it had been rejected by the Royal Academy), and displayed *Purple and Rose: The Lange Leizen of the Six Marks* and *Crepuscule in Flesh Colour and Green: Valparaiso* at Ernest Gambart's French Gallery in London in 1866 and 1867. During the 1870s and 1880s Whistler participated in group exhibitions at several London galleries including the artist-run Dudley Gallery (in 1871, 1872, 1873, and 1875), Paul Durand-Ruel's Society of French Artists (in 1872, 1873, 1875, and 1876), Sir Coutts Lindsay's Grosvenor Gallery (in 1877, 1878, 1879, 1881, 1882, 1883, and 1884), and at Galerie Georges Petit in Paris (in 1883 and 1887). Exhibition dates are from Andrew McLaren Young, Margaret F. MacDonald, Robin Spencer, and Hamish Miles, *The Paintings of James McNeill Whistler* (New Haven: Yale University Press, 1980), 1, xliii–lv, hereafter cited as YMSM. Geneviève Lacambre, "Whistler and France," in Richard Dorment and Margaret F. MacDonald, *James McNeill Whistler* (New York: Harry N. Abrams, 1995), 43, explains that the Society of French Artists was managed by Charles Deschamps but owned by Paul Durand-Ruel, who temporarily relocated to London during the Franco-Prussian War (1870–71).

7. For more details about Durand-Ruel, see Wildenstein , *One Hundred Years of Impressionism*.

8. According to Lacambre, "Whistler and France," 44, one of the unidentified paintings was titled "Harmony in Grey." This unidentified painting may well have been the Freer's *Symphony in Grey: Early Morning, Thames* (YMSM 98), which was titled "Harmony in Grey" when it was exhibited at Durand-Ruel's Society of French Artists in London in November 1872.

9. Ernest Chesneau, "Le Japonisme dans les arts," *Musée Universel* 2 (1873), 214–17, quoted and translated in Lacambre, "Whistler and France," 44. The fact that Whistler insisted on labeling the paintings probably means that Durand-Ruel did not publish a catalogue. In a January 18, 1873 letter to the private dealer George Lucas, Whistler explained that the paintings at Durand-Ruel "are not merely canvasses having interest in themselves alone, but are intended to indicate slightly to 'those whom it may concern' something of my theory in art—The *science* of color and *'picture pattern'* as I have worked it out for myself during these years." Whistler's letter to Lucas is reprinted in Nigel Thorp, ed., *Whistler on Art: Selected Letters and Writings of James McNeill Whistler* (Washington, D.C.: Smithsonian Institution Press, 1994), 47–49. Whistler's friend, Théodore Duret, coined the word "avant-garde" in his 1885 study of contemporary art and music, *Critique d'avant-garde* (Paris: G. Charpentier, 1885), which includes a chapter on Whistler.

10. Like other leading French dealers, Durand-Ruel resisted spending money on special designs for temporary installations. After hearing of Whistler's 1883 *Arrangement in White & Yellow* exhibition in London, the painter Camille Pissarro wrote to his son Lucien: "How I regret not to have seen the Whistler show: I would have liked to have been there as much for the fine dry-points as for the setting, which for Whistler has so much importance; he is even a bit too *pretentious* for me, aside from this I should say that for the room white and yellow is a charming combination. The fact is that we ourselves made the first experiments with colours: the room in which I showed was lilac, bordered with canary yellow. But we poor little rejected painters lack the means to carry out our concepts of decoration. As for urging Durand-Ruel to hold an exhibition in a hall decorated by us, it would, I think, be wasted breath. You saw how I fought with him for white frames, and finally I had to abandon the idea. No! I do not think that Durand can be won over." This letter is in, John Rewald, ed., *Camille*

Pissarro, Letters to his Son Lucien, (London: Kegan Paul, Trench, Trubner, 1943), 22–23.

11. Robin Spencer, "Whistler's First One-Man Exhibition Reconstructed," in Gabriel P. Weisberg and Laurinda S. Dixon, eds., *The Documented Image: Visions in Art History*, (Syracuse: Syracuse University Press, 1987), 27–48.

12. Spencer, "Whistler's First One-Man Exhibition," 41–44. Whistler could not have sold many of the paintings in the 1874 exhibition since most of the major ones were borrowed from his patrons, but he may have sold one or more of the nocturnes. For the evidence of this possible sale, see YMSM, 71, entry 117.

13. For more information on the Grosvenor Gallery, see Denny, *The Grosvenor Gallery*; Christopher Newall, *The Grosvenor Gallery Exhibitions: Change and Continuity in the Victorian Art World* (Cambridge: Cambridge University Press, 1995), and Linda Merrill, *A Pot of Paint: Aesthetics on Trial in Whistler v Ruskin* (Washington: Smithsonian Institution Press in association with the Freer Gallery of Art, Smithsonian Institution, 1992), 9–18.

14. For the December 1880 exhibition of Whistler's Venice etchings, see especially, Katharine A. Lochnan, *The Etchings of James McNeill Whistler* (New Haven: Published in association with the Art Gallery of Ontario by the Yale University Press, 1984), 211–16; Alastair Grieve, *Whistler's Venice* (New Haven and London: Yale University Press, 2000), 189–90; and Margaret F. MacDonald, *Palaces in the Night: Whistler in Venice* (Aldershot, Hampshire, England: Lund Humphries, 2001), 88–98.

15. Whistler to Marcus B. Huish, n.d. (ca. January 21–26, 1880). See also, Whistler to Helen [Nellie] Whistler, n.d. (ca. 20 February–March 1880): the pastels "are, and remain even in my present depression, lovely! Just think fifty—complete beauties!—and something so new in Art that every body's mouth will I feel pretty soon water—Tissot I daresay will try his hand at once—and others too." These letters are transcribed in MacDonald, *Palaces in the Night*, 143–44 and 146. The French painter James Tissot (1836–1902). For Whistler as a pastelist, see Robert H. Getscher, *James Abbott McNeill Whistler, Pastels* (New York: George Braziller, 1991). For the history of pastels, see Geneviève Monnier, *Pastels: From the Sixteenth to the Twentieth Century* (New York: SKIRA/Rizzoli, 1984); Anne F. Maheux, *Degas Pastels* (Ottawa: National Gallery of Canada, 1988); Dianne H. Pilgrim, "The Revival of Pastels in Nineteenth-Century America: The Society of Painters in Pastel," *American Art Journal* 10 (November 1978); and Marjorie Shelley, "American Pastels of the Late Nineteenth and Early Twentieth Centuries: Materials and Techniques," in *American Pastels in the Metropolitan Museum of Art* (New York: Metropolitan Museum of Art, 1989).

16. Deanna Marohn Bendix, *Diabolical Designs: Paintings, Interiors, and Exhibitions of James McNeill Whistler* (Washington, D.C.: Smithsonian Institution Press, 1995), 217–33. The most useful period reviews are E. W. Godwin, "Mr. Whistler's Venice Pastels," *British Architect and Northern Engineer* 4 (4 February 1881), PCB 4, p. 37; *Country Gentleman*, 5 February 1881, PCB 4, p. 47; and "Venice Pastels," *The Observer*, 6 February 1881, PCB 4, p. 45, reprinted in Robin Spencer, ed., *Whistler: A Retrospective* (New York: Hugh Lauter Levin, 1989), 176–77.

17. For an example of Whistler's standard late 1870s frames, see the frame for Whistler's *Arrangement in Grey: Portrait of the Painter* (*ca.* 1872; Detroit Institute of the Arts), reproduced in Eli Wilner, *American Antique Frames: Rediscovering a Lost Art* (San Francisco: Chronicle Books, 2000), 41. See also Whistler's letter to Helen [Nellie] Whistler, n.d. [20 February/March 1880], in which he exclaims, "Huish is preparing fifty frames! For the pastels." (Transcribed in MacDonald, *Palaces in the Night*, 146.) Two of the original 1881 Venice pastel exhibition frames are at the Freer Gallery of Art (F1905.123b and F1905.124b), both carry Grau's label on the reverse. Although the style of the frame for *Resting* derives from the frames Grau that made for the Fine Art Society in 1881, the frame was probably purchased through the Dowdeswells' gallery sometime in the later 1880s, and was probably made by Charles Mitchell May. For May's relation to the Dowdeswells, see Whistler to Charles William Dowdeswell, probably May 1884, LC–RC, vol. 1, doc. 41. The Grau and May frames are similar in appearance but have significant differences in construction. So far as I know, the first scholar to trace the origins of this style of frame to the 1881 pastel exhibition was MacDonald, *Palaces in the Night*, 99.

18. Godwin, "Mr. Whistler's Venice Pastels."

19. Bendix, *Diabolical Designs*, 223–31, and David Park Curry, "Total Control: Whistler at an Exhibition," in *Studies in the History of Art* 19 (1987), 67–84. All quoted phrases are from "Mr. Whistler's Latest 'Arrangement,'" *Pall Mall Gazette*, 19 February 1883, PCB, 8, p. 10. See also, Whistler to Waldo Story, ca. February 5, 1883, in Thorp, *Whistler on Art, 74–76*; and additional reviews in PCB.

20. Unsent examples of the invitation are in the Whistler Papers, numbers F88 and Whistler W765, GUL–WC.

21. The catalogues sold well and became an important ancillary source of income for Whistler, who received the profit from their sale. The catalogues cost a shilling apiece. In late March 1883, the gallery reported that almost two thousand had been sold, earning Whistler a little less than one hundred guineas. See P. Mugford to Whistler, 31 March 1883; and Whistler to Marcus Bourne Huish, 31 March or early April 1883—both in GUL–WC. By way of comparison, when Whistler was printing the etchings for the second Venice set, the Dowdeswells gave him an advance of two hundred guineas for the 960 impressions that made up the entire run of the set—about four-and-a-half shillings per impression. When the set was published in July 1886, the announced price was fifty guineas for each set of twenty-six etchings, about forty shillings per impression. See Whistler to Walter Dowdeswell, about March or April 1886; Walter Dowdeswell to Whistler, between April and December 1886—both in LC–RC; and Dowdeswell and Dowdeswells to Whistler, between July 1886 and July 1887, GUL–WC.

22. For other recent interpretations of the 1884 exhibition, see Bendix, *Diabolical Designs*, 232–36; and Lynne Bell, "Fact and Fiction: James McNeill Whistler's Critical Reputation in England, 1880–92" (Ph.D. diss.: University of East Anglia, 1987), 149–86.

23. James McNeill Whistler, *The Gentle Art of Making Enemies*, 2nd edn. (London: William Heinemann, 1892), 50–51.

24. The 1884 catalogue lists thirty-seven oils, twenty-seven watercolors, and three pastels. Two works in the catalogue, numbers 6 and 10, are titled *Violet and red*. Both are listed as oils, but a review in the *Globe*, 20 May 1884, discusses *Violet and red* in the context of several watercolors and specifically describes it as a watercolor. Number 43, *Yellow and grey* is also listed as an oil, but descriptions in "Mr. Whistler's Exhibition," *Standard*, 19 May 1884; and *The Builder*, 24 May 1884, suggests that it is a watercolor now known as *Note in Green* (Freer Gallery of Art). If we assume that *Yellow and grey* and one of the works titled *Violet and red* were watercolors, we get a count of one large oil painting, two medium-size oils, thirty-two small oils, and thirty-two drawings (twenty-nine watercolors and three pastels).

25. Parenthetical numbers refer to the numbers assigned in the catalogue to the 1884 exhibition, and to identifications I propose in this book. The Freer collection includes ten Venice pastels shown in the 1881 exhibition, most are approximately 8 x 12 inches. Mortimer Menpes describes the preparation of the panels Whistler used in St. Ives, in his memoir, *Whistler as I Knew Him* (London: Adam and Charles Black; New York: The MacMillan Company, 1904), 135–39.

26. *Standard*, 19 May, 1884.

27. *Kensington News*, 29 May 1884 and [Walter Dowdeswell], "Mr. Whistler and his Art," *Artist and Journal of Home Culture* 5 (1 June 1884), 164. That Dowdeswell was the unnamed author of this review was previously noted in Bell, "Fact and Fiction," 174.

28. E. W. Godwin, "To Art Students: Letter No. 9," *British Architect and Northern Engineer* 22 (11 July 1884), 13

29. Whistler to Charles William Dowdeswell, early May 1884, LC–RC, vol. 1, doc. 59.

30. *Green and opal—The Village* is probably the painting now known as *Green and Silver: The Devonshire Cottages* (YMSM 266), which measures $12^{5}/_{8}$ x $24^{1}/_{2}$ inches. *Nocturne; black and gold—No. 6, Rag Shop, Chelsea* (YMSM 204) measures $14^{1}/_{2}$ x 20 inches.

31. Menpes, *Whistler as I Knew Him*, 116.

32. About a dozen works in the show may have been completed between Whistler's return from Venice and the close of *Arrangement in White & Yellow*. Several of these were completed on short trips away from London. For example, *The Little Bay; blue and brown* (number 46), was painted during a brief working vacation to the Channel Islands in October 1881, and *Amsterdam in*

Winter (number 49) was drawn on a short trip to Holland in December 1882. *Scherzo in blue—The Blue Girl* was begun in early 1882 and was never finished to Whistler's satisfaction. Its current whereabouts are unknown, and Whistler probably destroyed it. For details about Whistler's trip to Guernsey and Jersey, see Whistler to Matthew Robinson Elden, 10 October 1881, and Whistler to Helen Euphrosyne Whistler, mid-October 1881, GUL-WC. For the Holland trip, see J. F. Heijbroek and Margaret F. MacDonald, *Whistler and Holland* (Zwolle: Uitgeverij Waanders; Amsterdam: Rijksmuseum, 1997), 53–54 and 137.

33. For the Fine Art Society's rebuff of Whistler's feeler, see Marcus B. Huish to Whistler, 25 October 1883 and 15 March 1884; and Whistler to Huish, ca. 16 March 1884, all three letters in GUL-WC. Whistler first mentions an upcoming exhibition in a January letter to the American sculptor Waldo Story. See Whistler to Waldo Story, late December 1883 or January 1884, Montclair Art Museum, Montclair, New Jersey.

34. Whistler to Edmund Hodgson Yates, published by December 27, 1883, reprinted in Whistler, *Gentle Art*, 111–12. Menpes describes his weeks with Whistler in St. Ives in, Menpes, *Whistler as I Knew Him*, 135–44. For the development of tourism in St Ives, see Bell, "Fact and Fiction," 152–58. See also five articles by Cyril Noall, published in the *St. Ives Times*, "Cyril Noall Starts the Fascinating Story of St. Ives' Picturesque 100-Year-Old Rail Line"(20 May 1977); "The Last of the Broad Gauge Lines: The Branch Railway" (27 May 1977); "The Story of the Branch Line (3): Open at Last—With Celebrations to Fit the Occasion" (10 June 1977); "The Early Days of St. Ives' Tourist Industry"(25 November 1977); and "St. Ives in the Year 1883" (6 January 1984). I want to thank Janet Axten and her colleagues at the St. Ives Archive Centre for supplying me with these newspaper clippings and a wealth of additional information and photographs relating to the development of the tourism industry in St. Ives.

35. The long quotations are from Whistler to James Alfred Chapman, 15 January 1884, Art Institute of Chicago, and Whistler to Waldo Story, January 1884, Montclair Art Museum, Montclair, New Jersey. He describes the new oils as "little games" in his 8 January 1884, letter to Charles W. Deschamps, LC-PC, box A, folder 23. Whistler describes them as "little things" in his 20 January 1884 letter to Ernest G. Brown and his 30 January 1884 letter to E. W. Godwin, both of which are in the GUL-WC, and in a late January 1884 letter to Elizabeth Lewis, Western Manuscripts Department, Bodleian Library, Oxford. Oil paintings in the 1884 exhibition that were completed in St. Ives include catalogue numbers 1, 32, 33, 36, 37, 38, 41, 45, 52, 54, 56, and probably 24 and 59. Numbers 1, 32, 56, and 59 are all approximately 3½ x 5½ inches. The only St. Ives watercolor definitely included in the Dowdeswell exhibition was *Sunrise; gold and grey*, (probably number 55, possibly number 47), which at 6 ⅞ x 4 15/16 inches is the smallest watercolor that is definitely known to have been in the show.

36. For Whistler's use of watercolor, see Ruth E. Fine, "Notes and Notices: Whistler's Watercolors," in John Wilmerding, ed., *Essays in Honor of Paul Mellon: Collector and Benefactor* (Washington, D.C.: National Gallery of Art, 1986), 111–35. See also YMSM, entry 472, and Andrew McLaren Young, *James McNeill Whistler* (London: Arts Council Gallery, 1960), entry 67. Whistler occasionally used watercolors to produce preparatory drawings or interior designs during the 1860s and 1870s, and made a wonderful series of monochrome wash drawings to illustrate the catalogue for the Murray Marks sale of Sir Henry Thompson's collection of blue and white porcelain in 1878, but he did not make much use of the medium until after his return from Venice. Thomas Way suggested that Whistler's interest was whetted by his friendship with the English watercolorist Charles Edward Holloway (1838–97), whom he met in the early 1880s. Most of Whistler's watercolors from the early 1880s are landscapes, produced in small numbers while sketching along the Thames or on short trips to Hastings, the Channel Islands, or Holland. Whistler included a few of his early watercolors in the 1884 exhibition, including catalogue numbers 9 and 46, but most of the watercolors in the show were drawn after the close of *Arrangement in White & Yellow*.

On the use of watercolors in Britain, see Andrew Wilton and Anne Lyles, *The Great Age of British Watercolours, 1750–1880* (London: Royal Academy of Arts, 1993); Jane Bayard, *Works of Splendor and Imagination: The Exhibition Watercolour, 1770–1870* (New Haven: Yale Center for British Art, 1981); and Martin Hardie, *Water-Colour Painting in Britain*, 3 vols. (London: Batsford, 1966–68).

37. Margaret F. MacDonald suggested the connection between Maud's illness and Milly's arrival in Margaret F. MacDonald, *James McNeill Whistler: Drawings, Pastels, and Watercolours: A Catalogue Raisonné* (New Haven: Yale University Press, 1995), entry 905, hereafter cited as M. Whistler mentions Milly in an early May letter to Charles William Dowdeswell, LC-RC, vol. 1, doc. 64; and in a late May 1884 letter to Waldo Story, LC-PC, box C, folder 30.

38. Whistler to Mortimer Menpes, early May 1884, Harry Ransom Humanities Research Center, University of Austin; and Whistler to Charles William Dowdeswell, early May 1884, LC-RC, vol. 1, doc. 47.

39. For the installation of the exhibition in the Dowdeswells' back parlor, see "Flesh Colour and Grey," *Queen*, 31 May 1884; *World*, 21 May 1884; and "Art Notes," *Liverpool Mercury*, 3 July 1884. For the color of the walls, see "Art Notes," *Liverpool Mercury*, 3 July 1884; "Causerie," *Court Circular*, 24 May 1884; and *The Builder*, 24 May 1884.

40. For the ceiling and blinds, see "Flesh Colour and Grey," *Queen*, 31 May 1884 and E. W. Godwin, "To Art Students," 11 July 1884. For the flooring, see *Globe*, 20 May 1884; *Manchester Guardian*, 20 May 1884; *Belle Life in London*, 24 May 1884; "Flesh Colour and Grey," *Queen*, 31 May 1884; and "Whistler's Criticism on the Art of Painting," *The Nation*, 26 June 1884, 549. For the azaleas, see *Globe*, 20 May 1884. For the chairs, see "Mr. Whistler's Gallery," *Standard*, 20 May 1884. For the fireplace hanging, see "Mr. Whistler's Gallery," *Standard*, 20 May 1884; "Whistles," *Topical Times*, 24 May 1884; and "Flesh Colour and Grey," *Queen*, 31 May 1884.

41. For the attendant, see *Queen*, 31 May 1884. Menpes, *Whistler as I Knew Him*, 121, describes Whistler signing the installation with his butterfly monogram.

42. On the deleterious effects of gaslight, see "Venice Pastels," *Daily Telegraph*, 1 February 1881.

43. "Flesh Colour and Grey," *Queen*, 31 May 1884, and "Whistles," *Topical Times*, 24 May 1884. See also, *World*, 21 May 1884; *Life* (?), 22 May 1884; *Whitehall Review*, 23 May 1884; and "Causerie," *Court Circular*, 24 May 1884. For Constance Lloyd and her marriage, see Richard Ellmann, *Oscar Wilde* (New York: Alfred A. Knopf, 1988), 249.

44. "Flesh Colour and Grey," *Queen*, 31 May 1884.

45. *Topical Times*, 24 May 1884.

46. Quotations from an unidentified period newspaper clipping in Freer's Whistler scrapbook 5, page 17, FGAA-FP.

47. Thomas Dartmouth, "International Art at Knightsbridge," *Art Journal*, August 1898, 250.

48. *The Nation*, 26 June 1884, reports that the color of the gilding ran from "Dutch gilt—a kind of buff silver," to "various tones of copper." An unidentified press-cutting, 24 May 1884 (PCB 3, p. 119), described "the oaken frames" as being "in every shade of gold, from pale yellow to almost bronze." *The Globe*, 20 May 1884, noted that some were "of a pale greenish gold, and others of a warmer tint." *Court Circular*, 24 May 1884, specified that sea pieces were generally "framed in green gold." Freer staff have just begun to research the Dowdeswell gallery frames in the collection, but have already discovered that many still have nineteenth-century pencil notations on the rabbet specifying what color the gilding was to be toned.

49. Widths for the molding that was used to frame the Venice pastels show at the Fine Art Society in 1881 are taken from two of the original frames, which are now at the Freer Gallery of Art—the frame for *The Old Marble Palace* (F1905.123, FAS no. 22) and the frame for *Beadstringers* (F1905.124, FAS no. 45). Both frames still have the original framer's label on the back (F. H. Grau) and both are stamped with the appropriate Fine Art Society catalogue number.

There are twenty-five frames at the Freer that almost certainly derive from the 1884 Dowdeswell exhibition. Twenty-two of these were included in the large group of paintings and drawings that Freer purchased from Henry Theobald in 1902. This purchase is discussed in the headnote to the reference catalogue. The other three works at the Freer in 1884 Dowdeswell frames are *Note en rouge: L'Éventail* (probably Dowdeswell 64), *Moreby Hall* (Dowdeswell 28), and *Amsterdam in Winter* (probably

Dowdeswell 49). Of these twenty-five works, all four of the tiny, 3½ x 5½ inch oil paintings at the Freer, including *Note en rouge: L'Éventail*, are in frames with a molding width of 4⅛ inches (nos. 44, 56, 59, and 64). With two exceptions, the other twenty-one works are all in frames with a molding width of 5⁹⁄₁₆ inches. Oil paintings in original Dowdeswell frames with moldings that are 5⁹⁄₁₆ inches wide are nos. 4, 25, 33, 45, 51, and the painting I have identified as probably being 23. Watercolors in original Dowdeswell frames with a molding width of 5⁹⁄₁₆ inches are Dowdeswell nos. 3, 10, 14, 16, 18, 19, 20, 28, 43, 53, 62, and the drawings I have identified as probably being 35 and 49. The two works that do not fall into either of these categories, are the 5¼ x 9¼ inch oil *Wortley; note in green* (no. 34), and the 9⅞ x 6⅞ inch oil *The Sea and Sand* (no. 36). Both of these paintings are in frames with a molding width of 4⅛ inches, which seem to be identical to the frames for three of the tiny oils (nos. 44, 56, and 59) — the frame for no. 64 has slight variations, suggesting it was made in a different shop.

Six of the frames with a molding width of 5⁹⁄₁₆ inches still have vintage Dowdeswell and Dowdeswells Gallery labels on them. These labels are on the frames for *Pink note — The Novelette* (no. 16), *Harmony in violet and amber* (no. 19), *Pink note — Shelling Peas* (no. 20), *Note in Opal: Breakfast* (probably no. 35), *Yellow and grey (A Note in Green)* (no. 43), and *Grey and silver — Pier, Southend* (no. 62). The Dowdeswells' gallery was at 133 New Bond Street from 1878 until 1888 when they moved the business to 160 New Bond Street. The six labels at the Freer give the gallery's address as 160 New Bond Street. However, each of these labels was pasted over an earlier label. Most of the under labels are completely covered, but the upper label on the frame for *Pink note — The Novelette*, has been partially removed, and clearly shows a Dowdeswells' gallery label with the earlier address of 133 New Bond Street.

Outside of the Freer collection, I have located one oil painting and three watercolors by Whistler in vintage frames made from the identical unusually wide molding. Two of these works were definitely in the 1884 Dowdeswell exhibition, the other two may have been. The oil painting is *Arrangement in Pink, Red, and Purple* at the Cincinnati Art Museum (probably no. 6 or 10, both titled *Violet and red*). Two of the watercolors were given by their first owner to the National Gallery of Ireland: *Nocturne in grey and gold — Piccadilly* (definitely no. 9), and *Sunrise: gold and grey* (definitely in the 1884 exhibition; probably no. 55, but possibly no. 47). The other watercolor, *Zuyder Zee*, is a possible match for *Blue and white — Dutch* (no. 29)

50. Menpes, *Whistler as I Knew Him*, 116. *Globe*, 20 May 1884.

51. The polemical meaning implied by Whistler's use of the same unusually wide frame for oil paintings, watercolors, and (I am assuming) pastels is clearly suggested by the subsequent history of the 1884 Dowdeswell frames at the Freer Gallery of Art. The Freer has twenty-five frames that can be traced back to the 1884 exhibition. All the oil paintings that were in their original Dowdeswell frames with a molding width of 5⁹⁄₁₆ inches when Charles Lang Freer acquired them are still in those frames. At an undetermined time, someone decided that those frames were inappropriately wide for watercolors and pastels. Watercolors and pastels that were in frames with a molding width of 5⁹⁄₁₆ when Freer acquired them were subsequently placed in reproduction Dowdeswell-style frames with a molding width of 3½ inches. Fortunately, although some of the 1884 watercolor and pastel frames with the wider molding have disappeared, most were kept.

52. *Globe*, 20 May 1884.

53. Whistler to Walter Dowdeswell, early April 1886, LC–RC, vol. 1, doc. 52.

54. Godwin, "To Art Students." That the installation stayed up at least until the late fall of 1884 is suggested by Whistler to William Booth Pearsall, November or December 1884, LC–PC, box C, folder 8.

Identifying Paintings and Drawings

1. Theobald purchased twenty-nine paintings and watercolors from the Dowdeswells on July 1, 1885, including most of the ones he subsequently sold to Freer. See Dowdeswell and Dowdeswells to Whistler, 1 July 1885,GUL–WC. The following September, Whistler wrote to Walter Dowdeswell, asking him to "arrange with the man who bought the lot that remained over after the exhibition of the 'Flesh color & grey,' to let his collection go with me to America." (Whistler to Walter Dowdeswell, 27 September 1885, LC–RC, vol. 1, doc. 24. The New York exhibition that Whistler hoped to arrange never happened, but Whistler did borrow paintings and watercolors from Theobald to show at the International Exposition of Painting and Sculpture in Paris in 1887, the International Art Exhibition in Munich in 1888, and in his large career retrospective at the Goupil Gallery in London in 1892. See Whistler to Theobald, 26 April 1887, LC–PC, box 15; Whistler to Theobald, 25 April 1888, Alexander volume, Department of Prints and Drawings, British Museum; and Whistler to Goupil Gallery, 20 May 1892, GUL–WC. Freer negotiated his purchase of the Theobald collection in May and early June 1902, while staying in London and having his portrait painted by Whistler. In a May 30, 1902, letter to Frank Hecker, his long-time business partner, Freer described the Theobald collection as the "most varied and beautiful and the finest single group" of Whistlers known. He gave Hecker a fuller description of the collection after closing the deal on June 3, 1902, writing that "they are all framed (the 31) and are undoubtedly the finest group of his small things in existence — added to the others I already own, they will, combined, help my collection very much." Freer to Frank Hecker, 30 May 1902 and 3 June 1902, FGAA–FP. See also Elizabeth R. Pennell and Joseph Pennell, *The Life of James McNeill Whistler*, 5th edn. (Philadelphia: J. B. Lippincott, 1911), 258, in which the Pennells report that Theobald told them that he had "purchased all that earlier buyers left on Messrs. Dowdeswell's hands."

2. Theobald mailed the now missing list to Freer in early June 1892, when Freer was still in London. In a cover letter, which does survive, Theobald explained, "It may interest you to have the enclosed scribble by Whistler. It is a list of the names he gave to 15 of the drawings you now possess — in 1887 when they were sent to Paris." Theobald to Freer, 6 June 1892, FGAA–FP. In April 1887 Whistler had written to Theobald, requesting the loan of "14 or 15 of the little things of mine you have on the staircase and in your dining room" so that he could send them to the Paris exhibition. Whistler to Theobald, 26 April 1887, LC–PC, box 15. In response to Whistler's request, Theobald lent at least nine of the 1884 Dowdewell paintings to the Galerie Georges Petit show: *Erith — Evening* (no. 14); *Pink note — The Novelette* (no. 16); *Pink note — Chelsea* (no. 23); *Nocturne; silver and opal — Chelsea* (no. 25); *Violet and silver — The Great Sea* (no. 33); *Wortley; note in green* (no. 34); *Red and pink, La Petite Mephisto* (no. 51); *Blue and grey — Unloading* (no. 56); and *Black and Emerald — Coal Mine* (no. 59). Theobald probably also lent *Nocturne; grey and gold — Canal; Holland* (no. 3). With only the 1887 exhibition catalogue to work from, it is impossible to determine whether Theobald lent others. From the tenor of Whistler's letters to Theobald, one can readily imagine Theobald telling Whistler he could have ten, 'but not one more.' For the complete catalogue to the 1887 exhibition, see "Exposition Internationale de Peinture et de Sculpture" (Paris: Galerie Georges Petit, May 8 – June 8, 1887).

3. As is indicated by Freer's note at the top of the sheet, price evaluations were added in May 1906. Freer had negotiated a single price for the entire Theobald collection (£3,000 or $15,000), so the detailed valuation of each object must have been intended for the benefit of Smithsonian officials, although it also indicates Freer's personal sense of the relative importance of each of the thirty-one pieces.

4. Titles on the 1906 inventory do not always correspond to current Freer Gallery of Art usage, but all works can be identified by their accession number. Accession numbers were assigned numerically according to the order established by the 1906 inventory, beginning with *Nocturne; silver and opal — Chelsea* (F1902.146), *Red and pink — La Petite Mephisto* (F1902.147), and *Violet and silver — The Great Sea* (F1902.148), and ending with *Resting* (F1902.176).

5. Andrew McLaren Young et. al. *The Paintings of James McNeill Whistler* (New Haven: Yale University Press, 1980), and Margaret F. MacDonald, *James McNeill Whistler: Drawings, Pastels, and Watercolours: A Catalogue Raisonné* (New Haven: Yale University Press, 1995).

6. *Globe*, 20 May 1884. The two larger works in narrower frames are *Wortley; note in green*, 5¼ x 9¼ in. (no. 34), and *The Sea and Sand*, 9⅞ x 6⅞ in. (no. 36).

List of Contemporary Exhibition Reviews Cited

Whistler's press-cutting books (PCB) are in the Whistler Papers at the University of Glasgow, and on microfilm at the Archives of American Art (AAA), Smithsonian Institution. Reviews which were consulted in the press-cutting books are cited by press-cutting book number and page, and by microfilm reel and frame. Newspaper reviews taken directly from the original source are cited by date. Magazine reviews taken directly from the original source are cited by volume, date, and page.

Yorkshire Post, 24 March 1884. PCB: 6:12; AAA 4687, fr. 508.
"Notes—Harmonies—Nocturnes," *Sunday Times*, 18 May 1884. PCB 8: no page number; AAA 4689, fr. 127.
The Echo, 19 May 1884. PCB 8: no page number; AAA 4689, fr. 127.
"Mr. Whistler's Exhibition," *Standard*, 19 May 1884. PCB 6:9; AAA 4687, fr. 505.
Globe, 20 May 1884. PCB 7:5; AAA 4689, fr. 132.
Manchester Guardian, 20 May 1884. PCB 6:8; AAA 4687, fr. 504.
"Mr. Whistler's Gallery," *Standard*, 20 May 1884. PCB 7:16; AAA 4687, fr. 593.
Unidentified Press Cutting, 21 May 1884. PCB 7:13; AAA 4689, fr. 130.
World, 21 May 1884. PCB 7:17; AAA 4687, fr. 594.
Country Life, 22 May 1884. PCB 6:53; AAA 4687, fr. 551.
Life (?), 22 May 1884. PC 6: 53; AAA 4687, fr. 551.
Society, 22 May 1884. PC 6: 52; AAA 4687, fr. 550.
Whitehall Review, 23 May 1884. PCB 6:52; AAA 4687, fr. 550.
Frederick Wedmore, "Mr. Whistler's Arrangement in Flesh Colour and Gray," *Academy*, vol. 25 (24 May 1884), 374.
Belle Life in London, 24 May 1884. PCB 6:53; AAA 4687, fr. 551.
The Builder, 24 May 1884. PC 6:57; AAA 4687, fr. 555 .
"Causerie," *Court Circular*, 24 May 1884. PCB 6:54; AAA 4687, fr. 552.
Court Journal, 24 May 1884. PCB 6:53; AAA 4687, fr. 552.
Figaro, 24 May 1884. PCB 6:57; AAA 4687, fr. 555.
Funny Folks, 24 May 1884. PCB 6:53; AAA 4687, fr. 551.
"Mr. Whistler's Exhibition," *Graphic*, 24 May 1884. PCB 6:57; AAA 4687, fr. 552.
Illustrated London News, 24 May 1884, p. 506. PCB 6:53; AAA 4687, fr. 551.
Land and Water, 24 May 1884. PCB 6:56; AAA 4687, fr. 554.
"Messrs. Dowdeswell's Gallery," *Morning Post*, 24 May, 1884. PC 6: 54; AAA 4687, fr. 552.
Morning Times, 24 May 1884. PCB 6:54; AAA 4687, fr. 552.
Cigarette, "Whistles," *Topical Times*, 24 May 1884. PC 6: 55; AAA 4687, fr. 532.
Unidentified newspaper, ca. 24 May 1884. PCB 3:119, AAA 4687, fr. 296.
Western Independent, 28 May 1884. PCB 8: no page number; AAA 4689, fr. 127.
Kensington News, 29 May 1884. PC 6:13; AAA 4687, fr. 509.
Yorkshire Post, 30 May 1884. PCB 6:12; AAA 4687, fr. 508.
"Flesh Colour and Grey," *Queen*, 31 May 1884. PCB 7:5; AAA 4689, fr. 132.
[Walter Dowdeswell], "Mr. Whistler and his Art," *The Artist and Journal of Home Culture*, 5 (1 June 1884), 164.
"Whistler's 'Notes,' 'Harmonies,' 'Nocturnes,' etc, in Bond Street," *Fun*, 4 June 1884. PCB 6:56; AAA 4687, fr. 554.
"Whistler's Criticism on the Art of Painting," *The Nation* 38 (26 June 1884), 549.
Philistine, "Mr. Whistler and His Artifices," *The Artist and Journal of Home Culture* 5 (1 July 1884), 199-201.
"Art Notes," *Liverpool Mercury*, 3 July 1884. PC 7: 13; AAA 4689, fr. 133.
E. W. Godwin, "To Art Students: Letter No. 9," *British Architect and Northern Engineer* 22 (11 July 1884), 13.
"The Private View at the Dublin Sketching Club," *Daily Express*, 12 January 1885. PCB 3:116; AAA 4687, fr. 293.
[Oscar Wilde], "The Butterfly's Boswell," *Court and Society Review* 4 (20 April 1887), 378.
"Etchings, Drawings, Pastels," *New York Times*, 3 March 1889.
New York Epoch, 8 March 1889. PCB 10:98; AAA 4687, fr. 920.
[New York] *Sun*, 10 March 1889. PCB 10:87; AAA 4687, fr 909.
Home Journal, 15 March 1889. PCB 10:87; AAA 4687, fr. 909.
[New York] *Evening Sun*, 16 March 1889. PCB 10:85; AAA 4687, fr. 907.
New York Evening News, 14 May 1889. PCB 10:86; AAA 4687, fr. 908.

Selected Bibliography

Bell, Lynne. "Fact and Fiction: Whistler's Critical Reputation in England 1880–1892." Ph.D. diss., University of East Anglia, 1987.

Bendix, Deanna M. *Diabolical Designs, Paintings, Interiors, and Exhibitions of James McNeill Whistler*. Washington, D.C.: Smithsonian Institution Press, 1995.

Casteras, Susan P., and C. Denny, eds. *The Grosvenor Gallery: A Palace of Art in Victorian England*. New Haven and London: Yale University Press, 1996.

Curry, David Park. *James McNeill Whistler at the Freer Gallery of Art*. Exh. cat. Washington, D.C.: Freer Gallery of Art, 1984.

—. "Total Control: Whistler at an Exhibition." In *James McNeill Whistler: A Reexamination*, edited by Ruth E. Fine, 67–84. Washington, D.C.: National Gallery of Art, 1987.

Dorment, Richard, and Margaret F. MacDonald. *James McNeill Whistler*. Exh. cat. London: Tate Gallery, 1994.

Fine, Ruth E. "Notes and Notices: Whistler's Watercolors." In *Essays in Honor of Paul Mellon: Collector and Benefactor*, edited by John Wilmerding, 111–35. Washington, D.C.: National Gallery of Art, 1986.

Getscher, Robert H., and Paul G. Marks. *James McNeill Whistler and John Singer Sargent, Two Annotated Bibliographies*. New York and London: Garland, 1986.

Heijbroek, J. F., and Margaret F. MacDonald. *Whistler and Holland*. Amsterdam: Rijksmuseum, 1997.

Kennedy, Edward G. *The Etched Work of Whistler*. 6 vols. 1910. Reprint, San Francisco: Alan Wofsy Fine Art, 1978.

Lochnan, Katherine A. *The Etchings of James McNeill Whistler*. New Haven and London: Yale University Press, 1984.

MacDonald, Margaret F. *James McNeill Whistler, Drawings, Pastels, and Watercolours, a Catalogue*

Raisonné. New Haven and London: Yale University Press, 1995.

MacDonald, Margaret F., Patricia de Montfort, and Nigel Thorp, eds. *The Correspondence of James McNeill Whistler, 1855–1903*. www.whistler.arts.gla.ac.uk/correspondence. Online centenary edition. Glasgow: University of Glasgow, Centre for Whistler Studies, 2003.

Menpes, Mortimer. *Whistler as I Knew Him*. London: Adam and Charles Black; New York: The MacMillan Company, 1904.

Merrill, Linda. *A Pot of Paint: Aesthetics on Trial in "Whistler v Ruskin."* Washington, D.C.: Smithsonian Institution Press, 1992.

Pennell, Elizabeth Robins, and Joseph Pennell. *The Life of James McNeill Whistler*. 2 vols. London: William Heinemann, 1908.

—. *The Life of James McNeill Whistler*. 5th ed. 2 vols. London: William Heinemann; Philadelphia: J. B. Lippincott, 1911.

Spencer, Robin. "Whistler, Manet, and the Tradition of the Avant-Garde." In *James McNeill Whistler: A Reexamination*, edited by Ruth E. Fine, 47–66. Washington, D.C.: National Gallery of Art, 1987.

—. "Whistler's First One-Man Exhibition Reconstructed." In *The Documented Image: Visions in Art History*, edited by Gabriel P. Weisberg and Laurinda S. Dixon, 27–49. Syracuse: Syracuse University Press, 1987.

—. "Whistler, Swinburne, and Art for Art's Sake." In *After the Pre-Raphaelites: Art and Aestheticism in Victorian England*, edited by Elizabeth Prettejohn, 59–88. New Brunswick: Rutgers University Press, 1999.

Thorp, Nigel. *Whistler on Art, Selected Letters and Writings, 1849–1903*. Washington, D.C.: Smithsonian Institution Press, 1994.

Way, Thomas Robert. *Memories of James McNeill Whistler, the Artist*. New York and London: John Lane, 1912.

Whistler, James McNeill. *The Gentle Art of Making Enemies*. London: William Heinemann, 1890.

Young, Andrew McLaren, et al. *The Paintings of James McNeill Whistler*. 2 vols. New Haven and London: Yale University Press, 1980.

Index of Works

Page numbers in *italic* include references to images.